Salesforce CRM: The Definitive Admin Handbook

Second Edition

A comprehensive guide for the setup, configuration, and customization of Salesforce CRM

Paul Goodey

[PACKT] enterprise
PUBLISHING   professional expertise distilled

BIRMINGHAM - MUMBAI

Salesforce CRM: The Definitive Admin Handbook
Second Edition

First published: October 2011

Second edition: July 2013

Production Reference: 1170713

Published by Packt Publishing Ltd.
Livery Place
35 Livery Street
Birmingham B3 2PB, UK.

ISBN 978-1-78217-052-5

www.packtpub.com

Cover Image by Suresh Mogre (suresh.mogre.99@gmail.com)

Credits

Author
Paul Goodey

Reviewers
Ankur Chopra
Sakthivel Thandavarayan

Acquisition Editor
Kunal Parikh

Lead Technical Editor
Azharuddin Sheikh

Technical Editors
Prasad Dalvi
Worrell Lewis
Larissa Pinto
Pushpak Poddar

Project Coordinator
Rahul Dixit

Proofreaders
Maria Gould
Paul Hindle

Indexer
Tejal Soni

Graphics
Abhinash Sahu

Production Coordinator
Pooja Chiplunkar

Cover Work
Pooja Chiplunkar

About the Author

Paul Goodey is the author of *Salesforce CRM Admin Cookbook* by *Packt Publishing*.

He has over 15 years' experience in developing web-technology solutions for companies of all sizes across a variety of industries, and has been building solutions with Salesforce CRM since 2006.

Paul has enjoyed a variety of roles while working with Salesforce CRM, having worked as a developer, business analyst, consultant, and as a system administrator to provide solutions for both in-house and consultancy-based end-users.

Based in the UK near London, Paul's professional qualifications include Salesforce. com Certified Developer DEV-401. In his spare time, he is a keen runner, having run several marathons and half-marathons since 2001.

Paul is a keen and active member of the salesforce.com administrator and developer online community and can be found at LinkedIn at `http://www.linkedin.com/in/paulgoodey`.

I enjoyed the time I spent working on the chapters in this book, and I am grateful to the people who have contributed toward the creation of the book.

My family and friends have been amazing; it is only with their help and support that I have been able to complete my part of this endeavor.

I would like to thank the team at salesforce.com for providing such an amazing product in the first place. Salesforce CRM is one of the very few business applications that is so easy and fun to work with. The application just goes from strength to strength with each new release and the amount of innovation, new feature development, and added business value that it brings is simply outstanding.

Next, I would very much like to thank everyone at Packt Publishing who have successfully orchestrated the completed work. From the time when I was first approached, to the time of editing and coordinating the final reviews, the team has been extremely supportive and highly professional throughout the writing process.

I would like to thank all the people who have contributed with feedback and suggestions. Instead of trying to name them all and risk not mentioning others, I would like to thank in general all the salesforce.com employees, professionals, and keen enthusiasts who help make the salesforce.com community such a productive and collaborative environment.

If you haven't participated in the salesforce.com online user communities such as success.salesforce.com (where you can post questions or ideas), developer.force.com, LinkedIn salesforce.com user groups, and Twitter (look out for hash tags #salesforce and #askforce), I would strongly recommend them, as they provide a truly valuable platform to exchange information.

Finally, I would like to thank YOU for purchasing the book. I sincerely hope you find it as enjoyable and useful to read as it has been to write!

About the Reviewers

Ankur Chopra is a Salesforce Certified Administrator and has been working on Salesforce for the past three years. He has rich experience in data migration, user training, and user adoption.

Ankur has worked with companies such as British Gas, VMware, RackSpace, and is currently employed with DMG :: Events in London. He can be reached on his e-mail ID ishchopra@gmail.com.

He states that this book is clearly a step forward to clear the Salesforce 201 certification.

> I would like to thank the writer of the book, Paul Goodey, and Packt Publishing for giving me this fantastic opportunity.

Sakthivel Thandavarayan, based in India (a Tamilian), has years of experience in MSSQL Sever database solutions for companies of all sizes across a variety of industries, and has been building solutions with Salesforce CRM since 2009.

He holds a Bachelor's degree in Electronics and Communication Engineering. He was always interested in computers, utilities, software, hacking, and tools. He got an opportunity to work in the IT field, became a database admin, and after some years, was suddenly attracted by cloud computing technology and Salesforce; he currently works with Salesforce CRM and is very passionate about it.

He maintains a blog at salesforceX.com, and can be reached on his e-mail ID admin@salesforcex.com.

He also owns and moderates the Hyperactive Salesforce Google+ Community, at https://plus.google.com/communities/112913878984525867679.

www.PacktPub.com

Support files, eBooks, discount offers and more

You might want to visit www.PacktPub.com for support files and downloads related to your book.

Did you know that Packt offers eBook versions of every book published, with PDF and ePub files available? You can upgrade to the eBook version at www.PacktPub.com and as a print book customer, you are entitled to a discount on the eBook copy. Get in touch with us at service@packtpub.com for more details.

At www.PacktPub.com, you can also read a collection of free technical articles, sign up for a range of free newsletters and receive exclusive discounts and offers on Packt books and eBooks.

http://PacktLib.PacktPub.com

Do you need instant solutions to your IT questions? PacktLib is Packt's online digital book library. Here, you can access, read and search across Packt's entire library of books.

Why Subscribe?

- Fully searchable across every book published by Packt
- Copy and paste, print and bookmark content
- On demand and accessible via web browser

Free Access for Packt account holders

If you have an account with Packt at www.PacktPub.com, you can use this to access PacktLib today and view nine entirely free books. Simply use your login credentials for immediate access.

Instant Updates on New Packt Books

Get notified! Find out when new books are published by following @PacktEnterprise on Twitter, or the *Packt Enterprise* Facebook page.

Table of Contents

Preface

As a leading Customer Relationship Management (CRM) application, Salesforce CRM helps enterprises, both big and small, to improve client relations. It greatly enhances sales performance and provides your business with a robust CRM system. In order to achieve optimum performance from the Salesforce CRM system, there are many areas for you to tackle as the Salesforce Administrator. This is the only book that provides a comprehensive guide to the administrative aspects of Salesforce CRM.

This book, *Salesforce CRM: The Definitive Admin Handbook Second Edition*, will give you all the information you need to administer this powerful CRM application. It is the definitive guide to implementing Salesforce CRM. Whether you are looking to enhance the core features or you have already started customizing your Salesforce CRM system and are looking for guidance on advanced features, this book will show you how to get the maximum benefit from this exciting product.

What this book covers

Chapter 1, Organization Administration, shows you how to set up the organization-wide settings that affect the look and feel of the system and how to provide access to features for all users within the system.

Chapter 2, User Management in Salesforce CRM, describes how to manage and administer user records and password policies. It also describes how profiles and permission sets affect the permissions for individual users.

Chapter 3, Configuration in Salesforce CRM, covers the various methods for configuring and tailoring the system to suit the way information is used within the organization through the use of objects and fields. It also looks at custom field governance.

Chapter 4, Data Management, looks in detail at the data-access security models in Salesforce CRM and the mechanisms for controlling access such as Organization-wide Sharing Defaults (OWD) and sharing mechanisms.

Chapter 5, Data Analytics with Reports and Dashboards, discusses and describes the analytics building blocks within Salesforce CRM.

Chapter 6, Implementing Business Processes in Salesforce CRM, discusses the various methods for automating business activities and approval mechanisms to align with business processes.

Chapter 7, Salesforce CRM Functions, looks at the core functional areas within Salesforce CRM such as Marketing Administration, Salesforce Automation, Customer Service, and Salesforce Chatter. It also describes how you can administer and measure the process from campaign to customer and beyond.

Chapter 8, Extending Salesforce CRM, explains how Visualforce coding can be used to extend the standard page functionality in Salesforce CRM, and provides an example walk-through on setting up an enterprise mash-up between a web utility and a Salesforce CRM Visualforce page.

Chapter 9, Best Practices for Enhancing Productivity, looks at methods to improve the experience of users in Salesforce CRM and the ways to measure user adoption. AppExchange Marketplace is covered along with best practices for app selection and a walk-through of the process of installing an app from the AppExchange.

What you need for this book

The pre requisite for this book is a computer with an Internet connection with one of the following supported browsers: Microsoft Internet Explorer, Mozilla Firefox, Google Chrome, or Apple Safari. You will need either an Enterprise, Unlimited, or a Developer edition of Salesforce CRM, along with System Administrator permission.

Who this book is for

This book is for administrators who want to develop and strengthen their Salesforce CRM skills in the areas of configuration and system management. Whether you are a novice or a more experienced admin, this book aims to enhance your knowledge and understanding of the Salesforce CRM platform. By the end of the book, you will be ready to configure and administer a Salesforce CRM system in a real-world environment that fully supports your business needs.

Conventions

In this book, you will find a number of styles of text that distinguish between different kinds of information. Here are some examples of these styles, and an explanation of their meaning.

Code words in text are shown as follows: "If a user's password is pa$$word, and their security token is xxxxxx, then the user must enter pa$$wordxxxxxx as the password to log in."

New terms and **important words** are shown in bold. Words that you see on the screen, in menus or dialog boxes for example, appear in the text like this: "In the **Tools** area, click on **Mass Mail Merge** to start the mass mail merge wizard."

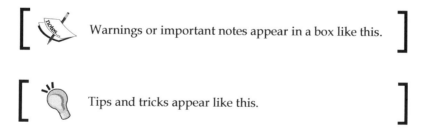

Warnings or important notes appear in a box like this.

Tips and tricks appear like this.

Reader feedback

Feedback from our readers is always welcome. Let us know what you think about this book—what you liked or may have disliked. Reader feedback is important for us to develop titles that you really get the most out of.

To send us general feedback, simply send an e-mail to feedback@packtpub.com, and mention the book title via the subject of your message.

If there is a topic that you have expertise in and you are interested in either writing or contributing to a book, see our author guide on www.packtpub.com/authors.

Customer support

Now that you are the proud owner of a Packt book, we have a number of things to help you to get the most from your purchase.

Errata

Although we have taken every care to ensure the accuracy of our content, mistakes do happen. If you find a mistake in one of our books—maybe a mistake in the text or the code—we would be grateful if you would report this to us. By doing so, you can save other readers from frustration and help us improve subsequent versions of this book. If you find any errata, please report them by visiting http://www.packtpub.com/submit-errata, selecting your book, clicking on the **errata submission form** link, and entering the details of your errata. Once your errata are verified, your submission will be accepted and the errata will be uploaded on our website, or added to any list of existing errata, under the Errata section of that title. Any existing errata can be viewed by selecting your title from http://www.packtpub.com/support.

Piracy

Piracy of copyright material on the Internet is an ongoing problem across all media. At Packt, we take the protection of our copyright and licenses very seriously. If you come across any illegal copies of our works, in any form, on the Internet, please provide us with the location address or website name immediately so that we can pursue a remedy.

Please contact us at copyright@packtpub.com with a link to the suspected pirated material.

We appreciate your help in protecting our authors, and our ability to bring you valuable content.

Questions

You can contact us at questions@packtpub.com if you are having a problem with any aspect of the book, and we will do our best to address it.

1
Organization Administration

Application security is always important, and even more so when the application is delivered across a public network, such as the Internet. Salesforce.com has developed various mechanisms to secure the platform and reduce the chances of unauthorized people accessing your company data. This chapter describes the way login attempts to the system are controlled and the features available to help you manage your users' access to the Salesforce CRM application.

In this chapter, you will also look at establishing your company profile within Salesforce and how core information, such as the details that are provided when your company first signs up with Salesforce.com, can be managed.

You will also be introduced to the settings available for organization-wide customizing of the application's user interface along with a detailed description of the searching facilities offered by the Salesforce CRM application.

Throughout this chapter, notes and tips are provided that are intended to offer further guidance within the areas of functionality, and have been generated from the practical results and experience of Salesforce CRM system administration.

In this chapter, we will cover:

- User login and authorization
- Company profile
- User Interface
- Search options

To start, we will look at how users' login requests are verified and authorized by the Salesforce CRM application.

User login and authorization

Organizations have several methods of accessing the Salesforce CRM application. Access can be gained from either the user interface (using a web browser), the API (for example, using an integrated client application or the Apex Data Loader), a desktop client (for example, Salesforce for Outlook), or from a mobile client application.

Whenever a login attempt is made to Salesforce using any of these preceding methods, the user's login request is authorized by the system using the following sequence of checks:

- Does the user's profile have any login restrictions?
- Does the user's IP address appear within the organization's trusted IP address list?
- Has the user been activated from this IP address before?
- Does the user's web browser have a valid browser cookie stored from Salesforce?

If the user's login is from neither a trusted IP address nor a browser with a valid Salesforce cookie, the login is denied. To gain access to Salesforce, the user's identity must be confirmed by successfully completing the computer activation process.

Does the user's profile have any login restrictions?

Login hour and IP address restrictions can be set for the user's profile. If these are set and there are login attempts from a user outside the specified hours or from an unknown IP address, access is denied.

Login hour restrictions

If login hour restrictions are set for the user's profile, any login attempt outside the specified hours is denied.

To navigate to the **Profile** menu, go to **Your Name | Setup | Administration Setup | Manage Users | Profiles**. Now select a profile and click on **Edit** in the **Login Hours** related list.

Set the days and hours when users with this profile can login to Salesforce.com.

The login hours that are set are based on the default time zone of the organization, as described later in this chapter. Navigate to **Your Name | Setup | Administration Setup | Company Profile | Company Information** and select the required time zone from the **Default Time Zone** picklist.

The login hours that are set apply strictly to that exact time, even if a user has a different personal time zone or if the organization's default time zone is changed.

To allow users to login at any time, click on **clear times** as shown in the following screenshot:

 To prevent users from accessing the system on a specific day, set the start time and end time to the same value, for example, **Start Time** to **8:00 AM** and **End Time** to **8:00 AM** (as in the **Saturday** and **Sunday** example setting in the previous screenshot).

IP address restrictions

If IP address restrictions are defined for the user's profile, any login attempt from an unknown IP address is denied.

To restrict the range of valid IP addresses through the **Profile** menu, navigate to **Your Name | Setup | Administration Setup | Manage Users | Profiles**. Now select a profile and click on the **New in the Login IP Ranges** related list.

Enter a valid IP address in the **Start IP Address** field and a higher IP address in the **End IP Address** field.

The start and end addresses specify the range of IP addresses from which users can login. To allow a login from a single IP address, enter the same address in both fields.

For example, to allow a login from only **88.110.54.113**, enter **88.110.54.113** as both the start and end IP addresses as follows:

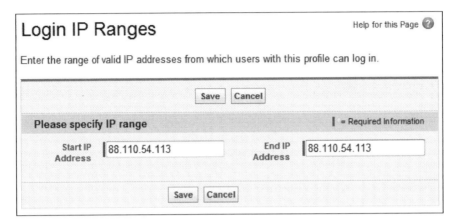

Does the user's IP address appear within your organization's trusted IP address list?

This check is performed if profile-based IP address restrictions are not set.

If the user's login is from an IP address listed in your organization's trusted IP address list, the login is allowed.

Trusted IP range

To navigate to the **Trusted IP range** settings, go to **Your Name | Setup | Administration Setup | Security Controls | Network Access**.

Click on **New** and enter a valid IP address in the **Start IP Address** field and a higher IP address in the **End IP Address** field.

The start and end addresses specify the range of IP addresses from which users can login. To allow a login from a single IP address, enter the same address in both fields.

For example, to allow a login from only **88.110.54.113,** enter **88.110.54.113** as both the start and end addresses as follows:

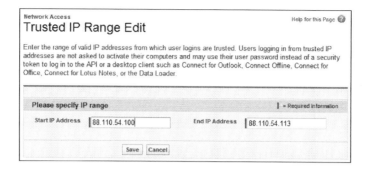

Has the user been activated from this IP address before?

Each user has a list of IP addresses from which they've been activated. If the user has previously been activated from this IP address, then this IP address is added to the user's personal list and is never challenged again.

 This list is not currently visible within the Salesforce application.

Does the user's web browser have a valid cookie stored from Salesforce?

The browser will have the Salesforce cookie if the user has previously used that browser to login to Salesforce and has not cleared the browser cookies.

So, if the user's login is from a browser that includes a Salesforce.com cookie, the login is allowed.

A **cookie** is a small file containing a string of characters that is sent to your computer when you visit a website. Whenever you visit the website again, the cookie allows that site to recognize your web browser.

Computer activation process

If the user's login is from neither a trusted IP address nor a browser with a Salesforce cookie, the login is denied and becomes blocked, and Salesforce must verify the user's identity.

A trusted, genuine user can access the Salesforce CRM application using the following means:

- User interface (using a web browser)
- API (for example, using an integrated client application or the Apex Data Loader)
- Desktop client (for example, Salesforce for Outlook)

User Interface

For access through the user interface, the user is prompted to click on the **Email me a verification code** button to send an activation e-mail to the address specified in the user's Salesforce user record as follows:

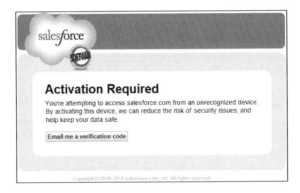

On clicking the **Email me a verification code** button, a new screen is presented to allow the entering of a verification code as shown in the following screenshot:

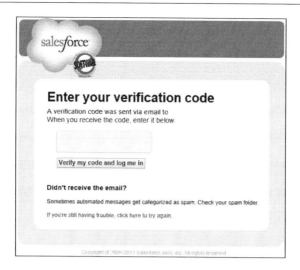

Salesforce sends the verification code e-mail to the e-mail address associated with the user's record in Salesforce. Here, the following screenshot shows an e-mail example:

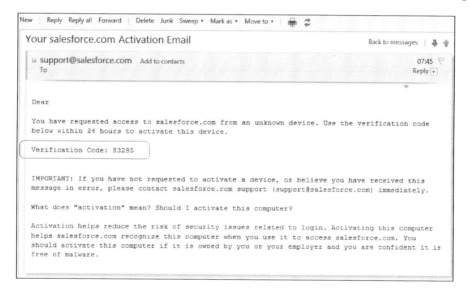

The e-mail instructs the user to enter the verification code into browser to activate laptop for login to Salesforce.

The activation code within the e-mail is valid for up to 24 hours from the time the **Email me a verification code** button was clicked. After 24 hours, the activation link will expire and the user must repeat the activation process.

Confusion can occur if your company has remote users that connect to Salesforce away from the company network such as from home or from public Internet connections. The remote users are likely to have dynamically assigned IP addresses set as their computer identity. Hence, whenever they attempt to login, Salesforce will identify it as an unknown IP address, prompt for verification, and the remote user will have to click on the verification button.

The remote user will then have to access the e-mail associated to their Salesforce user record to retrieve the activation e-mail, and it is here where confusion can occur. If the remote user has to access corporate web e-mail using a **VPN (Virtual Private Network)** connection, the clicking of the activation link may not work because the IP address that is being validated may now no longer be the same IP address used by the browser. This is because the VPN connection may likely be using a web proxy.

 It is recommended that you establish a policy to ensure the user clicks on the verification button while connected to the VPN, or can access non-VPN-based web mail (if this is permitted in your company) to ensure the validated IP addresses are the same.

API or a desktop client

For access using the API or a desktop client (for example, using the Apex Data Loader), the user must add his/her security token at the end of the password in order to log in. A security token is an automatically generated key from Salesforce. For example, if a user's password is pa$$word, and their security token is XXXXXX, then the user must enter pa$$wordXXXXXX.

Users can obtain their security token by changing their password or resetting their security token via the Salesforce.com user interface by navigating to **Your Name** | **Setup** | **Personal Setup** | **My Personal Information** | **Reset My Security Token** and then clicking on the **Reset Security Token** button.

When a user changes their password or resets their security token, Salesforce sends a new security token to the e-mail address associated to their Salesforce user record. The security token is valid until a user resets their security token, changes their password, or has their password reset by a system administrator.

Do not enter a security token within your password when accessing Salesforce from a web browser.

It is recommended that you obtain your security token via the Salesforce user interface from a trusted network prior to attempting access from a new IP address.

When a user's password is changed, the user's security token is automatically reset. The user will experience a blocked login until they add the security token to the end of their password or enter the new password after you have added their IP address to the organization's trusted IP range.

Establishing your company profile within Salesforce

The company profile contains core information for your organization within Salesforce, some of which is captured during the initial system sign-up, and includes:

- Company information and primary contact details
- Default language, locale, and time zone
- License information
- Fiscal year settings
- Currencies and exchange rates
- My Domain

Company information and primary contact details

When your company signs up with Salesforce, the information provided is displayed on the **Company Information** page. This page can be accessed by navigating to **Your Name | Setup | Administration Setup | Company Profile | Company Information**.

From the **Company Information** page, you can edit the company default localization settings and primary contact details:

Default language, locale, and time zone

The company information settings for language, locale, and time zone can affect how key data is handled for the organization.

However, individual users can set their own language, locale, and time zone which will override the organization-wide setting by navigating to **Your Name | Setup | Personal Setup | My Personal Information | Personal Information**.

Default language

This is the primary language for the organization. All interface text and online help is displayed in this language. Individual users can, however, set their own language which will override the organization-wide setting.

For global organizations, it is recommended that you consider how the setting of language impacts, user's ability to access and share information, and whether a common language is preferred to aid reporting and system administration.

You can use the feature called **Language Settings** (described later) to restrict the languages that your users can set in their personal information language setting.

Default locale

The default locale setting affects the format of date, date/time, and number fields.

For example, a given date in the **English (United States)** locale would appear as **07/27/2012**, and in the **English (United Kingdom)** locale as **27/07/2012**.

Time in the **English (United States)** locale is displayed using a twelve hour clock with AM and PM (for example, 3:00 PM), whereas in the **English (United Kingdom)** locale, they display using a twenty-four hour clock (for example, 15:00).

Numbers in the **English (United States)** locale would be displayed as **1,000.00** and in the **German** locale as **1.00,000**.

However, individual users can set their own locale which will override the organization-wide setting.

Default time zone

This is the primary time zone in which your organization is located, for example, the head-office location. However, individual users can set their own time zone which will override the organization-wide setting.

The **Company Information** page also displays all of the base licenses, active users, and feature licenses that have been purchased by your organization.

License information

A user license entitles a user to different functionality within Salesforce and determines the profiles available to the user. A feature license entitles a user to an additional Salesforce feature, such as **Marketing** or **Connect Offline**.

 Salesforce bills an organization based on the total number of licenses and not on active users.

Currencies and conversion rates

Currency settings are organization-wide within Salesforce and can be set using either a single currency option using the **Currency Locale** setting on **Company Profile**, or as a multiple currencies option where you can add currencies and set conversion rates using the **Manage Currencies** link within, **Company Profile** section.

Multiple currencies can only be enabled by a request to Salesforce customer support. When activated, the **Currency Locale** field and its value is passed to a new field, **Corporate Currency**, also on **Company Profile**.

The corporate currency reflects the currency in which your company reports revenue, and is used as the rate that all other currency conversion rates are based on. This is initially set by Salesforce.com when the Salesforce application is activated.

All organizations, whether using single or multiple currencies, are by default with only one currency at **Company Profile** accessed by navigating to **Your Name | Setup | Administration Setup | Company Profile | Company Information,** and setting either the **Currency Locale** field or the **Corporate Currency** field respectively.

Single currency

In a single currency organization, you set the organization-wide currency locale for your company and your Salesforce users cannot set individual currency locales.

Multiple currencies

In a multiple currency organization, you set the corporate currency instead of the currency locale, and your Salesforce users can also set their individual currency by navigating to **Your Name | Setup | Personal Setup | My Personal Information | Personal Information**.

 Multiple Currencies activation is available by a request to Salesforce customer support.

Your Salesforce user's individual currency is used as the default currency in their own reports, quotas, forecasts, and any records that contain currency amounts, such as opportunities.

 Currency becomes a required field on records where it has been added or was originally defined, and so must be considered when activating the **Multiple Currencies** option and then importing data or custom object creation.

Users can also create opportunities (and all other data records that contain currency amounts) using any other available active currency.

Only active currencies can be used in currency amount fields.

Active currencies

The list of active currencies represents the countries or regions in which your company trades. Only an active currency can be set by you, as the system administrator on the organization profile, or by your users on their individual user records or on data records in the currency field.

Manage Currencies

The **Manage Currencies** section enables you to maintain the list of active currencies and their conversion rates in relation to the corporate currency, and can be accessed by navigating to **Your Name | Setup | Administration Setup | Company Profile | Manage Currencies**.

 The **Manage Currencies** option appears when your organization has enabled **Multiple Currencies**, currently available by request to Salesforce customer support.

Changing the conversion rates will update all existing records with the new conversion rates, even the closed opportunities. As a result, you will not be able to measure financial changes due to the effects of currency fluctuations unless you have implemented **Advanced Currency Management**, which stores dated exchange rates.

Dated exchange rates

Dated exchange rates allow you to track conversion rates when an opportunity closes, enabling the accurate reporting of opportunity converted amounts based on the rate that was set at the opportunity's close date. This is made possible because the historic conversion rates are stored, and rate changes after that close date can be tracked. Therefore, reports can include the opportunity amount based on the conversion rate at the close date instead of the rate at the time that the report is run.

Updating currency conversion rates will not change the original opportunity amounts, only the converted amounts. Accounts and their associated contacts must use the same default currency.

Account and contact records may be imported using active or inactive currencies. However, importing lead records must use active currencies only.

A lead is a potential sales opportunity or prospect, which has either expressed interest or has been identified as someone who may have an interest in your company's offerings.

Dated exchange rates are activated by setting the **Advanced Currency Management** option, and are used for opportunities, opportunity products, opportunity product schedules, campaign opportunity fields, and reports related to these objects and fields.

Dated exchange rates are not currently used in forecasting.

When **Advanced Currency Management** is first enabled, your existing exchange rates automatically become the first set of dated exchange rates.

These exchange rates will be valid until you set another set of exchange rates by navigating to **Your Name | Setup | Administration Setup | Company Profile | Manage Currencies, Manage Dated Exchange Rates**.

If you enable **Advanced Currency Management**, you cannot create roll-up summary fields that calculate currency on the opportunity object. Any existing currency related roll-up summary fields on the opportunity object will be disabled and their values will no longer be calculated.

How do you convert currency amounts automatically using the Data Loader?

In a Salesforce organization with multi-currency enabled, when you change the currency on a record via the browser, currency amounts on that record are not updated. Thus, if you change the currency of an opportunity whose amount is 5000 from USD to EUR, the amount remains 5000 and is not converted from USD 5000 into EUR 3900 (based on a USD:EUR exchange rate of 1:0.76).

However, currency amounts are converted when you change record currency using the Data Loader. This means that changes to the currencies of records will cause a mass recalculation of any currency fields on those records.

To change the currency of records using the Data Loader, update the **CurrencyIsoCode** field with the three-letter ISO code of the currency you want to set. For example, USD for US Dollars, EUR for Euros, and so on.

Fiscal year settings

The fiscal year settings in Salesforce can be set by navigating to **Your Name |
Setup | Administration Setup | Company Profile | Fiscal Year**.

Standard fiscal years

The fiscal year settings in Salesforce by default use the Gregorian calendar year
(twelve month structure) starting from January 1 and ending on December 31. If
your organization follows the twelve month structure, you can use the standard
fiscal years. Standard fiscal years can start on the first day of any month, and you can
specify whether the fiscal year is named for the starting or ending year. For example,
if your fiscal year starts in April 2012 and ends in March 2013, your fiscal year setting
can be either 2012 or 2013.

Custom fiscal years

If your fiscal year is more complicated than this, you can define these periods
using custom fiscal years. For example, as part of a custom fiscal year, you can
create a 13-week quarter represented by three periods of 4, 4, and 5 weeks, instead
of calendar months.

If you use a fiscal year structure, such as a 4-4-5 or a 13-period structure, you can
define a fiscal year by specifying a start date and an included template. If your
fiscal year structure is not included in the templates, you can modify a template.
For example, if you use three fiscal quarters per year (a trimester) instead of four,
delete or modify the quarters and periods to meet your needs. These custom fiscal
periods can be named based on your standards. For example, a fiscal period could
be called P12 or December.

Fiscal years can be modified any time you need to change their definition.
For example, an extra week could be added to synchronize a custom fiscal year
with a standard calendar in a leap year. Changes to fiscal year structure take effect
immediately upon being saved.

My Domain

My Domain allows you to set a custom Salesforce.com subdomain name as your
Salesforce login as well as navigation URLs to uniquely identify your company.

Using a custom domain name provides benefits such as increased security
and better support for single sign-on (a way to authenticate login using your
company network). This feature can be set by navigating to **Your Name | Setup |
Administration Setup | Company Profile | My Domain**.

You enter the name you want to use (anything up to 40 characters) and then click on **Check Availability** to see if it is available. For example, the login URL for a company called **WidgetsXYZ** could be set as `https://widgetsxyz.my.salesforce.com`.

You will receive an e-mail when your domain name is ready (after 24 hours to 72 hours), and included in the e-mail is the URL to log in to Salesforce with the new domain name.

There is a Salesforce site called trust.Salesforce.com that lists live system performance and maintenance details for various regional servers known as instances (a subdomain of the standard `XXX.salesforce.com` URL).

To get this instance information from your new domain name, navigate to `http://trust.salesforce.com` and click on the **System Status** tab. Enter your domain name in the **My Domain Lookup** search field (on the top-right of the page) to find your system instance and check the status.

Scroll to the **System Maintenance** table and look for entries for your instance.

Language settings

The **Language settings** feature allows you to specify the acceptable languages that can be used within the Salesforce CRM application.

This feature can be set by navigating to **Your Name | Setup | Administration Setup | Company Profile | Language Settings**.

You then choose the languages that you want to make available to users by selecting them from the **Available Languages** pick list and then clicking on **Add**.

In the following example, we have added **Spanish** and **French** along with **English**, and these appear in the **Displayed Languages** list:

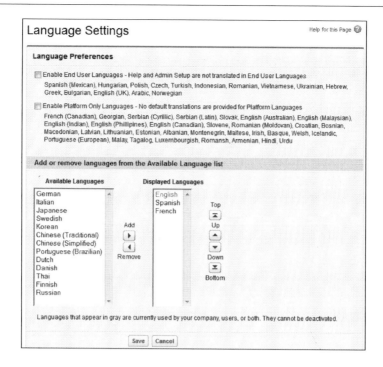

The languages that appear in the **Displayed Languages** list are now shown as available options in the **Language** picklist section on user's **Personal Information** pages as shown in the following screenshot:

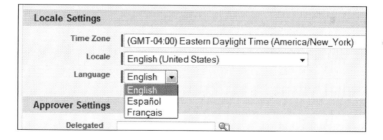

User Interface

Salesforce currently has two user interface themes: the **Classic Theme** and the **New Theme**. Starting with the summer 2010 edition (released in June 2010), all new organizations are enabled by default with the new user interface theme.

All screen image capture and setup in this book has been undertaken using the new user interface theme. The difference in themes can be seen in the following screenshot, which appears when you attempt to change from the **Classic** to **New theme**:

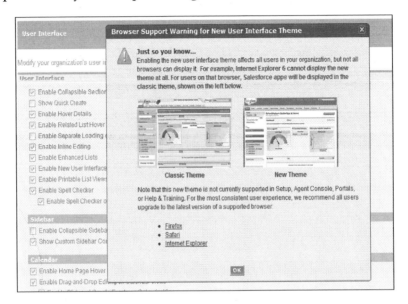

Not only does the new user interface theme change the look and feel of Salesforce, but it also positions some key links such as **Setup** and **Logout** under the user name for each user in your organization.

> The new user interface theme is seen only by users with supported browsers. Supported browsers include Microsoft Internet Explorer (IE) 7, 8, 9, and 10, Firefox (the most recent stable version), Apple Safari Version 5.1.x for Mac OS X, and Google Chrome (the most recent stable version).
>
> Neither IE 6 nor the Metro Version of IE 10 is supported. Safari on iOS is not supported.
>
> Some newer functional areas are dependent on the **New Theme** and cannot be provided when the **Classic Theme** is activated, such as Chatter (a collaboration application suite). Therefore, to enable Chatter, you must first activate the **New Theme**.

Along with the user interface theme, there are many other aspects of the user interface that can be set up in Salesforce to present the optimum user experience for the users in your organization.

Additional user interface options include, **User Interface** settings (such as collapsible detail page sections and inline field editing), **Sidebar** settings (**Collapsible Sidebar** settings and **Custom Sidebar Components on All Pages**), and **Calendar** settings (such as **Home Page Hover Links for Events** and **Drag-and-Drop Editing on Calendar Views**).

There are also some administrator-specific settings that can improve your experience with the application located under the **Setup** settings. It also includes the **Enhanced Page Layout Editor** and **Enhanced Profile List Views** settings.

The selection of the **User Interface** option can be carried out by navigating to **Your Name | Setup | App Setup | Customize | User Interface**.

 The **User Interface** option is the final option on the **Customize** section on the left-hand setup sidebar.

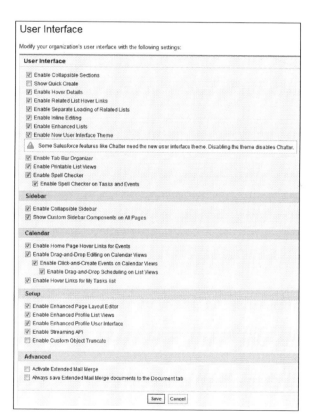

User Interface settings

In the following sections, we will look through the various **User Interface** settings. Let's look at the various **User Interface** settings one by one:

Enable Collapsible Sections

Collapsible Sections enables your users to collapse or expand sections on record detail pages using the arrow icon next to the section heading. Sections remain expanded or collapsed until the user changes their settings for that section. Salesforce will store a different setting for each record type if the record types have been set up as follows:

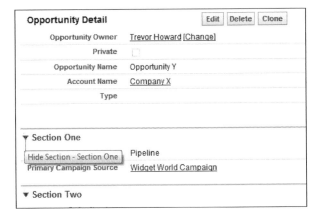

 When enabling collapsible sections, you need to ensure that the section headings have been entered on the page layouts.

Clicking on the triangle icon toggles between showing and hiding the section, as shown in the following screenshot:

Show Quick Create

The **Show Quick Create** option adds the **Quick Create** fields section to the sidebar on a **Record** tab page to enable users to create a new record using minimal data fields as follows:

The **Show Quick Create** option also controls whether users can create new records from within the lookup dialogs. With the setting enabled, users see a **New** button in the lookup dialog screen. The following example shows the creation of a new account within the account lookup dialog while working with an opportunity record:

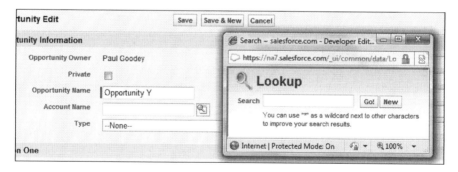

Clicking on the **New** button reveals the fields that are available for creating the new record:

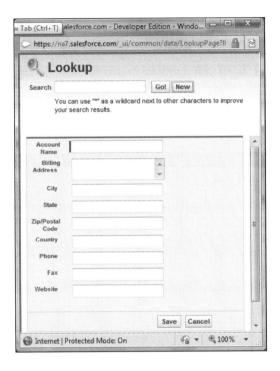

The option to create new records and the display of the **New** button in the lookup dialog is only available for accounts and contacts. Also, users still need the appropriate **Create user profile** permission to enter data with **Quick Create** in spite of whether the entry fields are displayed.

Enable Hover Details

The **Enable Hover Details** option allows users to view interactive information for a record by hovering the mouse pointer over a link to that record in the **Recent Items** list on the sidebar or in a lookup field on the record detail page. The fields displayed in the hover details are determined by the record's mini page layout which is set at the page layout edit screen.

 The **Enable Hover Details** option is selected by default.

In the following screenshot, we are hovering the mouse pointer over a link to a record in the **Recent Items** list on the sidebar:

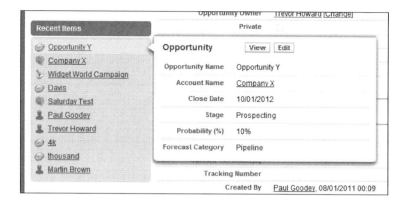

In the following screenshot, we are hovering the mouse pointer over a lookup field on the record detail page:

 To view the hover details for a record, users require the appropriate sharing access to the record and field level security to the fields in the mini page layout, which is set at the page layout edit screen (see *Chapter 3, Configuration in Salesforce CRM*).

Enable Related List Hover Links

This option enables related list hover links to be displayed at the top of standard and custom object record detail pages. It allows users to view the related list and its records by hovering the mouse pointer over the related list link. Users can also click on the related list hover link to jump down directly to the **Related List** section without having to scroll down the page.

The **Enable Related List Hover Links** option is selected by default.

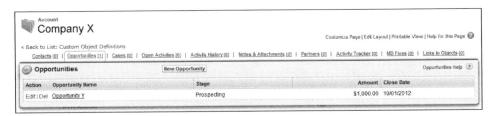

Enable Separate Loading of Related Lists

This option enables a separate loading of record detail pages. First, the primary record detail data loads, and then the related list data. This option serves to improve the display performance for organizations with a large number of related lists on record detail pages. When the page is loaded, the record details are displayed immediately and afterwards, the related list data loads during which the users see a progress indicator for the related list.

You will see that the related list sections are not yet loaded. They appear as [...] while the primary record detail (for the account example) is loaded immediately, as follows:

After the primary record detail has loaded (the account page), the related lists are then loaded. You can see that the number of records for the **Contacts** related list is now displayed as **[2]**.

This option does not apply to pages for which you cannot control the layout (such as user pages or Visualforce pages).

 The **Enable Separate Loading of Related Lists** option is disabled by default.

Enable Inline Editing

This option allows users to change field values directly within the record detail page, avoiding the need to load the record edit page first. By double-clicking on the field to be edited within the detail page, the field changes to become editable. The new value can then be entered and saved or the action can be undone using the undo button.

First, the field is highlighted by hovering over it with the mouse to reveal the pencil icon indicating that the field is editable, as follows:

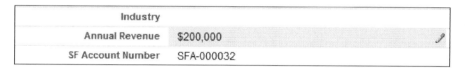

Then double-clicking the field causes the field to switch from a view mode to an edit mode to allow a new value to be entered, as follows:

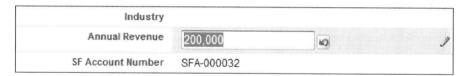

After a new value has been entered, the value is displayed in orange text and the user has the option to undo the change using the undo button as follows:

The changed value and the detail page can then be saved in the standard way using the **Save** button, as follows:

Account Detail	Save Cancel
Account Owner	Paul Goodey [Change]
Account Name	Company X [View Hierarchy]
Parent Account	
Account Number	
Account Site	
Type	
Industry	
Annual Revenue	350,000
SF Account Number	SFA-000032

To check if inline editing is enabled for your organization and to discover which value can be edited, you can hover over a value with your mouse and note the following result:

- It represents an editable field displayed by a pencil icon
- It represents a non-editable field displayed by a lock icon

This option is enabled by default. Certain fields cannot be changed using inline editing, such as **System Fields** (created by, last modified by, and so on), **Calculated Fields** (formula, auto number, roll-up summary, and so on), **Read-Only Fields,** and **Special Fields** (such as owner and record type).

 Also, fields on detail pages for documents and forecasts are not currently editable using inline editing.

Enable Enhanced Lists

This option provides the user with the ability to view, customize, and edit list data, which is the resulting data section that is rendered from **Views**. When enabled along with the **Enable Inline Editing** setting, users can also edit records directly within the list without having to move away from the page, as shown in the following screenshot:

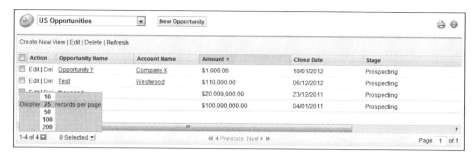

With enhanced lists enabled, users can:

1. Create a new view or edit, delete, or refresh the existing view.

2. Navigate through the list results by clicking the first page, previous, next, and last page links at the bottom of the list. You can jump directly to a specific results page by entering a number in the textbox in the lower-right corner. You can also change the width of a column by dragging the right side of the column heading with the mouse. Changes made to column widths apply to that specific list only and are recalled whenever that list is viewed. Please note that when columns are added or removed from a list, any column width setting for that list is discarded.

3. Change the order in which a column is displayed by dragging the entire column heading with your mouse to the desired position. For your users who have the permission to edit the list definition, the changes are saved for all who see the list. For your users without permission to edit the list definition, their changes are discarded after leaving the page.

4. If inline editing is enabled for your organization, values can be entered directly into the list by double-clicking on individual field values. Users who have been granted the **Mass Edit from Lists** option on their profile can edit up to 200 records at a time.

> The **Mass Edit from Lists** option only appears on the profile if inline editing is enabled.

A mass edit is performed by first selecting the records to be edited using the checkboxes and then clicking on one of the fields that is to be edited.

Upon clicking on the field, a new pop-up window is displayed to prompt whether the change is to be done to just the selected record or to all the records that have been selected. In the following screenshot, we see an example where two account records have been selected, and where one of the record's billing street fields has been clicked:

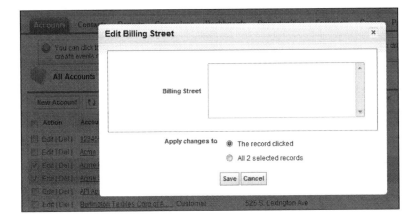

 This feature only allows mass edit. Users cannot mass delete.

 Remind users that they cannot mass delete records

As a system administrator you may need to remind users that they cannot mass delete records, as occasionally users may try to mass delete using the only visible **Delete** link, which is in fact the link to delete the **View** as shown in the following screenshot.

Communication of this fact will hopefully save you from having to recreate any views that have been deleted in error.

On **Account**, **Contact**, and **Lead List** views, there is an **Open Calendar** link at the bottom of the page to display a weekly view of a calendar underneath the list. A record can be dragged from the list to a time slot on the calendar to create an event associated with the record.

 To perform inline editing on an enhanced list, **Advanced Filter** options must be turned off in the list view filter criteria.

Some standard fields do not support inline editing. For example, **Case Status, Opportunity Stage**, and several of the **Task** and **Event** fields can only be edited from the record edit page.

The number of records displayed can be changed per page by setting the view for **10**, **25**, **50**, **100**, or **200** records at a time. When this setting is changed, navigation is set to the first page of list results as shown in the following screenshot:

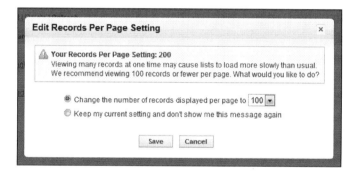

 If users change the number of records to be displayed per page, that setting is applied to all the lists (not just the current list).

Also, if the option of displaying 200 records is selected, a warning message appears, as it can reduce performance.

Enable the New User Interface Theme

The **New User Interface Theme** changes the look and feel of Salesforce from the **Classic Theme** to the **New Theme**. It also houses the links, such as **Setup, Developer Console**, and **Logout**, under the user name for users in your organization.

There are still some older browsers (such as IE 6) that cannot render the **New User Interface Theme** and should be avoided.

Enable Tab Bar Organizer

Tab Bar Organizer automatically arranges users' tabs in the tab bar to control the width of the CRM application pages and prevent horizontal scrolling. It dynamically measures how many of the application tabs can be displayed and puts tabs that extend beyond the browser's current width into a drop-down list presented on the right-hand side of the tab bar as shown in the following screenshot:

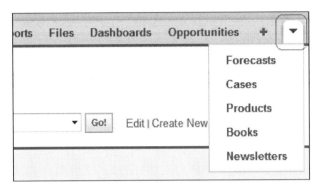

 This setting is only enabled when the **New User Interface Theme** is activated. If your organization is not using the **New User Interface Theme,** you can enable the feature, but the **Tab Bar Organizer** will not be activated for your users until the new theme is also enabled.

Enable Printable List Views

This option allows users to easily print list views.

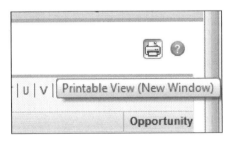

If enabled, users can click on the **Printable View** link (the printer logo) located in the top-right corner on any list view to open a new browser window. Within the new window, the current list view is displayed in a print-ready format, as follows:

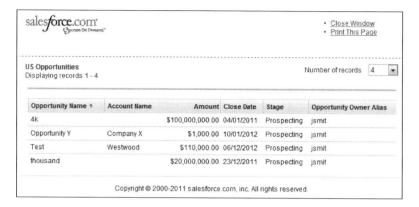

This option allows users to click on the **Printable View** link from any list view, which opens a new browser window displaying the current list view in a print-ready format.

Enable Spell Checker

When this option is selected, the **Check Spelling** button appears in certain areas of the application where text is entered, such as sending an e-mail, or when creating cases, notes, and solutions. Clicking on this button checks the spelling of your text as shown in the following screenshot:

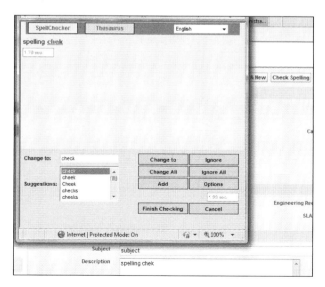

The **Spell Checker** option is not supported for all languages in Salesforce and does not appear where the language is for example, Thai, Russian, Japanese, Korean, or Chinese.

Enable Spell Checker on tasks and events

This option enables the appearance of the **Check Spelling** button when users create or edit tasks or events. Spelling is checked in the **Description** field on events and the **Comments** field on tasks.

Sidebar

The settings for the sidebar options are as follows:

Enable Collapsible Sidebar

The collapsible sidebar gives users the ability to show or hide the sidebar on every Salesforce page where the sidebar is included. When this option is selected, the collapsible sidebar becomes available to all users in your organization. However, each user can set their own preference for displaying the sidebar. Users can set the sidebar to be permanently displayed or they can collapse the sidebar and show it only when needed.

Show Custom Sidebar Components on All Pages

If you have custom home page layouts that include components in the sidebar, this option displays the sidebar components on all pages in Salesforce and for all users. If only certain profiles are allowed to view sidebar components on all pages, you can assign a **Show Custom Sidebar on All Pages** permission to just those profiles.

 If the **Show Custom Sidebar Components on All Pages** user interface setting is enabled, the **Show Custom Sidebar on All Pages** permission is not available within the profile permissions.

Calendar settings

The following options are available to help users view and edit information on calendar sections and views:

Enable Home Page Hover Links for Events

This option enables hover links in the calendar section of the **Home** tab and allows users to hover the mouse over the subject of an event to see interactive information for that event.

 This setting controls the **Home** tab only, as hover links are always displayed in other calendar views. Also, this option is enabled by default.

Enable Drag-and-Drop Editing on Calendar Views

This option enables your users to drag-and-drop existing events around their daily and weekly calendar views to reschedule events without having to navigate from the page to the event creation page. The loading performance of the calendar control may suffer with this option enabled. Drag-and-drop editing is not available for either multi-day events or on console calendar views. Also, this option is enabled by default.

Enable Click-and-Create Events on Calendar Views

This option enables the creating of events on daily and weekly calendar views by double-clicking on a specific time slot and entering the details of the event in an interactive section. The fields presented in the interactive section are set using the mini page layout on the **Event** page layout screen.

 Recurring events and multi-person events cannot be created using the **Click-And-Create Events On Calendar Views** option.

Enable Drag-and-Drop Scheduling on List Views

This option enables users to create events by dragging the record to be linked from the list view onto the weekly calendar view. Upon dropping, an interactive section for the event detail is displayed where the fields available are set using the mini page layout.

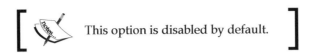

[This option is disabled by default.]

Enable Hover Links for My Tasks List

This option enables hover links for tasks in the **My Tasks** section of the **Home** tab and on the calendar day view, and allows users to hover the mouse over details of the task in an interactive section.

Setup settings

There are administrator-specific user interface settings that can improve your experience with the application located under the **Setup** settings for the following:

Enable Enhanced Page Layout Editor

This option enables the **Enhanced Page Layout Editor** for your organization for editing page layouts with a feature-rich **WYSIWYG (What You See Is What You Get)** editor.

Enable Enhanced Profile List Views

This option enables the enhanced list views and inline editing on the profiles list page, which allows you to manage multiple profiles at once.

To navigate to the **Profile** menu, go to **Your Name | Setup | Administration Setup | Manage Users | Profiles**. Now select a profile and click on **Create New View** as shown in the following screenshot:

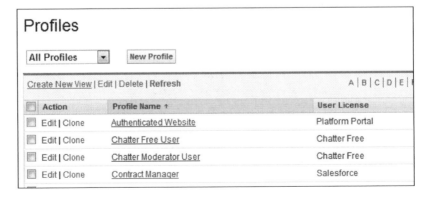

Following are the three steps to produce the list of profiles that allow you to modify multiple profile settings at once:

1. **Enter View Name**
2. **Specify Filter Criteria**
3. **Select Columns to Display**

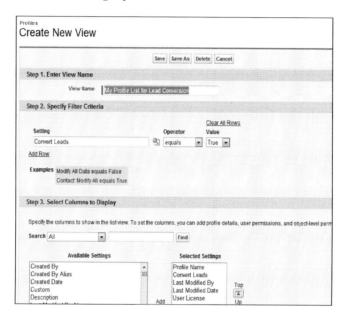

Now that the profile view has been created, we can select multiple profiles to manage all at once as shown in the following screenshot:

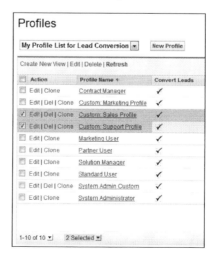

You can display the multiple lists of profiles that can be selected and actioned as follows:

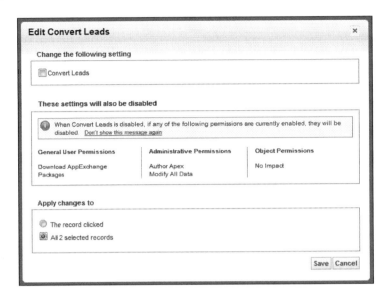

You can also modify the multiple profile selection to apply the setting to all the profiles as shown in the following screenshot:

The **Advanced** settings of **User Interface** set up the screen currently related to the **Extended Mail Merge** features.

Enable Enhanced Profile User Interface

This option allows you to enable the **Enhanced Profile User Interface**, which then offers the following features to help you:

- **Find permissions and settings**. Here, you can start typing a specific permission or setting name in the **Find Settings** box and then choose from a list of matching results.

- **Edit profile properties**. Here, you can change the name or description of a profile.

- Find out who belongs to a profile by clicking on the **Assigned Users** button to see a list.

- **Browse permissions and settings, for both, app and system properties**. Here, the app-related and system permissions and settings are grouped on individual pages where the profile overview page provides the descriptions and links.

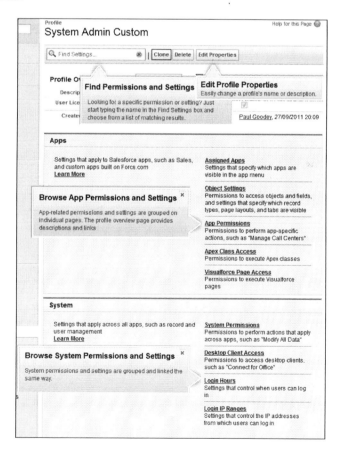

Enable Custom Object Truncate

Select the **Enable Custom Object Truncate** checkbox to activate truncating custom objects, which permanently removes all of the records from a custom object while keeping the object and its metadata intact for future use.

 When this option is enabled, a **Truncate** button appears in the list of edit buttons within the custom object setup page.

Truncating custom objects is a quick way to permanently delete all of the records from a custom object, for example, if a custom object has been created and filled with test records. When testing is complete and the test data is no longer required, you can truncate the object to remove the test records, but keep the object ready to be deployed into production. This is much quicker than batch-deleting records and having to recreate the custom object.

 Truncating a custom object permanently removes all of its records, and you cannot recover the records from the **Recycle Bin**. A copy of the truncated object appears in the **Deleted Objects** list for 15 days, during which the object and its records continue to count towards the organization data limits. The copied object and its records are then permanently deleted after 15 days.

Advanced settings

Advanced settings provides the activation of two features, namely the activation of **Extended Mail Merge** and the option to **Always save Extended Mail Merge documents to the Documents tab**.

 The **Advanced** settings option appears when your organization has enabled **Extended Mail Merge**, currently available by request to Salesforce customer support.

Activate Extended Mail Merge

This option enables the **Mass Mail Merge** link to be available in the **Tools** area on the home pages for accounts, contacts, and leads.

When enabled, this option also sets single mail merges requested from the **Activity History** related list on a record to be created with the **Extended Mail Merge** function. The **Extended Mail Merge** function is activated using a wizard comprising of the following steps:

1. In the **Tools** area, click on **Mass Mail Merge** to start the mass mail merge wizard. Choose a list view from the **View** drop-down list and select the records to include in the mail merge. Selecting the checkbox in the column header will select all records currently displayed on the page.

2. Select the types of Word documents to generate from the multiple selections of documents, envelopes, and labels. Select the optional **Log an activity...** checkbox to log the creation of these mail merge documents, which adds a completed task to each record.

3. Select the appropriate mail merge templates. For documents, choose whether to create one Word document that includes all the outputs or a separate Word document for each record. Click on the optional **Preview Template** button to review the preloaded mail merge template.

Although the document preview is editable, do not edit in Word as the changes will not be saved to your current mail merge request. You have to make a new mail merge template and upload this first.

> With **Extended Mail Merge**, the mail merge operation cannot exceed 1000 records; the selected mail merge template's total size cannot be greater than 1 Mbytes, and the number of records multiplied by the combined size of the mail merge templates cannot be greater than 50 Mbytes.
>
> Also, **Extended Mail Merge** is available by sending a request to Salesforce customer support.

Always save Extended Mail Merge documents to the Documents tab

This option stops the sending of the mail merge documents as e-mail attachments, and instead stores them in the user's personal documents folder on the **Documents** tab. Users are still sent e-mails as confirmation when their mail merge requests have completed, and these e-mails contain links to the documents in the **Documents** tab.

These documents count against your organization's storage limits.

The Salesforce user interface includes pop-up windows, therefore, pop-up blockers must be disabled for the Salesforce domain.

A way to check that a user's browser allows pop-up windows is as follows:

Click on **Your Name** | **Setup** | **My Personal Information** | **Reminders**, and then click on **Preview Reminder Alert**.

Search overview

Salesforce.com uses custom algorithms that consider the following within searches:

- The search terms
- Ignored words in search terms (for example, the, to, and for)
- Search term stems (for example, searching for speaking returns items with speak)
- Proximity of search terms in a record
- Record ownership and most recently accessed records

A user might therefore not have the same search results as another user performing the same search because searches are configured for the user performing the search. For example, a user recently viewed a record, the record relevancy increases, and the record moves higher in their search results list. Records that are owned by the user also move higher in their search results. There are currently three types of search, as follows:

Sidebar Search

From the **Sidebar Search** box, users can search a subset of record types and fields. Wildcards and filters can be used to help refine the search.

A wildcard is a special character or token that can be used to substitute for any other character or characters in a string. For example, the asterisk character (*) substitutes for zero or more characters. More information about the wildcard characters can be found using the following link: http://en.wikipedia.org/wiki/Wildcard_character

Advanced Search

The **Advanced Search** in the sidebar allows searching for a subset of record types in combination and offers more fields including custom fields and long text fields, such as descriptions, notes, task, and event comments. Wildcards and filters can be used to help refine the search.

Global Search

From the **Global Search** box, users can search more types of records, including articles, documents, products, solutions, chatter feeds, and groups. Users can also search more fields, including custom fields and long text fields such as descriptions, notes, tasks, and event comments. Wildcards and filters can be used to help refine the search.

> To enable **Global Search**, you must enable **Chatter**. If **Global Search** is enabled, **Sidebar Search** and **Advanced Search** are disabled.
>
> **Global Search** is not supported in **Partner Portal** or **Customer Portal**.
>
> Only users with supported browsers can use **Global Search**, as it has indirect dependencies on the **New Theme** user interface.

Searching in Salesforce.com

Your search term must have two or more characters. Special characters, such as ", ?, *, (, and) are not included in the character count. For example, a search for **m*** will fail to return any search results.

Search terms are not case-sensitive. For example, a search for martin returns the same results as the search for Martin.

Finding phone numbers can be done by entering part or all of a number. For example, to find (512) 757-6000, enter 5127576000, 757, or 6000. To search for the last seven digits, you must enter the punctuation, such as 757-6000.

In Chinese, Japanese, and Korean, you can find a person by entering the last name before the first name; searching for howard trevor returns any person named Trevor Howard.

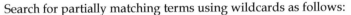

If you're using **Advanced Search** or **Global Search**, refine your search using operators such as AND, OR, and AND NOT.

If you're using **Advanced Search** or **Global Search**, search for exact phrases by selecting the **Exact phrase** checkbox, or by putting quotation marks around multiple keywords; for example, "phone martin brown" returns results with phone martin brown, but not martin brown phoned or phone martina browning.

If you're using **Sidebar Search**, your search string is automatically treated as a phrase search.

Search for partially matching terms using wildcards as follows:

Asterisks match one or more characters at the middle or end (not the beginning) of your search term. For example, a search for brown* finds items that start with variations of the term brown, such as browning or brownlow. A search for ma* brown finds items with martin brown or mandy brown. If you're using **Sidebar Search**, an * is automatically appended at the end of the search string.

If you're using **Global Search**, question marks match only one character in the middle (not the beginning or end) of your search term. For example, a search for ti?a finds items with the term tina or tika, but not tia or tinas.

If using **Sidebar Search** or **Advanced Search**, question marks match only one character in the middle or end (not the beginning) of your search term.

Search Settings

There are various search options that can be customized to change the way information can be searched by your users in Salesforce. These options either present enhanced search features that are visible as a part of the user interface, or are non-visible and used to optimize searching behind the scenes. The search settings can be set by navigating to **Your Name | Setup | App Setup | Customize | Search | Search Settings**.

The following screenshot shows the search settings that are available if Chatter is not activated in your Salesforce CRM application:

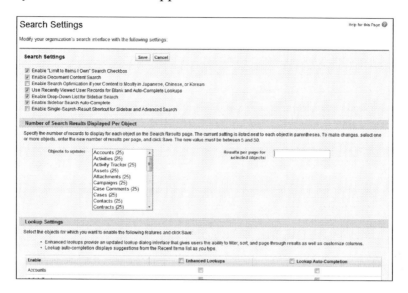

By activating Chatter, the **Global Search** setting is automatically enabled and provides the following reduced set of options:

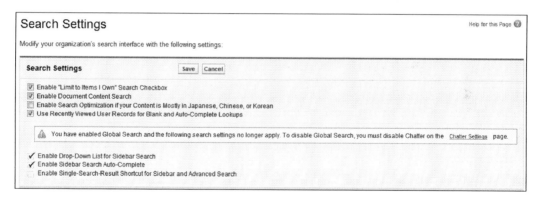

In the following sections, you will see how to work with various search settings:

Enable "Limit to Items I Own" Search Checkbox

The **Limit to Items I Own** option allows your users to restrict the search results to find only the records of which they are the record owner when searching in the sidebar.

 The **Limit to Items I Own** checkbox that is available for the **Advanced Search** is always displayed, regardless of this option setting.

Enable Document Content Search

This option allows users to perform a full text search of a document. When new documents are uploaded or an existing document is updated, its contents are available as search terms to retrieve the document.

Enable Search Optimization if your Content is Mostly in Japanese, Chinese, or Korean

This option optimizes searching for Japanese, Chinese, and Korean language sets. It affects **Sidebar Search** and the account search for **Find Duplicates** on a lead record in **Sidebar Search** and **Global Search**.

 This option should not be selected if you expect content and searches to be mostly in other languages.

Use Recently Viewed User Records for Blank and Auto-Complete Lookups

This option causes the list of records returned from a user autocomplete lookup and from a blank user lookup to be generated from the user's recently viewed user records. By not enabling this option, the dialog shows a list of recently accessed user records from across your organization.

Enable Drop-Down List for Sidebar Search

This option creates a drop-down list in the **Search** section to appear that allows users to limit searches by the type of record.

Enable Sidebar Search Autocomplete

This option provides the functionality that when users start typing search terms, the **Sidebar Search** displays a matching list of recently viewed records.

 The **Global Search** feature includes autocomplete as a standard feature and does not require a specific autocomplete option to be set.

Enable Single-Search-Result Shortcut

This option allows users to skip the search results page and navigate directly to the record detail page if their search produces a single result.

Number of Search Results Displayed Per Object

The **Number of Search Results Displayed Per Object** area allows you to configure the number of items that are returned for each object in the **Search Results** page. The current setting is in brackets next to each object where the new value must be between 5 and 50.

Lookup Settings

The **Lookup Settings** section of the **Search Settings** page allows you to enable enhanced lookups and lookup autocompletion for **Accounts**, **Contacts**, **Users**, and custom objects.

Enhanced lookups

Enhanced lookups provides an enhanced interface for your users to sort and filter search results by any field that is available in regular search results, as shown in the following screenshot:

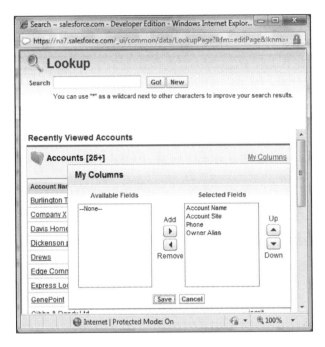

With enhanced lookups enabled, users can hide and reorganize the columns that are displayed in the results window. Enhanced lookups return all records that match the search criteria and allow you to page through large sets of search results.

After enabling enhanced lookups, you must specify which fields users can use to filter lookup search dialog results. This is set by accessing search layouts and choosing the fields from the **Lookup Dialog Fields** layout.

For custom objects, this is done by navigating to **Your Name | Setup | Create | Objects**. Choose the object you want to modify, scroll down to the **Search Layouts** related list, and choose the fields from the **Lookup Dialog Fields**.

For **Accounts**, **Contacts**, or **Users**, this is done by navigating to **Your Name | Setup | App Setup | Customize**, go to **Accounts**, **Contacts**, or **Users**, and then **Search Layouts**. Then, choose the fields from the **Lookup Dialog Fields** as shown in the following screenshot:

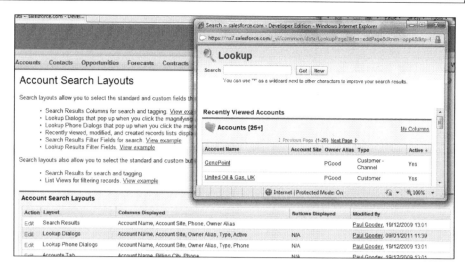

Currently, only **Accounts**, **Contacts**, **Events**, **Users**, **Chatter** objects, and custom objects can be enabled to use the enhanced lookup settings.

Lookup Autocompletion

When the **Lookup Autocompletion** option is enabled, your users are shown a dynamic list of matching recently used records when they edit a lookup field. This feature is available for **Accounts**, **Contacts**, **Users**, and custom object lookups.

> Currently, only **Accounts**, **Contacts**, **Events**, **Users**, **Chatter** objects, and custom objects can be enabled to use the **Lookup Autocompletion** option.

Summary

This chapter looked at the mechanisms in place to help manage login access to the Salesforce CRM application and how organization-wide settings can be set to determine your company-specific information within Salesforce.com.

The options to configure the look and feel of the application were identified along with details of the methods for searching for information in Salesforce.

Notes and tips gained from the experience of Salesforce CRM system administration were outlined to help guide the understanding and improve the implementation of these features.

Having looked at these core customization feature sets, we will now look at how profiles and sharing in Salesforce CRM govern what functionality and access permissions a user has throughout the application.

2
User Management in Salesforce CRM

In the previous chapter, we looked at user authentication and how user login access is authorized by the Salesforce application. We were introduced to the concept of a user being assigned a profile that could be set to control certain permissions. The user profile login permissions we looked at were restrictions on login hours and IP addresses, which allow you to control when and from where users log in to the Salesforce application.

In this chapter, we will look at how users can be managed in more detail and understand how some of the key profile settings are used within the Salesforce CRM application.

We will start to look into the ways in which a user's profile controls both access to objects and also governs what features are available to that user.

Generally speaking, objects represent database tables that contain your organization's information and are discussed in detail in *Chapter 3, Configuration in Salesforce CRM*. For example, one of the key objects in the Salesforce CRM application represents account information.

Along with profiles, this chapter also begins to look at the concept of record sharing and provides a high-level look at sharing features within Salesforce. It also describes how these features control access to records for users.

The term record describes a particular occurrence of an object. A specific record could be "American Express" or "Google" that is represented by an account object in our preceding example. We will now look at the following:

- Introduction to record ownership, profiles, and sharing
- Managing users in Salesforce

Introduction to record ownership, profiles, and sharing

Before looking at the features available to manage users, we start with a brief introduction to the concepts of record owner, profiles, and sharing in Salesforce CRM.

Record owner

The terminology "record owner" is reflected throughout Salesforce and for each and every data record there can be one and only one record owner.

Only users that are active in Salesforce can have records assigned to them.

When a user is marked inactive in Salesforce CRM, he/she no longer has access to the application. However, any records that this inactive user owns remain in the application and continue to show the inactive user as the record owner.

The record owner setting generally determines if access to that record is available to other users within the organization, and is enabled using either profile or sharing settings.

Profiles and sharing

Profiles, sharing, and the optional role hierarchy setting work together and should be considered as a whole when setting up record ownership and data access for users. An overview of the relationship between users, profiles, and the sharing settings can be pictured as follows:

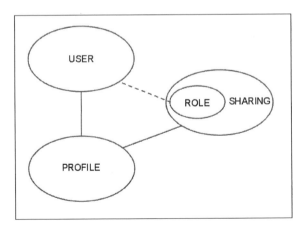

All users in Salesforce must be assigned a profile. The profile is a control mechanism used to determine which functions the user can perform, which types of data they can access, and which operations they can carry out on that data.

All users are associated with sharing mechanisms in Salesforce, which determine the actual records the user can access. Controlling the level of record access can be achieved using options ranging from default sharing, which is set at the organization level, to role hierarchy and beyond using advanced sharing mechanisms. A user does not have to be assigned to a role in Salesforce.

The sharing rules are briefly outlined as follows and covered in far more detail later in this book.

Profiles

Some of the key controls of the profile are to identify the type of license specified for the user, any login hours or IP address restrictions, and control access to objects. If the appropriate object-level permission is not set on the user's profile, the user will be unable to access the records of that object type in the application.

Profiles never override your organization's sharing model or role hierarchy. For example, a profile may be set to allow a user access to create, edit, and delete leads. However, a user with this profile cannot edit or delete other users' leads if your organization's lead sharing model is read only.

In the next chapter, we will look in detail at the features that the profile controls, which include tabs, object-level security, field-level security, Apex/Visualforce page accessibility, console layout, application selections, and administrative and general user permissions.

There are two types of profile in Salesforce—standard and custom—with each standard or custom profile belonging to exactly one user license type.

Standard profiles and custom profiles are similar in nature. The difference being that for standard profiles, the following settings cannot be applied: administrative permissions, general user permissions, and object-level permissions, plus notably the **Password Never Expires** setting, which means you are not required to change your password after a certain amount of time (this is a part of the password policies, which are described later). Hence, you must create a custom profile if you want to enable any of these features.

There are six standard profile types which are as follows:

- Contract manager
- Marketing user
- System administrator
- Solution manager
- Standard user

 Read-only standard profiles have their uses, but it is wise to limit that use to cloning them to create custom profiles. It is not unknown for Salesforce to change the settings for standard profiles when a new release is rolled out, which can result in an undesired outcome for any user assigned with that profile.

Sharing

Sharing settings control the default access for each object across the organization. Sharing rules per object can grant access beyond the default sharing settings; they cannot restrict access. The default sharing settings are as follows:

- **Controlled by Parent**
- **Private**
- **Public Read Only**
- **Public Read/Write**
- **Public Read/Write/Transfer**
- **Public Full Access**
- **Grant Access Using Hierarchies**

When the **Grant Access Using Hierarchies** setting is enabled, the role of the record owner determines visibility throughout the organization. Users in higher roles in the hierarchy will have full access (view/edit/delete) to all records owned by those at a lower level in the role hierarchy.

If **Grant Access Using Hierarchies** is not enabled, all roles are treated equally regardless of the hierarchy.

 Grant Access Using Hierarchies is only applicable for custom objects since they cannot be disabled for standard objects.

Roles

Roles are the principal elements in sharing rules. Users can be grouped into roles based upon their need for access to data, according to how they fit into the role hierarchy. Creating a role for every user's job title is not required.

Roles are accessed throughout the application and are particularly important for reporting. For instance, if you have two departments, "Operations" and "Sales", you can run comparative reports on both roles.

Roles generally report to another role and are used to maintain the role hierarchy. It is a one-to-many hierarchical relationship with the hierarchy, allowing managers to see the data of the users that report to them. Users at any given role level are always able to view, edit, and report on all data owned by or shared with users below them in the hierarchy.

 You can create up to 500 roles for your organization.

Role hierarchies do not need to specifically match your organization chart. Instead, each role in the hierarchy should represent a level of data access required by users.

Permission sets

Permission sets allow you to further control access to the system for the users in your organization. They can be considered as a method to fine-tune the permissions for selected individuals and enable access in a similar way to the setting up of profiles.

 Permission sets allow you to grant further access but not to restrict or deny access.

While an individual user can have only one profile, you can assign multiple permissions and permission sets to users. For example, you can create a permission called *Convert Leads* that provides the facility for converting and transferring the leads and assign it to a user who has a profile, which does not provide lead conversion. You can create a permission called *Edit Contacts* and assign it to a user who has a profile that does not provide contact editing. You can also group these permissions into a permission set to create specific profile-like permissions without actually having to create or clone complete profiles, which are often unnecessary.

 You can create up to 1,000 permission sets for your organization.

Permission sets are an ideal mechanism to apply system access for your users without affecting all other users that have the same profile and without having to create one-off profiles, which sometimes lead to an increase in the amount of maintenance.

A common use for permission sets is to grant additional permissions in addition to the settings listed in a profile to individuals without changing their profile. For example, to provide more rights than their profile currently allows.

Creating Permission sets

To create a permission set, navigate to **Your Name | Setup | (Administration Setup) | Manage Users | Permission Sets**. Click on **New**. Enter a label, API name, and description.

If you plan to assign the permission set to users that all have the same type of user license, a best practice is to associate that user license with the permission set. However, if you plan to assign the permission set to users that currently have different licenses (or may have different licenses in the future), it is probably best to create an organization-wide permission set.

To continue creating the permission set (as outlined previously), either select a user license or select the option **--None--** (to create an organization-wide permission set). Now finally, click on **Save**.

When you clone an existing permission set, the new permission set has the same user license and enabled permissions as the permission set it is cloned from.

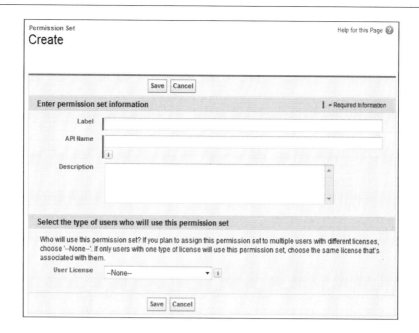

Managing users in Salesforce CRM

All users in your organization with access to Salesforce CRM require a username, an e-mail address, a password, and a profile along with an active user license.

Depending on the features your organization has purchased, you may have user options such as Marketing, Service Cloud, and Mobile, which give particular users the ability to access other features that are only available with a specific user license. A user can be assigned to one or more of these options.

You can also create and manage other types of users outside your organization by applying the appropriate licenses that provide limited access to your Salesforce organization.

In association with the user license, you can govern all users' access to data using the options available in either the profile settings or the sharing features.

Profile settings control access to applications and objects while sharing features control access to specific records.

To navigate to the user detail page, go to **Your Name | Setup | Administration Setup | Manage Users | Users**.

The user detail page shows a list of all the users in your organization as well as any portal users:

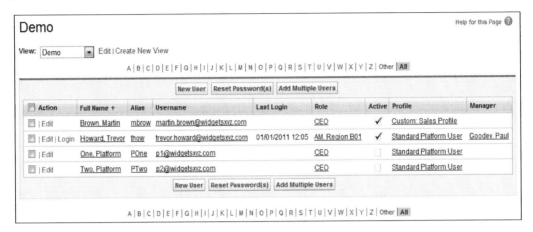

To show a filtered list of users, select a predefined list from the **View** drop-down list or click on **Create New View** to define your own custom view.

For example, you can create a view with search criteria of **Last Login, less than, LAST 28 DAYS** to show all users that have not logged in for 28 days as shown in the following screenshot:

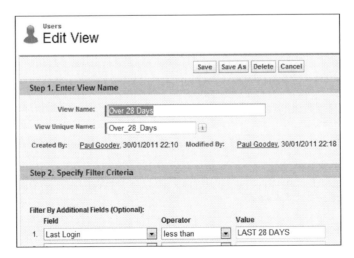

As the system administrator for Salesforce CRM, you can perform various user management actions such as creating new users, resetting passwords, and even delegating user administration tasks to other users within your organization. The following list of user actions will be covered:

- Creating new users
- Viewing and editing user information
- Password management
- Logging in as another user
- Creating custom user fields

Creating new users

The steps for creating a new user are as follows:

1. Click on **New User**.
2. Enter fields in the **General Information** and **Locale Settings** sections.
3. Check the box **Generate new password and notify user immediately**.
4. Save the new user details.

To create a new user for your organization, navigate to the user detail page. This page displays the list of all the users in your organization. To navigate to the **New User** page, go to **Your Name | Setup | Administration Setup | Manage Users | Users**. Now click on the **New User** button.

Looking at the top section of the page, you will see the **General Information** section:

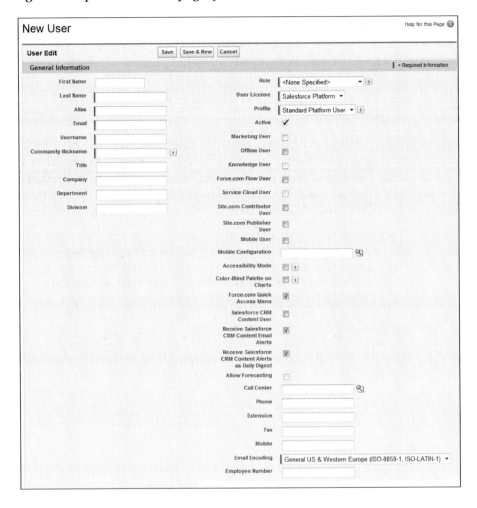

Enter the user's first name, last name, and e-mail address.

 The length of users' passwords cannot exceed 16,000 bytes.

The e-mail address automatically becomes the username, but you can change it if you require prior to saving.

Restricting the domain names of users' e-mail addresses

You can restrict the domain names of users' e-mail addresses to a list of values such as xxx@WidgetsXYZ.com, yyy@CompanyXYZ.com, and so on. After which, attempts to set a user's e-mail address to an unlisted domain (such as xxx@MyNonCompanyWebMail.com) will result in an error.

This feature can only be enabled by request to Salesforce customer support.

Then select a user license, noting that some further options become unavailable depending on the license type you choose. For example, the **Marketing User** and **Allow Forecasting** options are not available for Force.com user licenses because the **Forecasts** and **Campaigns** tabs are not available to users with that license. Now select a profile from the available list, which depends on the user license you have chosen.

You should consider the username that is entered. After the username is saved, it becomes a unique setting throughout the Salesforce.com universe, hence you will not be able to use that same username in any other Salesforce CRM application.

You can enable additional features by selecting one or more of the following checkboxes:

- **Marketing User**
- **Offline User**
- **Knowledge User**
- **Force.com Flow User**
- **Service Cloud User**
- **Site.com Publisher User**
- **Mobile User** (this checkbox displays if you have purchased Salesforce Mobile feature licenses)
- **Salesforce CRM Content User**

You will not be able to select these features if they are not supported by your user license type. Also, you will be unable to save the new user record if you do not have any remaining licenses available for these features.

At the bottom of the page, there are further sections, which include the **Locale Settings** section:

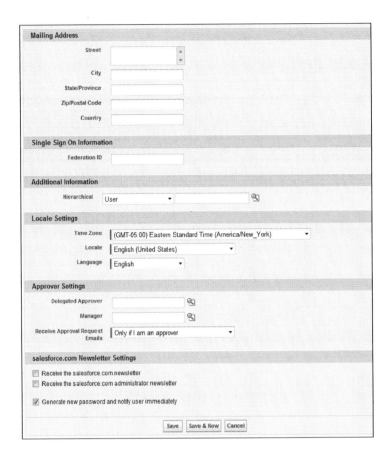

Complete the required information and then check the **Generate new password and notify user immediately** checkbox and save the details by clicking on the **Save** button. Upon saving, the user's login name and a temporary password are e-mailed via Salesforce.com to the new user.

Junk e-mail folder

If you have generated the new password to be sent, but the new user cannot see the e-mail notification from Salesforce.com in his/her inbox you may need to have the user check his/her junk e-mail folder.

The following table lists the key standard user fields with the required fields shown in bold:

First Name	Last Name	Alias	E-mail	Username
Community Nickname	Title	Company	Department	Division
Role	User License	Profile	Active	Grant Checkout Access
Marketing User	Offline User	Knowledge User	Service Cloud User	Mobile User
Mobile Configuration	Accessibility Mode	Color-Blind Palette on Charts	Salesforce CRM Content User	Receive Salesforce CRM Content Email Alerts
Receive Salesforce CRM Content Alerts as Daily Digest	Allow Forecasting	Call Center	Phone	Extension
Fax	Mobile	Email Encoding	Employee Number	Mailing Address Fields
Time Zone	Locale	Language	Delegated Approver	Manager
Receive Approval Request Emails	Newsletter	Admin Newsletter	Development Mode	Send Apex Warning Emails

The **Send Apex Warning Emails** field is used to send an e-mail to the user when an application that invokes an Apex script experiences issues. This feature can be used during Apex script development to test the amount of resources being used at runtime.

Grant Checkout Access provides a user with access to **Checkout**. Using **Checkout**, the user can purchase Salesforce.com licenses, AppExchange application licenses, and other related products. Additionally, within **Checkout**, the user can view the organization's quotes, installed products, orders, invoices, payments, and contracts.

After saving the **User Edit** page, you are presented with the details page for the user where you can view the information that was entered:

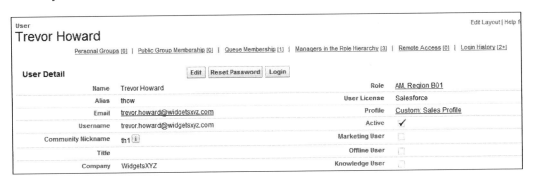

In the **View User Detail** page, the following read-only fields and related lists can be seen:

- **Used Data Space**
- **Used Data Space**
- **Last Login**
- **Last Password Change or Reset**
- **Checkout Enabled**

Do not overwrite active or inactive user records with new user data

Salesforce recommends not overwriting inactive user records with new user data. Doing so prevents you from tracking the history of past users and the records associated with them.

There are also situations where you may feel it appropriate to recycle an active user record, but it is better to deactivate users when they are no longer using Salesforce and create a new record for each new user.

A typical real-world example of recycling a user record, and one to avoid, is sometimes encountered when a sales team is organized into sales territories.

The sales team user records in Salesforce are stamped with a territory indicator and any account records that are located in their particular territory are assigned to the user record (set as the record owner). In this way, the user record simply acts as a container for the territory.

Managing user records in this way results in both audit and maintenance issues. For example, if Tina Fox changes sales territory her personal information (username, password, e-mail, address, phone number, and so on) all has to be transferred to a new user record requiring Tina to reactivate a new password, re-enter both personal details, and all her personal preferences in the Salesforce application.

The issue worsens if the user record (or territory) that Tina is reassigning to, is held by, say, Timothy Little as he would also need to reset his personal details.

This approach leads to a technically complex method of territory reassignment and a very disappointing user experience for your sales team. Fortunately, Salesforce provides features such as criteria-based sharing rules, sales teams, and territory management to better manage the organization of sales territories.

Adding multiple users

If you have several users to add, you can add more than one at a time. To add multiple users, navigate to **Your Name | Setup | Administration Setup | Manage Users | Users**. Now click on the **Add Multiple Users** button.

As you can see, this can be a quick method for creating users since not all required fields have to be entered in this page:

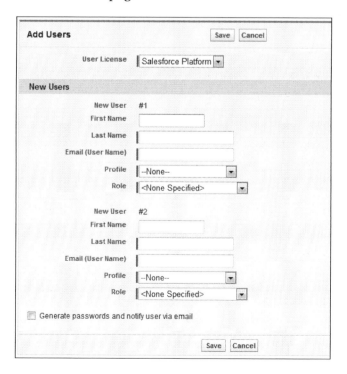

If, however, after the initial saving of multiple user records, you attempt to edit a user record, via the user edit screen, you will be prompted to fill up all mandatory fields.

Delegation of user management

If you have an organization with a large number of users or a complex role hierarchy, you can delegate aspects of user administration to users who are not assigned with the system administrator profile.

This allows you to focus on tasks other than managing users for every department or structure that your company has within Salesforce. This provides further benefits for global organizations that encounter time zone and cultural differences as it allows a user based in that region with local knowledge to create the users, which saves time and results in a better user experience.

For example, you may want to allow the manager of the Asia Pacific Operations team to create and edit users in the Asia Pacific Operations Team Leader role and all subordinate roles.

There are currently two options for providing this delegated user management access:

- Create a profile with the **Manage Users** permission
- Use delegated administration

Creating a profile with the Manage Users permission

This option is not recommended and should be very carefully considered as it allows a much greater range of system administration functions to be carried out by the user.

In addition to creating and managing users, the **Manage Users** permission also allows the user to perform the following:

- Expire all passwords
- Clone, edit, or delete profiles
- Edit or delete sharing settings
- Edit user login hours

By providing users with the **Manage Users** permission, as you can see, there are many other permissions that are switched on, which introduce security risks.

Using delegated administration

Delegated administration is a more secure method for providing delegated user management access as it allows you to assign limited administrative privileges to the selected non-administrator users in your organization.

Delegated administrators can perform the following tasks:

- Creating and editing users, and resetting passwords for users in specified roles and all subordinate roles
- Assigning users to specified profiles
- Logging in as a user who has granted login access to his/her administrator

To create delegated groups, navigate to **Your Name | Setup | Administration Setup | Security Controls | Delegated Administration**. Now click on the **New** button or select the name of an existing delegated administration group:

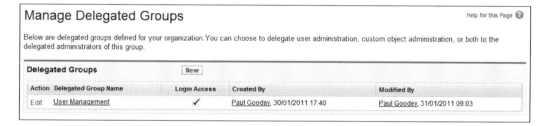

Here we look at the existing group that has been named **User Management**:

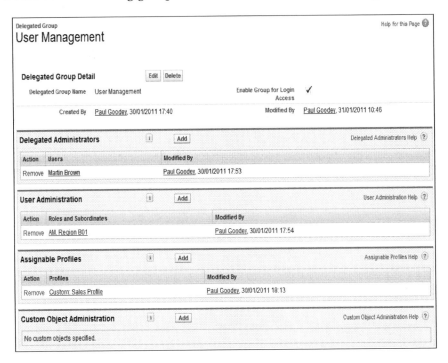

The **Delegated Administrators** section allows you to select and add the users that are to be given the delegated administration permission.

The **User Administration** section allows you to select and add roles which the delegated administrators can assign to the users they create and edit. They can assign users for the stated roles and all subordinated roles.

The **Assignable Profiles** section allows you to select and add profiles which the delegated administrators can assign to the users they create and edit.

To enforce security, profiles with the **Modify All Data** permission (such as the **System Administrator** profile) cannot be assigned by a delegated administrator. See the following example message shown when attempting to allow the delegated administrator to assign the **System Administrator** profile:

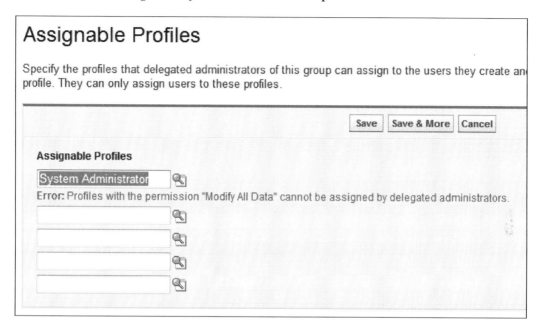

 If a user is a member of more than one delegated administration group, be aware that he/she can assign any of the assignable profiles to any of the users in roles he/she can manage.

Select the **Enable Group for Login Access** option, if you want to allow delegated administrators in this group to log in as users who have granted login access to their administrators and are in the roles selected for the delegated administrator group:

To look at how users can grant login access to their administrators, refer to the section *Logging in as another user* towards the end of this chapter.

Agreement in using active user licenses by delegated user administrators

If you have established delegated user management in your organization, you will need to have some agreement between yourself and the delegated user administrators about how many of the available licenses can be used for each area of the organization. You cannot automatically limit the number of active users that can be created by users with these permissions.

Viewing and editing user information

To view or edit user information, navigate to **Your Name | Setup | Administration Setup | Manage Users | Users**. Now, click on **Edit** next to a user's name. Change the necessary information and click on **Save**.

Users can also change or add to their own personal information after they log in.

If you change a user's e-mail address and do not select the **Generate new password and notify user immediately** option, a confirmation message will be sent to the new e-mail address that you entered to verify the change of e-mail. The user must click on the link provided in that message for the new e-mail address to take effect.

If you change a user's e-mail and reset the password for a user at the same time, the new password is automatically sent to the user's new e-mail address, and e-mail verification is not required.

Click on **Unlock** to unlock a user that is locked out of Salesforce.

The **Unlock** button is only available when a user is locked out.

Searching for users

You can use the search features (described in the previous chapter) to search for any user in your organization, regardless of the user's status. However, when using a lookup dialog from fields within records, the search results return active users only.

Deactivating users

You cannot remove users from the system, but you can deactivate their records so that they can no longer access the application. To deactivate users, navigate to **Your Name | Setup | Administration Setup | Manage Users | Users**. Now, click on **Edit** next to a user's name, disable the **Active** checkbox, and then click on **Save**.

If the user is a member of account, sales, or case teams, you are prompted to remove the user from those teams:

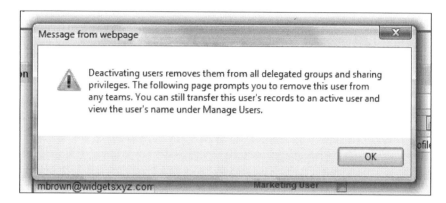

When deactivating users, there are some considerations that ought to be made, such as:

- Deactivating users with **Run as specified user** dependencies set on dashboards causes those dashboards to stop displaying. Each dashboard has a running user, whose security settings determine which data to display in a dashboard. You need to reassign **Run as specified user** to an active user with the appropriate permissions.

- As mentioned in *Chapter 1, Getting Started with the Salesforce CRM Application: Organization Administration*, in the *License information section*, Salesforce bills an organization based on the total number of licenses and not on active users.

- If **Chatter** is enabled and a user who has been included in either the **Following** or **Followers** list is deactivated and the user is removed from the list. However, he/she is restored to the lists if he/she is re-activated.

Password management

You have the following options for resetting passwords for users in Salesforce CRM:

- Resetting passwords
- Expiring passwords

Resetting passwords

If users have forgotten their password, they can click on the **Forgot your password?** link on the Salesforce CRM login page to have a new password link e-mailed to them:

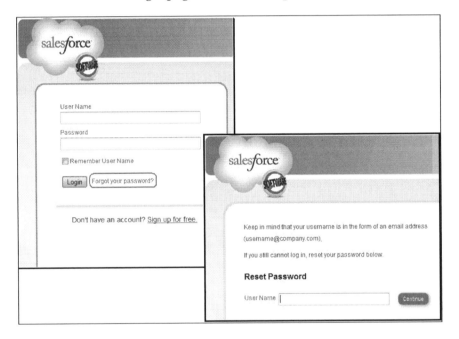

The user will need to answer a previously set security question such as *Where were you born?* before their password is reset and they can log in to Salesforce.

To reset a user's password, navigate to **Your Name | Setup | Administration Setup | Manage Users | Users**. Now select the checkbox next to the user's name.

Optionally, to change the passwords for all currently displayed users, check the box in the column header to select all rows.

Click on **Reset Password** to have a new password e-mailed to the user(s).

 After you reset users' passwords, some users may need to re-activate their computers to successfully log in to Salesforce (see the previous chapter).

Expiring passwords

You can expire passwords for all users any time to enforce extra security for your organization. After you expire passwords, users may need to activate their computers to successfully log in to Salesforce (see the previous chapter).

 This includes system administrators if they don't have **Password Never Expires** on their profile (or permission set), however, the standard **System Administrator** profile has the **Password Never Expires** setting activated by default.

To expire passwords for all users, except those with the **Password Never Expires** permission, navigate to **Your Name | Setup | Administration Setup | Security Controls | Expire All Passwords**. Now, select the **Expire all user passwords** checkbox and then click on **Save**.

The next time each user logs in, he/she will be prompted to reset their password.

 After you expire passwords, some users may need to reactivate their computers to successfully log in to Salesforce (see the previous chapter).

Password policies

There are several password and login policy features that help you to improve your organization's security. To set these password policies, navigate to **Your Name | Setup | Administration Setup | Security Controls | Password Policies**. Select the required settings and then click on **Save**:

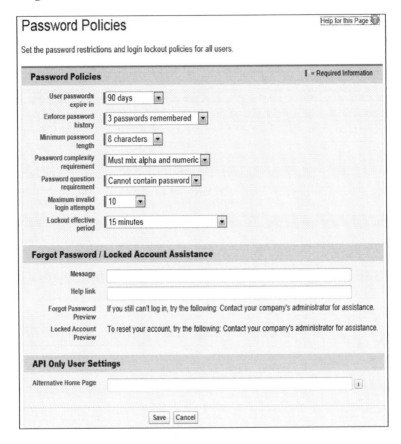

Let's look at each of the policies.

User passwords expire in

This sets the length of time until all user passwords expire and must be changed. Users with the **Password Never Expires** permission are not affected by this setting.

 The options are **30 days**, **60 days**, **90 days**, **180 days**, **One Year**, and **Never Expires**.

Enforce password history

This setting is used to remember users' previous passwords so that they must always enter a previously unused password. Password history is not saved until you set this value. You cannot select the **No passwords remembered** option unless you select the **Never expires** option for the **User passwords expire in** field.

 The options are either **No passwords remembered** or a number between one and fifteen passwords remembered.

Minimum password length

This sets the minimum number of characters required for a password. When you set this value, existing users are not affected until the next time they change their passwords.

 The options are five characters, eight characters, or ten characters.

Password complexity requirement

This sets a restriction on which types of characters must be used in a user's password. The options are **No Restriction** and **Must mix alpha and numeric**, which requires at least one alphabetic character and one number.

 The **Must mix alpha and numeric** option is the default option.

Password question requirement

This setting requires that a user's answer to the password hint question does not contain the password itself. The option is either set or not set.

 The policy that a user's answer to the password hint question does not contain the password itself is the default setting.

Maximum invalid login attempts

This sets the number of incorrect login attempts allowed by a user before they become locked out. The options are **No limit**, **3**, **5**, and **10**.

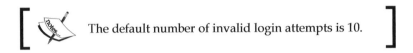

The default number of invalid login attempts is 10.

Lockout effective period

This sets the duration of the login lockout. The options are **15 minutes**, **30 minutes**, **60 minutes**, and **Forever** (must be reset by admin).

The default lockout effective period is 15 minutes.

If a user becomes locked out, he/she can either wait until the lockout effective period expires or you can view the user's information and click on **Unlock**. The **Unlock** button is only displayed when a user is locked out.

Forgot Password or Locked Account Assistance

The following sections discuss the available options.

Message

By setting this message, the text will appear in the lockout e-mail that users receive whenever they need you to reset their password. Your users will also see the message text in the confirm identity screen and e-mail that they receive whenever their password is reset. This is useful to add your contact details and a personal message.

Help link

Setting this link results in the text above this option appearing as a web URL, which when clicked will allow your users to navigate to a separate page such as a custom help page, which you have available.

API Only User settings

API Only Users will be redirected to this URL after they have confirmed a user management change (such as resetting a password).

Logging in as another user

To assist other users, you can log in to Salesforce as another user. If you have been granted access, you will see a **Login** button on their user record if they have granted login access to their administrator.

System administrators can also log in as any user in their organization without asking users to grant login access.

 This feature is only available by request to Salesforce.com support to have this in your organization.

If you have had this feature activated by Salesforce, you can enable login access by navigating to **Your Name | Setup | Administration Setup | Security Controls | Login Access Policies**. On the **Login Access Policies** page, enable **Administrators Can Log in as Any User**. Finally, click on **Save**.

To log in as another user, navigate to **Your Name | Setup | Administration Setup | Manage Users | Users**. Now click on the **Login** link next to the user who has granted you access:

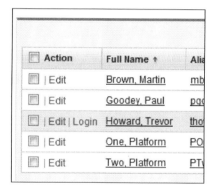

You can also log in as another user from the **User Detail** page using the **Login** button as shown in the following screenshot:

The **Login** link or button only appears for users who have granted login access to an administrator. After you have logged in as another user, you will notice a message at the top-right corner of all Salesforce pages that display the message **You are currently logged in as**.

To return to your administrator account, click on the logged in user's name (the user who has granted you access, Trevor Howard in this example). Then click on the **Logout** option:

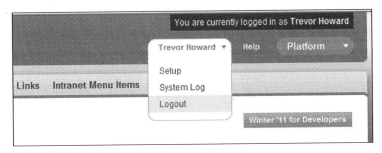

 Regardless of the login access policy, whenever an administrator logs in as another user, the login and logout events are recorded in the setup audit trail.

How-to guide to help users grant login access to you

There are many occasions when it is useful for you to log in as one of the users in your organization. This could be, say, to check data access from their role or profile or to check reports or dashboards and so on.

Rather than instructing individuals one-by-one, you can save time for both yourself and the users in your organization by preparing a how-to guide to help users grant login access to you. Produce a how-to guide that lists the steps that they need to take to make the required setting; the following is an example:

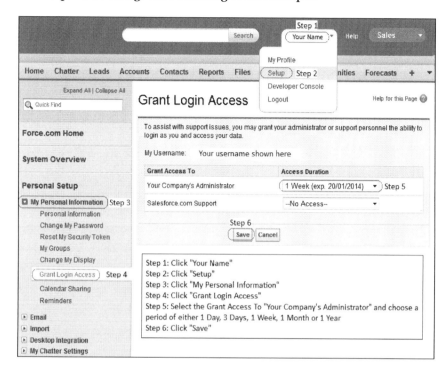

When the **Administrators Can Log in as Any User** feature is enabled, users will no longer have the option to grant login access to administrators, but they can still grant login access to Salesforce.com support.

Where additional apps have been installed, the list of entities that users can select to grant access may increase. For example, if your organization has installed the Non Profit Starter Pack app published by the Salesforce.com Foundation (see `http://www.salesforcefoundation.org/nonprofitstarterpack`), you will see the option to grant access to this organization's support team as shown in the following screenshot:

Creating custom user fields

You can create custom fields for users and set custom links that appear on the user detail page. To navigate to the user field's page, go to **Your Name | Setup | App Setup | Customize | Users | Fields** and then scroll down to the **User Custom Fields** section:

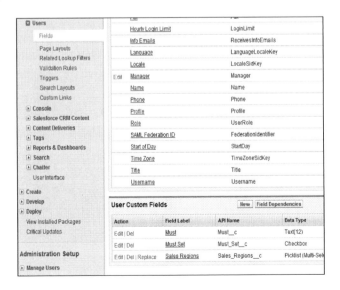

The User object can be considered as a special object in Salesforce as there are restrictions on what can be configured. For example, there can be only one record type and page layout for the User object.

Summary

In this chapter, we described the features for managing users within Salesforce CRM.

We looked at how user information can be accessed and the mechanisms for managing users' passwords.

We were introduced to the concepts of record ownership, profiles, and sharing, and discussed at a high-level how these concepts are used to control the application and record permissions for users.

We discussed other features to help with the administration of users using features such as granting login access to administrators and enabling delegated user administration.

In the next chapter, we will look in detail at the mechanisms for controlling access to data and the features that provide data management and record sharing.

3
Configuration in Salesforce CRM

In *Chapter 1, Organization Administration* and *Chapter 2, User Management in Salesforce CRM*, we were introduced to the profile feature in Salesforce, which is a controlling mechanism. Profiles are used to determine the functions users can perform, which type of data they can access, and what operations they can carry out on that data.

In this chapter, we will describe in detail the Salesforce CRM record storage features and user interface that can be customized, such as objects, fields, and page layouts. In addition, we will see an overview of the relationship that exists between the profile and these customizable features that the profile controls.

This chapter looks at the methods for configuring and tailoring the application to suit the way your company information can be best represented within the Salesforce CRM application.

We will look at the mechanisms for storing data in Salesforce and at the concepts of objects and fields. The features that allow this data to be grouped and arranged within the application are then considered by looking at apps, tabs, page layouts, and record types. Finally, we take a look at some of the features that allow views of data to be presented and customized, by looking in detail at related lists and list views.

The relationship between a profile and the features that it controls

The following diagram describes the relationship that exists between a profile and the features that it controls:

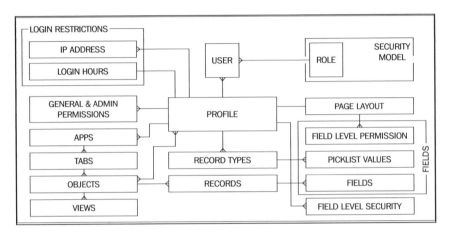

The profile is used to:

- Control access to the type of license specified for the user and any login hours or IP address restrictions that are set. This was covered in detail in *Chapter 1, Organization Administration*.

- Control access to objects and records using the role and sharing model. If the appropriate object-level permission is not set on the user's profile, then the user will be unable to gain access to the records of that object type in the application. This was introduced in *Chapter 2, User Management in Salesforce CRM*, and will be covered in detail in *Chapter 4, Data Management*.

In this chapter, we will look at the configurable elements that are set in conjunction with a profile. These are used to control the structure and the user interface for the Salesforce CRM application.

Objects

Objects are a key element in Salesforce CRM as they provide a structure for storing data and are incorporated in the interface, allowing users to interact with the data.

Similar in nature to a database table, objects have properties such as:

- Fields, which are similar in concept to a database column
- Records, which are similar in concept to a database row
- Relationships with other objects
- Optional tabs, which are user-interface components to display the object data

Standard objects

Salesforce provides standard objects in the application when you sign up; these include **Account, Contact, Opportunity**, and so on. These are the tables that contain the data records in any standard tab, such as **Accounts, Contacts**, and **Opportunities**.

In addition to the standard objects, you can create custom objects and custom tabs.

Custom objects

Custom objects are the tables you create to store your data. You can create a custom object to store data specific to your organization. Once you have the custom objects and have created records for these objects, you can also create reports and dashboards based on the record data in your custom object.

Fields

Fields in Salesforce are similar in concept to a database column; they store the data for the object records. An object record is analogous to a row in a database table.

Standard fields

Standard fields are predefined fields that are included as standard within the Salesforce CRM application. Standard fields cannot be deleted but non-required standard fields can be removed from page layouts, whenever necessary.

With standard fields, you can customize visual elements that are associated to the field, such as field labels and field-level help, as well as certain data definitions such as picklist values, the formatting of auto-number fields (which are used as unique identifiers for the records), and setting of field history tracking. Some aspects, however, such as the field name, cannot be customized and some standard fields (such as **Opportunity Probability**) do not allow the changing of the field label.

Custom fields

Custom fields are unique to your business needs and can not only be added and amended, but also deleted. Creating custom fields allow you to store the information that is necessary for your organization.

Both standard and custom fields can be customized to include custom help text to help users understand how to use the field:

Object relationships

Object relationships can be set on both standard and custom objects and are used to define how records in one object relate to records in another object. Accounts, for example, can have a one-to-many relationship with opportunities; these relationships are presented in the application as related lists.

Apps

An app in Salesforce is a container for all the objects, tabs, processes, and services associated with a business function.

There are standard and custom apps that are accessed using the **App** menu located at the top-right corner of the Salesforce page, as shown in the following screenshot:

When users select an app from the **App** menu, their screen changes to present the objects associated with that app. For example, when switching from an app that contains the **Campaign** tab to one that does not, the **Campaign** tab no longer appears. This feature is applied to both standard and custom apps.

Standard apps

Salesforce provides standard apps such as **Sales**, **Call Center**, and **Marketing**.

Custom apps

A custom app can optionally include a custom logo.

Both standard and custom apps consist of a name, a description, and an ordered list of tabs.

Tabs

A tab is a user-interface element that, when clicked, displays the record data on a page specific to that object.

Hiding and showing tabs

To customize your personal tab settings, navigate to **Your Name | Setup | My Personal Settings | Change My Display | Customize My Tabs**. Now, choose the tabs that will display in each of your apps, by moving the tab name between the **Available Tabs** and the **Selected Tabs** sections and click on **Save**. The following screenshot shows the section of tabs for the **Sales** app:

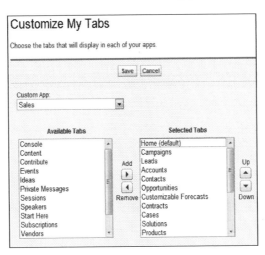

To customize the tab settings of your users, navigate to **Your Name | Setup | Administration Setup | Manage Users | Profiles**. Now, select a profile and click on **Edit**. Scroll down to the **Tab Settings** section of the page, as shown in the following screenshot:

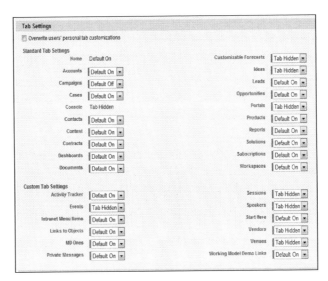

Standard tabs

Salesforce provides tabs for each of the standard objects that are provided in the application when you sign up. For example, there are standard tabs for **Accounts**, **Contacts**, **Opportunities**, and so on:

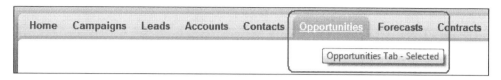

 Visibility of the tab depends on the setting on the **Tab Display** setting for the app.

Custom tabs

You can create three different types of custom tabs: **Custom Object Tabs**, **Web Tabs**, and **Visualforce Tabs**.

Custom Object Tabs allow you to create, read, update, and delete the data records in your custom objects. **Web Tabs** display any web URL in a tab within your Salesforce application. **Visualforce Tabs** display custom user-interface pages created using Visualforce.

Creating custom tabs:

- The text displayed on the custom tab is set using the **Plural Label** of the custom object, which is entered when creating the custom object. If the tab text needs to be changed, this can be done by changing the **Plural Label** stored on the custom object.

- Salesforce.com recommends selecting the **Append** tab to users' existing personal customizations checkbox. This benefits your users as they will automatically be presented with the new tab and can immediately access the corresponding functionality without having to first customize their personal settings themselves.

- It is recommended that you do not show tabs—by setting appropriate permissions—so that the users in your organization cannot see any of your changes until you are ready to make them available.

- You can create up to 25 custom tabs in the Enterprise Edition and as many as you require in the Unlimited Edition.

To create custom tabs for a custom object, navigate to **Your Name | Setup | App Setup | Create | Tabs**. Now, select the appropriate tab type and/or object from the available selections, as shown in the following screenshot:

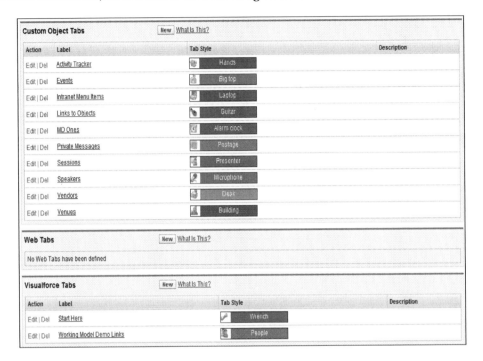

Renaming labels for standard tabs, standard objects, and standard fields

Labels generally reflect the text that is displayed and presented to your users in the user interface and in reports within the Salesforce application.

You can change the display labels of standard tabs, objects, fields, and other related user interface labels so they can reflect your company's terminology and business requirements better. For example, the **Accounts** tab and object could be changed to **Clients**; similarly, **Opportunities** to **Deals**, and **Leads** to **Prospects**. Once changed, the new label is displayed on all user pages.

The **Setup Pages** and **Setup Menu** sections cannot be modified and do not include any renamed labels and continue. Here, the standard tab, object, and field reference continues to use the default, original labels. Also, the standard report names and views continue to use the default labels and are not renamed.

To change standard tab, objects, and field labels, navigate to **Your Name | Setup | App Setup | Customize | Tabs Names and Labels | Rename Tabs and Labels**. Now, select a language, and then click on **Edit** to modify the tab names and standard field labels:

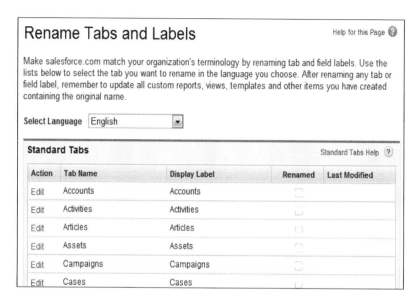

Click on **Edit** to select the tab that you wish to rename.

 Although the screen indicates that this is a change for the tab's name, this selection will also allow you to change the labels for the object and fields in addition to the tab name. To change field labels, click through to step 2. Enter the new field labels.

Here, we are going to rename the **Accounts** tab to **Clients**. Enter the **Singular** and **Plural** names and then click on **Next**:

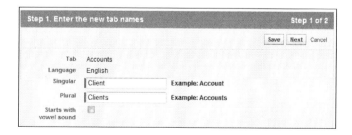

Only the following standard tabs and objects can be renamed:

Accounts, Activities, Articles, Assets, Campaigns, Cases, Contacts, Contracts, Documents, Events, Ideas, Leads, Libraries, Opportunities, Opportunity Products, Partners, Price Books, Products, Quote Line Items, Quotes, Solutions, Tasks.

Tabs such as **Home, Chatter, Forecasts, Reports,** and **Dashboards** cannot be renamed.

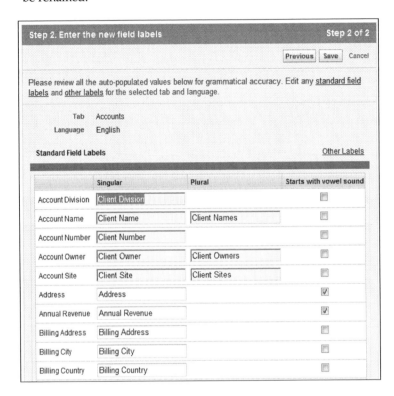

Salesforce looks for the occurrence of the **Account** label and displays an auto-populated screen showing where the **Account** text would be replaced with **Client**. This auto-population of text is carried out for the standard tab, the standard object, and the standard fields. Review the replaced text, amend as necessary, and then click on **Save**.

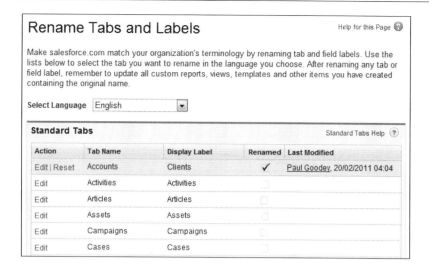

After renaming, the new labels are automatically displayed on the tab, in reports, in dashboards, and so on.

 Some standard fields, such as **Created By** and **Last Modified By**, are prevented from being renamed because they are audit fields that are used to track system information.

You will, however, need to carry out the following additional steps to ensure consistent renaming throughout the system as these may need manual updates:

- Check all list view names as they do not automatically update and will continue to show the original object name until you change them manually.

- Review standard report names and descriptions for any object that you have renamed.

- Check the titles and descriptions of any e-mail templates that contain the original object or field name, and update them as necessary.

- Review any other items that you have customized with the standard object or field name. For example, custom fields, page layouts, and record types may include the original tab or field name text that is no longer relevant.

If you have renamed tabs, objects, or fields, you can also replace the Salesforce online help with a different URL. Your users can view this replaced URL whenever they click on any context-sensitive help link on an end-user page or from within their personal setup options.

Creating custom objects

Custom objects are database tables that allow you to store data specific to your organization, in `salesforce.com`. You can use custom objects to extend Salesforce functionality or to build new application functionality.

 You can create up to 200 custom objects in the Enterprise Edition and 2000 in the Unlimited Edition.

Once you have created a custom object, you can create a custom tab, custom-related lists, reports, and dashboards for users to interact with the custom object data.

To create a custom object, navigate to **Your Name** | **Setup** | **App Setup** | **Create** | **Objects**. Now click on **New Custom Object**, or click on **Edit** to modify an existing custom object. The following screenshot shows the resulting screen:

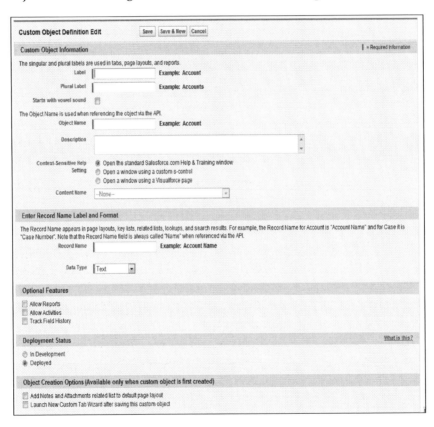

On the **Custom Object Definition Edit** page, you can enter the following:

- **Label**: This is the visible name that is displayed for the object within the Salesforce CRM user interface and shown on pages, views, and reports, for example.

- **Plural Label**: This is the plural name specified for the object, which is used within the application in places such as reports and on tabs (if you create a tab for the object).

- **Gender** (language dependent): This field appears if your organization-wide default language expects gender. This is used for organizations where the default language settings are, for example, Spanish, French, Italian, German, among many others. Your personal language-preference setting does not affect whether the field appears or not. For example, if your organization's default language is English but your personal language is French, you will not be prompted for gender when creating a custom object.

- **Starts with a vowel sound**: Use of this setting depends on your organization's default language and is a linguistic check to allow you to specify whether your label is to be preceded by an "an" instead of a "a"; for example, resulting in reference to the object as "an Order" instead of "a Order".

- **Object Name**: A unique name used to refer to the object. Here, the **Object Name** field must be unique and can only contain underscores and alphanumeric characters. It must also begin with a letter, not contain spaces, not contain two consecutive underscores, and not end with an underscore.

- **Description**: An optional description of the object. A meaningful description will help to explain the purpose of your custom objects when you are viewing them in a list.

- **Context-Sensitive Help Setting**: Defines what information is displayed when your users click on the **Help for this Page** context-sensitive help link from the custom object record home (overview), edit, and detail pages, as well as list views and related lists. The **Help & Training** link at the top of any page is not affected by this setting; it always opens the Salesforce **Help & Training** window.

- **Record Name**: This is the name that is used in areas such as page layouts, search results, key lists, and related lists, as shown next.

- **Data Type**: This sets the type of field for the record name. Here the data type can be either text or auto-number. If the data type is set to be **Text**, then when a record is created, users must enter a text value, which does not need to be unique. If the data type is set to be **Auto Number**, it becomes a read-only field whereby new records are automatically assigned a unique number:

Enter Record Name Label and Format
The Record Name appears in page layouts, key lists, related lists, lookups, and search results. For example, th "Case Number". Note that the Record Name field is always called "Name" when referenced via the API.

Record Name		Example: Account Name
Data Type	Auto Number ▾	
Display Format		Example: A-{0000} What Is This?
Starting Number		

- **Display Format**: As in the preceding example, this option only appears when the **Data Type** field is set to **Auto Number**. It allows you to specify the structure and appearance of the **Auto Number** field. For example: {YYYY}{MM}-{000} is a display format that produces a 4-digit year, 2-digit month prefix to a number with leading zeros padded to three digits. Example data output would include: **201203-001; 201203-066; 201203-999; 201203-1234**.

  It is worth noting that although you can specify the number to be three digits, if the number of records created becomes over 999, the record will still be saved but the automatically incremented number becomes 1000, 1001, and so on.

- **Starting Number**: As described, **Auto Number** fields in Salesforce CRM are automatically incremented for each new record. Here, you must enter the starting number for the incremental count (which does not have to be set to start from 1).

- **Allow Reports**: This setting is required if you want to include the record data from the custom object in any report or dashboard analytics.

> Such relationships can be either a lookup or a master-detail.
>
> Lookup relationships create a relationship between two records so that you can associate them with each other. A master-detail relationship creates a relationship between records where the master record controls certain behaviors of the detail record such as record deletion and security.

When the custom object has a master-detail relationship with a standard object or is a lookup object on a standard object, a new report type will appear in the standard report category. The new report type allows the user to create reports that relate the standard object to the custom object, which is done by selecting the standard object for the report type category instead of the custom object.

- **Allow Activities**: Allows users to include tasks and events related to the custom object records, which appear as a related list on the custom object page.

- **Track Field History**: Enables the tracking of data-field changes on the custom object records, such as who changed the value of a field and when it was changed. Fields history tracking also stores the value of the field before and after the fields edit. This feature is useful for auditing and data-quality measurement and is also available within the reporting tools.

- **Deployment Status**: Indicates whether the custom object is now visible and available for use by other users. This is useful as you can easily set the status to **In Development** until you are happy for users to start working with the new object.

- **Add Notes & Attachments**: This setting allows your users to record notes and attach files to the custom object records. When this is specified, a related list with the **New Note** and **Attach File** buttons automatically appears on the custom object record page where your users can enter notes and attach documents.

The **Add Notes & Attachments** option is only available when you create a new object.

Launch the New Custom Tab Wizard: Starts the custom tab wizard after you save the custom object.

The **New Custom Tab Wizard** option is only available when you create a new object.

Object Limits

You can access **Object Limits** pages when planning how to customize a particular object, or to monitor the current usage and limits, such as the number of custom fields or rules applied.

Standard objects

To access the standard **Object Limits** page, navigate to **Your Name | Setup | (App Setup) | Customize**. Click on the name of the desired standard object, and then click on the limits, as shown in the following screenshot (for the **Account** object):

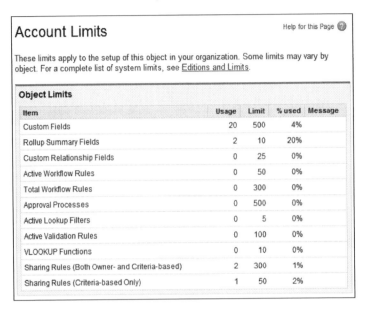

Here, you can see usage details for the following: **Custom Fields, Rollup Summary Fields, Custom Relationship Fields, Active Workflow Rules**, Total **Workflow Rules, Approval Processes, Active Lookup** Filters, **Active Validation Rules, VLOOKUP Functions, Sharing Rules (Both Owner- and Criteria-based)**, and **Sharing Rules (Criteria-based Only)**.

Custom objects

To view information about the usage of various fields and rules that have been created on a custom object, you can access the **Object Limits** window displayed on a custom object definitions related list at the bottom of a custom object definition page.

> When an item reaches 75 percent or more of the limit allowed for the object, a warning message appears that identifies what can be done to reduce the amount of usage. The object limit percentages display values that are truncated, and not rounded up. For example, if your organization reaches 79.55 percent of the limit for an item, the limit percentage displays 79 percent.

Creating custom object relationships

Considerations to be observed when creating object relationships are as follows:

- Create the object relationships as a first step before starting to build the custom fields, page layouts, and any related list

- The **Related To** entry cannot be modified after you have saved the object relationship

 Each custom object can have up to two master-detail relationships and up to 25 total relationships.

- When planning to create a master-detail relationship on an object, be aware that it can only be created before the object contains record data

- Clicking on **Edit List Layout** allows you to choose columns for the key views and lookups

- The **Standard Name** field is required on all custom object-related lists and also on any page layouts

Creating custom fields

Before you begin to create custom fields, it is worth spending some time to first plan and choose the most appropriate type of field to create. You can create many different custom field types in Salesforce CRM, including text, number, currency, as well as relationship types that enable lookup, master-detail, and hierarchical relationships.

Adding custom fields can be carried out by navigating to the field's area of the appropriate object:

- For standard objects, navigate to **Your Name** | **Setup** | **App Setup** | **Customize**. Now, select the appropriate object from the **Customize** menu, click on **Fields**, and then click on **New** in the **Custom Fields & Relationships** section of the object page.

- For custom task and event fields, navigate to **Your Name** | **Setup** | **App Setup** | **Customize** | **Activities** | **Activity Custom Fields**. Now, click on the **New** button.

- For custom objects, navigate to **Your Name** | **Setup** | **App Setup** | **Create** | **Objects**. Now, select one of the custom objects in the list. Next, click on **New** in the **Custom Fields & Relationships** section of the page.

Field dependencies and field history tracking

From these pages, you can set field dependencies and field history tracking for the objects. Field history tracking captures information for the date, time, nature of the change, and who made the change. A dependent field is a picklist field for which the valid values depend on the value of another field. Field dependencies and field history tracking is not available for task and event fields, as described later in this chapter.

Whenever history tracking is set, a separate history data object is created for the object. This history data comprises the record ID and the history-tracked field names whose value has been changed. Here, both the old and the new record values are recorded.

Choose a data type for the field to be created. The following screenshot shows the first page (step 1) where a full list of data types (which are described in detail later) are available to choose from:

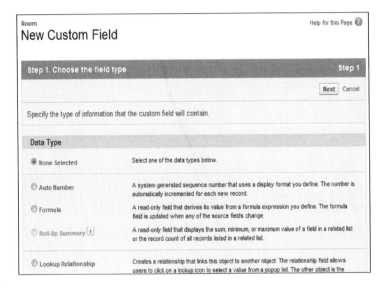

Field types not listed in custom field types may appear if your organization installed a package from AppExchange that uses those custom field types.

Some data types are only available for certain configurations. For example, the **Master-Detail Relationship** option is available only for custom objects when the custom object does not already have a master-detail relationship. The **Roll-Up Summary** option is only available for objects defined as **Master** in master-detail relation and is used to record an aggregate of the child records, using functions such as SUM, MAX, MIN (these are described in detail later).

Click on **Next** and enter a **Field Label**. **Field Name** is a mandatory field and must be unique within the Salesforce CRM application. There are also some restrictions on what can be entered. Here, you can only enter alphanumeric characters and underscores. In addition, the text must start with a letter; it cannot include spaces, it cannot contain two consecutive underscores, and the final character must not be an underscore.

Make both the custom field name and label unique in your application

Ensure that the custom field name and label are unique and not the same as any existing standard or custom field for that object. Creating identical values may result in unexpected behavior when you reference that name in a merge field. If a standard field and custom field have matching names or labels, the merge field displays the value of the custom field. If two custom fields have matching names or labels, the merge field may not display the value of the field you expect. For example, if you create a field label called Phone, the field name automatically populates as Phone__c. If you also have a standard field with the label Phone, the merge field may not be able to distinguish between the standard and custom field names. Make the custom field name and label unique by adding a suffix to each, such as Phone_Custom and Phone_Custom__c, respectively.

For relationship fields, choose the object that you want to associate with it:

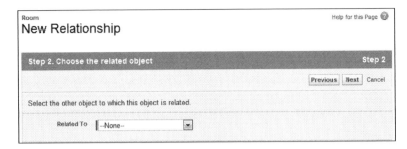

 The number of custom fields allowed per object is 500 for both Enterprise and Unlimited Editions of Salesforce. Relationship fields count towards these custom-field limits.

Enter any field attributes. In this example, a new checkbox field is set as **Checked** by default:

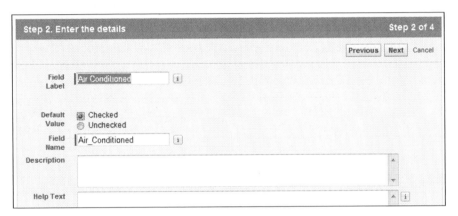

Object relationship fields allow you to create a lookup filter that can be used to further control the associated returned records and lookup dialog results for the field. These are available for **Lookup**, **Master-detail**, and **Hierarchical** relationship fields. Here, you can select multiple fields and selection criteria to restrict the results. This is presented in an additional step of the field-creation process and is available at the bottom section **Lookup Filter** available from the **Step 3. Enter the label and name for lookup field** setup page.

Click on **Next** to continue and specify the field's access settings for each profile:

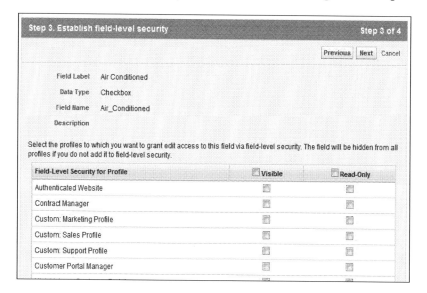

To set the field-level security, enable the following settings:

The Visible checkbox	The Read-Only checkbox	Result
Checked	Not Checked	Users can view and edit the field
Checked	Checked	Users can view but not edit the field

Click on **Next** and choose the page layouts that you would want to add the new field to:

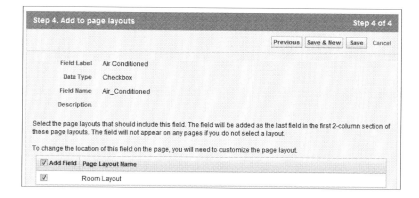

The new field is automatically positioned on the page layout as the final field in the first two-column section. However, there is an exception for **Text Area (Long)** and **Text Area (Rich)** fields. These fields, due to their double width, are placed as the final field on the first one-column section on the page layout.

> For user custom fields, the field is automatically added to the bottom of the user detail page.
>
> For universally required fields, you cannot remove the field from page layouts or make it read only.

Click on **Save** to finish, or on **Save & New** to create more custom fields.

For relationship fields, choose whether to create a related list that displays information about the associated records. You can choose to put the related list on any page layout for that object.

To change the label of the custom-related list as it will appear on the page layouts of the associated object, edit the **Related List Label** field. This is covered later in this chapter in the sections on page layouts and related lists.

To add the new related list to page layouts that users have already customized, check the Append-related list to users' existing personal customizations.

Custom-field data types

When creating a custom field, the first step is to select the appropriate type for the field. There are many different field types available in Salesforce that allow the storage of records of various data types, such as numbers, dates, and percentages. The following sections describe the data types that are available.

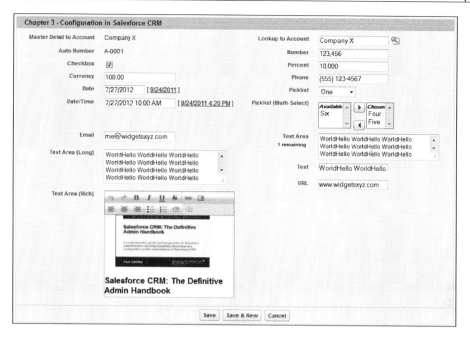

Auto Number

An **Auto Number** field produces a unique number that is automatically incremented for each saved record. As such, this is a read-only field where the maximum length is 30 characters, of which 20 are reserved for further prefix or suffix text that you can specify.

Checkbox

A **Checkbox** allows your users to set or unset a value to mark the attribute as either true or false.

> When using a checkbox field in a report, use True for values that are checked values and False for unchecked values. The import wizards and the weekly export tool use 1 for checked values and 0 for unchecked values.

Currency

Salesforce provides a **Currency** field to specifically capture a monetary value. Here, the Salesforce CRM application applies currency-related codes, which are applied when working with that field record.

Values lose precision after 15 decimal places.

Date

A **Date** field provides a way for your users to either pick a date from a pop-up calendar or to manually key the date. Your users can also enter the current date by clicking on the date link positioned to the right of the field.

Date/Time

A **Date/Time** field provides a way for your users to either pick a date from a pop-up calendar or to manually key the date and the time of day. Your users can also enter the current date and time by clicking on the date and time link positioned to the right of the field. Here, the time of day includes the A.M.-P.M. notation.

Email

An **Email** field provides us with the capability to store an individual's e-mail address. The Salesforce CRM application provides a very robust method of verifying the correct format of e-mail addresses before they are allowed to be saved. If this field is specified for contacts or leads, users can choose the address when clicking on **Send an Email**.

You cannot use custom e-mail addresses for mass e-mails.

Formula

A **Formula** field enables a method to automatically calculate a value that is obtained from other fields or values stored within Salesforce CRM. These referenced fields are known as merge fields. Formula fields are very powerful and flexible mechanisms. However, a formula field cannot be set to reference itself within a formula irrespective of whether the reference is made directly or indirectly. Further information concerning formulas is covered later in this chapter under the *Building Formulas* section. Salesforce uses the, round-half up, tie-breaking rule for numbers in formula fields. For example, 12.345 becomes 12.35 and −12.345 becomes −12.34.

Geolocation

The geolocation custom field allows you to identify locations by their latitude and longitude, and calculate the distance between locations.

> Geolocation is a compound field that counts toward an organization's limits as three custom fields: one for latitude, one for longitude, and one for internal use.

You can then use the geolocation field with the `DISTANCE` and `GEOLOCATION` formula functions to calculate distance between locations. For example, you can calculate the distance between two geolocation fields (such as between the warehouse and an account-shipping address), or between a geolocation field and any fixed latitude-longitude coordinate.

> The geolocation field is currently in beta release and so has the following limitations:
> - History tracking is not available on geolocation fields
> - Geolocation fields cannot be used on custom settings
> - Geolocation fields cannot be included in reports, dashboards, validation rules, Visual workflow, workflow, or approvals
> - Geolocation fields cannot be searched
> - Geolocation fields cannot be accessed within the Schema Builder
> - DISTANCE and GEOLOCATION formula functions are available only when creating formula fields or using them in Visual Workflow

Lookup relationship

The lookup relationship field creates a relationship between two records so you can associate them with each other. For example, opportunities have a lookup relationship with cases that enable you to associate a specific case with an opportunity.

A lookup relationship creates a field that allows users to click on a lookup icon and select another record from a pop-up window. On the associated record, you can display a related list to show all of the records that are linked to it, and you can create lookup relationship fields that link to the following: users, and custom or standard objects. See the **Building Relationship Fields** section for further options, discussed later in this chapter.

Master-detail relationship

This field creates a parent-child type relationship between records, where the master record controls certain behaviors, such as security and record deletion, of the detail record.

Master-detail relationship fields can only be created on custom objects that relate to a standard object and not the other way round. If the master record is deleted then all detail records are also deleted. You can create up to two master-detail relationship fields per custom object. See the **Building Relationship Fields** section for further options, discussed later in this chapter.

 As a best practice, salesforce.com recommends that you do not exceed 10,000 child records for a master-detail relationship.

Hierarchical relationship

This field type forms a hierarchical lookup relationship between relevant objects. For the user hierarchical relationship, users can use a lookup field to associate one user with another. For example, you can create a custom hierarchical relationship field to store each user's direct manager. See the **Building Relationship Fields** section for further options, discussed later in this chapter.

 This type of lookup relationship is available only for the user object.

Number

The **Number** field (data type) can be used to enter any number, with or without a decimal place (the number of decimal places can be specified), and saved as a real number with any leading zeros removed.

Percent

With **Percent** fields in Salesforce CRM, a percentage sign is automatically appended to the entered number.

 Fields values lose precision after 15 decimal places. If the decimal value is greater than 15 and a percent sign is added to the number, a runtime error occurs.

Phone

The **Phone** field allows the users in your organization to enter any telephone number. While saving the record, the Salesforce CRM application will attempt to format it into a known phone format.

When your users enter phone numbers in **Phone** fields, Salesforce keeps the phone number format that has been entered. However, if the **Locale** field is set to **English (United States)** or **English (Canada)**, 10-digit phone numbers and 11-digit numbers that start with 1 are automatically formatted as **(800) 555-1234** when you save the record. If you do not want this formatting for a 10- or 11-digit number, you can enter a + before the number, for example, **+44 117 123 4567**.

 If you are using Salesforce CRM Call Center, custom phone fields are displayed with the button, allowing click-to-dial functionality. Consequently, salesforce.com recommends that you do not use a custom phone field for fax numbers.

Picklist

The **Picklist** field allows users to choose a value from a set of predefined text values. The maximum length of the text values is 255 characters.

Picklist (Multi-select)

The **Picklist (Multi-select)** field allows users to choose more than one picklist value from a set of predefined text values. The maximum length of the text values is 255 characters. When saving and viewing, the data is stored as text along with semi-colons, which are used to separate the individual picklist values.

Roll-Up Summary

A **Roll-up Summary** field (or RUS) is used to automatically display the summarized values of the related records. This can be a record count of related records or a calculation of the sum, minimum, or maximum value of the related records.

 The records must be directly related to the selected record and on the detail side of a custom master-detail relationship with the object that contains the roll-up summary field. For example, a custom account field called **Total Number of Branches** displays the number of branches the custom object records in the branch-related list for **Accounts**.

Text

The **Text** field allows users to enter any combination of alphanumeric characters. The maximum length of the text value is 255 characters.

Text (Encrypted)

The **Text (Encrypted)** field allows users to enter any combination of alphanumeric characters. The text is then stored in an encrypted form (this data type can be availed by sending a request to Salesforce support).

 For encrypted text, you can set a maximum length of up to 175 characters.

Encrypted fields are encrypted with 128-bit master keys and use the **Advanced Encryption Standard (AES)** algorithm.

 Your master encryption key can be archived, deleted, and imported using the Master Encryption Key Management feature, which is made available by sending a request to Salesforce customer support.

Text Area

The **Text Area** field allows users to enter alphanumeric characters on separate lines. The maximum length of the text value is 255 characters and a warning is displayed when the number is about to be reached (as shown before).

Text Area (Long)

The **Text Area (Long)** field provides for the storage of up to 32,000 characters that display on separate lines, similar to a **Text Area** field. However, you can specify a lower maximum length of this field type, between 256 and 32,000 characters.

 Every time you press *Enter* within a long text area field, a line break and a return character are added to the text. These two characters count towards the 32,000 character limit.

This data type is not available for activities or products, on opportunities. Only the first 254 characters in a rich-text area or a long-text area are displayed in a report.

Text Area (Rich)

Using the **Text Area (Rich)** data type, your users are provided with a text field with an embedded toolbar. This toolbar allows simple formatting of the text and provides for the adding of images and URL web links.

 The maximum size for uploaded images is 1 MB and only GIF, JPEG, and PNG file types are currently supported.

Also, the toolbar allows your users to undo, redo, bold, italicize, underline, strike-out, add a hyperlink, upload or link to an image, and add a numbered or non-numbered list.

The maximum field size is 32,000 characters, which is inclusive of all the formatting and HTML tags and only the first 254 characters in a rich text area or a long text area will be displayed in a report.

URL

The **URL** field allows users to enter a web link.

 The **URL** field can store up to 255 characters. However, only the first 50 characters are displayed on the record detail pages.

When the web link is clicked, the Salesforce CRM application opens a new browser window to show the web page.

 When entering a value in currency or numbers fields

Whenever your users enter values into either a currency amount or a number field, they can use the shortcuts k, m, or b, to indicate thousands, millions, or billions. For example, when you enter 7k, it is displayed as 7,000.

Dependent picklists

Dependent picklists are picklists (including multi-select picklists) in which the values available in the picklist depend on the value of another field, which is called the controlling field.

 Controlling fields can be any picklist or checkbox field within the same record.

Controlling fields that are picklists are fields with at least one and fewer than 300 values. These are used to help with efficient, accurate data entry and help to achieve consistent data.

- To define a dependent picklist, navigate to the field's area of the appropriate object.

- For standard objects, this is carried out by navigating to **Your Name | Setup | (App Setup) | Customize |** (select the appropriate standard object) **| Fields**. Click on **Field Dependencies**.

- For custom objects, navigate to **Your Name | Setup | (App Setup) | Create | Objects |** (select the appropriate custom object). Click on **Field Dependencies**.

Now click on **New**, choose a controlling field and dependent field, and then click on **Continue**.

Use the field-dependency matrix to specify the dependent picklist values that are available when a user selects each controlling field value, as shown in the following screenshot:

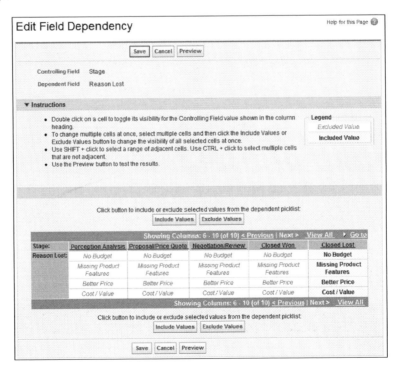

Finally, click on **Save**.

Please note the following points:
- Checkbox fields can be controlling fields but not dependent fields
- You can set default values for controlling fields but not for dependent picklists
- Multi-select picklists can be dependent picklists but not controlling fields
- Standard picklist fields can be controlling fields but not dependent fields
- Custom picklist fields can be either controlling or dependent fields
- The maximum number of values allowed in a controlling field is 300

Building relationship fields

When building lookup and master-detail relationship fields, there are various options and settings that you can set, which will enforce data integrity. These options and settings are covered in the next section.

Lookup relationship options

When you create a lookup field on an object, you can choose whether the lookup field is required or optional. If it is set as optional, you can choose one of the following three actions to occur if the lookup record is deleted:

- Clear the value of this field
- Don't allow deletion of the lookup record that's part of a lookup relationship
- Delete this record also

Clear the value of this field

This is the default option and is a good choice when the field does not have to contain a value from the associated lookup record.

Don't allow deletion of the lookup record that's part of a lookup relationship

This option prevents the lookup record from being deleted and is a good choice to restrict deletions if you have dependencies, such as workflow rules, based on the lookup relationship.

Delete this record also

This option works similar to the master-detail relationship and deletes the record whenever the lookup record is deleted. However, such a deletion on a lookup relationship is known as a cascade-delete and bypasses security and sharing settings. As a result, users can delete records when the lookup record is deleted even if they do not have access to the related records.

 The cascade-delete feature is disabled by default and is available only by sending a request to Salesforce support.

This option is a good choice when the lookup field and its associated record are highly coupled and you need to delete related data whenever the lookup data is removed.

 This option is only available within custom objects and is not available for standard objects. However, the lookup field object can be either a standard or custom object.

Master-detail relationship options

When you create a **Master-detail** field on an object, you can choose **Allow Reparenting Option**.

Allow Reparenting Option

By default, records in master-detail relationships cannot be reparented. However, you can allow child records in a master-detail relationship to be reparented to a different parent by selecting **Allow Reparenting Option** in the master-detail relationship definition.

Lookup filters

Lookup filters are used to restrict the values and lookup dialog results for **Lookup**, **Master-detail**, and **Hierarchical** relationship fields.

You can specify the restrictions by configuring filter criteria that compare fields and values based on:

- The current record
- The related object (via the **Lookup**, **Master-detail**, or **Hierarchical** field)
- The current user's record, permissions, and role
- The records directly associated to the related object

As an example, you can:

- Restrict the **Contact Name** field on an **Account** record to allow only those contacts that have a custom status of active, filtering out inactive contacts

- Restrict the **Contact Name** field on a case record to allow only those contacts that are associated with the **Account** record specified in the **Account Name** field on the **Case** record

- Restrict the **Account Name** field on an **Opportunity** record to allow only those users who have an **International** profile to create or edit **Opportunity** records, for accounts outside the United States

You can optionally click on **Insert Suggested Criteria** to choose from a list of lookup filter criteria that the Salesforce CRM system suggests based on the defined relationships between the objects in your organization.

You can make lookup filters either required or optional.

For fields with required lookup filters, only values that match the lookup filter criteria appear in the lookup dialog. Non-valid values manually entered into the field also prevent the record from saving Salesforce CRM displays an error message, which you can set.

For fields with optional lookup filters, only values that match the lookup filter criteria appear in the lookup dialog initially. However, users can click on the **Show all** results link in the lookup dialog to remove the filter and view all search result values for the lookup field. Optional lookup filters also allow users to save values that do not match the lookup filter criteria.

Building formulas

Custom formula fields require additional settings as specified by the Salesforce CRM application, which are carried out using the following actions and steps:

1. Create the **Formula** field.
2. Choose the data type for the field, based on the output of the calculation.
3. Enter the number of decimal places for currency, number, or percent data types.

The setting for the number of decimal places is ignored for currency fields in multi-currency organizations. Instead, the decimal places for your currency setting apply. Salesforce uses the, round-half up, tie-breaking rule for numbers in formula fields. For example, 12.345 becomes 12.35 and −12.345 becomes −12.34.

4. Click on **Next** to display the formula creation screen.

Basic formula

To create a basic formula that passes specific Salesforce data, select the **Simple Formula** tab, choose the field type in the **Select Field Type** drop-down list, and choose one of the fields listed in the **Insert Field** drop-down list.

To insert an operator, choose the appropriate operator icon from the **Insert Operator** drop-down list. Here, you can select from the following operators: **+ Add, - Subtract, * Multiply, / Divide, ^ Exponentiation, (Open Parenthesis,) Close Parenthesis, & Concatenate, = Equal, <> Not Equal, < Less Than, > Greater Than, <= Less Than or Equal, >= Greater Than or Equal, && And,** and **| | Or.**

Advanced formula

The basic formula feature is quite restricted and you will likely seek to create more complicated formulas which can be performed by selecting the **Advanced Formula** tab.

Within this tab, click on **Insert Field**, choose a field, and then click on **Insert**.

You can now include merge fields along with advanced operators as well as functions, which are prebuilt Salesforce CRM formulas that you can invoke and pass your input values to.

 Function description and example usage

Select a function and click on **Help** to view a description and examples of formulas using that function.

1. Click on **Check Syntax** to check your formula for errors.
2. Enter a description of the formula in the **Description** box.
3. If your formula references any number, currencies, or percent fields, choose an option for handling blank fields. To give any blank fields a zero value, choose **Treat blank fields as zeros**. To leave these fields blank, choose **Treat blank fields as blanks**.

4. Click on **Next**.

5. Set the field-level security to determine whether the field should be visible for specific profiles or not, and click on **Next**.

6. Choose the page layouts that should display the field. The field is added as the last field in the first two-column section on the page layout. For user custom fields, the field is automatically added to the bottom of the user detail page.

 Formula fields are automatically calculated. Therefore, they are not visible on edit pages and are read-only on record detail pages. Formula fields do not update last-modified date fields.

7. Click on **Save** to finish, or on **Save & New** to create more custom fields.

 Formula fields have character and byte size limits and cannot contain more than 3,900 characters.

Building formulas – best practices

Some best practices and methods to improve the creation and maintenance of formula fields are as follows:

- Formatting with carriage returns and spacing
- Commenting

Formatting with carriage returns and spacing

Consider the following formula:

```
Sales Tax (Percent) =
IF(TEXT(Account.Market__c) = "US", IF(TEXT(Account.State__c) =
"California", 0.0925, IF(TEXT(Account.State__c) = "Nevada", 0.081,
IF(TEXT(Account.State__c) = "Utah", 0.0835, 0) )) , 0)
```

To improve the readability of formula fields, you can add spacing and carriage returns. The preceding formula can be made far easier to understand, simply by adding spaces and carriage returns, as follows:

```
Sales Tax (Percent) =
  IF( TEXT(Account.Market__c) = "US",
    IF(TEXT(Account.State__c) = "California", 0.0925,
    IF(TEXT(Account.State__c) = "Nevada", 0.081,
    IF(TEXT(Account.State__c) = "Utah", 0.0835, 0) ))
  , 0)
```

Commenting

Salesforce CRM allows you to put comments in your formulas. These are sections of text that are not run as part of the formula and are typically used to make notes about the formula code, especially if it is particularly complicated. Comments must start with a forward slash followed by an asterisk (/*), and finish with an asterisk followed by a forward slash (*/).

Comments are useful for explaining specific parts of a formula to other system administrators viewing the formula definition. Look at the following code block as an example:

```
Sales Tax (Percent) =
/* value only set for US opportunities */
  IF( TEXT(Account.Market__c) = "US",
/* Check for the US State of the Account record and set accordingly */
    IF(TEXT(Account.State__c) = "California", 0.0925,
    IF(TEXT(Account.State__c) = "Nevada", 0.081,
    IF(TEXT(Account.State__c) = "Utah", 0.0835, 0) ))
  )
  , 0)
```

Carefully using comments to prevent parts of the formula from being activated allows you to test and verify the syntax as you construct and iron out bugs in the formula. However, if you try to comment out the entire formula as syntax, an error is shown. Also, you will experience a syntax error if you try to place comments within other comments because this is not supported in the Salesforce CRM application:

```
/* /* comment */ */
```

 Including comments and formatting with carriage returns and spacing adds to the number of characters used and therefore counts against the character and byte size limits.

Building formula text and compiled character size limits

There is a text character and byte size limit of 3,900 characters, and a limit of 5,000 characters for the compiled characters for formulas.

When this limit is reached, you will be unable to save the formula field and will be presented with the following error:

```
Compiled formula is too big to execute (7,085 characters). Maximum
size is 5,000 characters.
```

It is common to encounter these limits when building complicated formula field calculations and particularly so when building formulas that reference other formula fields. While there is no way to increase this limit, there are some methods to help avoid and workaround these limitations, listed as follows:

- Use the CASE function for branch conditions
- Use algebra

For formulas that use multiple branch conditions to derive the values, as in the preceding example formula, check if the market is US and the state is California, Nevada, or Utah. You can replace the nested IF statements and instead use the CASE statement.

Nested IF statements often result in larger compiled sizes where the IF function is used multiple times, as in our example:

```
IF(TEXT(Account.State__c) = "California", 0.0925,
IF(TEXT(Account.State__c) = "Nevada", 0.081,
IF(TEXT(Account.State__c) = "Utah", 0.0835, 0) ))
```

Using the CASE statement can provide better logic and often results in a smaller compiled size for the formula:

```
IF( TEXT(Account.Market__c) = "US",
  CASE(Account.State__c,
    "California", 0.0925,
    "Nevada", 0.0685,
    "Utah", 0.0475, 0) ,
  0)
```

Using algebra

The compiled size of formula fields increases as you increase the number of fields that are referenced. This is compounded when you are referencing fields that are themselves formula fields. A way to reduce the overall size is to use algebra to avoid the need to reference fields, wherever possible. The following example shows how the Item_Price__c and Support_Price__c fields are used multiple times:

```
Total Price =
(Item_Price__c + (Item_Price__c * Sales_Tax__c)) +
(Support_Price__c + (Support_Price__c * Sales_Tax__c))
```

To reduce the compiled size, use simple algebra to avoid multiple uses of the Item_Price__c and Support_Price__c fields, as in the following example:

```
Total Price =
(Item_Price__c * (1 + Sales_Tax__c)) +
(Support_Price__c * (1 + Sales_Tax__c))
```

Formula field size limit workarounds

There may be situations where the logic that is required for a formula is simply too complex for the current size limitations in formula fields. The proven methods to overcome this are to implement a solution using either of the following:

- Workflow field updates
- Apex trigger updates

There are two ways in which workflow field updates can help to provide the formula logic workaround. Firstly, larger and more complex formulas can be saved using the formula-building function within the workflow mechanism. Secondly, large formula logic can be decomposed into smaller functions of resulting data. For example, you could create simple formulas that get the data fed from fields that have been updated by multiple workflow field updates.

Workflows are covered in detail later in this book. However, the general approach for implementing a workflow field update to provide a solution to the formula field limit is to:

- Create a non-formula field on the object, such as a currency or number field, in place of the desired formula field. Administrators often identify this field with a suffix to indicate it is a workflow field—for example, **Total Price (workflow)**. This field is then set as read-only on page layouts as the field can be considered a system field (as it should not be available for manual updating).
- Create a workflow rule that will always fire.
- Create a field update with an appropriate formula to update the workflow field—**Total Price (workflow)** in our preceding example.

Any subsequent formulas can reference the populated field. The disadvantages to this workaround are that creating many workflows can add to the complexity of the application and may eventually introduce performance issues. Also, whenever an object has multiple complex workflows assigned, the order in which the workflows are evaluated cannot always be guaranteed, which if not properly maintained can lead to subtle data discrepancies.

Custom field governance

Controlling the creation of fields is necessary to avoid adding unnecessary new fields in Salesforce. Without appropriate field creation governance, there is a risk of producing an application with a complex data structure that provides a poor user experience.

This issue can often be observed due to the ease of creating new custom fields. However, there are other causes such as:

- Configuring spontaneous responses to end-user field creation requests without gathering full requirements

- Lack of specification or understanding of reporting requirements for field usage

- Creation of fields that are too specific for common uses, thus driving the need to create ever more fields

- Lack of knowledge or awareness of existing fields that could be used rather than creating new ones

As the number of unnecessary fields increases, users will find it ever more difficult to enter the correct data into the correct fields. Therefore, the amount of entered data is reduced along with users' satisfaction because the application requires less effort to work with. It is all too easy for your users to become dissatisfied and this can lead to less overall usage and hence poor data quality due to lack of user participation.

Addressing the issue

Create new fields with care because as each new custom field is added, your application structure increases in complexity. As a system administrator, you are responsible for knowing which fields are used, where they appear on **Page Layouts**, and which fields are required for reporting.

If the benefits and long-term use for a new field cannot be easily understood, it is unlikely to be of much use. One method to help determine its use is to consider where and how the proposed new field would be used. If it is never going to be reported, it may be worth querying its purpose and value. The following considerations can be made when creating new fields.

More generic field names

Try to make your field names more generic so that they can serve multiple purposes. In some situations, different business units share objects but track different information. Although they may have different requirements, they can often share fields. Here you need to be proactive, forward-thinking, and reach out to the business and propose fields that can be used across multiple business units.

Field history tracking

Often there are unnecessary date fields that are used to track milestones or data-processing dates. With native field history tracking, these milestones can be tracked and reported without the need to always create new fields.

Field history tracking can be applied on certain custom and standard fields for custom objects and the following core standard objects: **Accounts, Cases, Contacts, Contracts, Leads,** and **Opportunities** using the **Set History Tracking** button, as shown in the following screenshot:

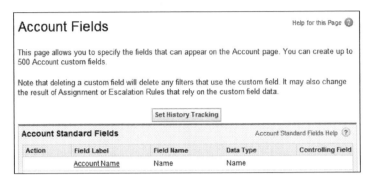

Upon clicking on the **Set History Tracking** button, a page appears, displaying the activation of fields history tracking and selection of the fields to be tracked, as shown in the following screenshot:

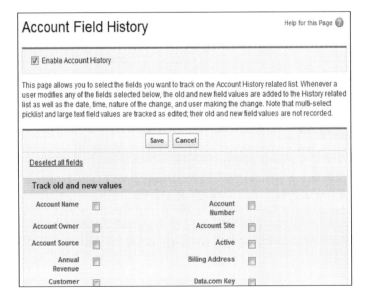

Changes to fields that have been set up for field history tracking will see a new entry to the object's history-related list whenever changes are made to records (where that field is modified). All entries include the date, time, details of the change, and the name of the user that made the change as shown here.

> Not all field types can have their history tracked. Changes to field types greater than 255 characters are tracked as edited; their old and new values are not recorded.
>
> Field history data does not count against your organization's storage limit, however. Salesforce auto-deletes field history data that is 18 months old or older for organizations created after 12:00 A.M. on June 2, 2011.
>
> You can request the disabling of the auto-delete mechanism by contacting Salesforce support.

Milestone objects

Create milestone objects and related lists to avoid hard-coding date fields on a record. For example, avoid creating fields to track dated historical financial information within an object. Here, you may have to create redundant fields for each year. For example, 2011 Budgets, 2012 Budgets, and so on. Instead, create a `Financials` object with one set of fields and a corresponding date field where you can create a new record each year. This can result in fewer fields and far better display and reporting.

Chatter

Consider the use of Chatter to eliminate unnecessary fields. Often, text-area boxes are used to track conversation flows such as support comments and internal review. These may no longer be necessary after Chatter is established. Chatter is covered later in *Chapter 7, Salesforce CRM Functions*.

Page layouts

Page layouts are used to organize the display of fields, custom links, and related lists on an object detail or edit page. They are used to establish unique layouts for different business scenarios.

The displayed fields within a related list are controlled by the page layout; the name of the related list is determined by the lookup/master-detail relationship on the related object.

Page layouts are comprised of sections. Within each section, the user interface can be set to make a field required or read only, as shown in the following screenshot:

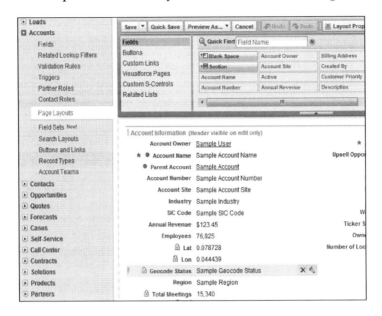

The enhanced page-layout editor showing read-only settings, as indicated with the padlock icons, is shown in the following screenshot:

In the corresponding **Account Edit** page, the read-only fields are displayed with no edit capabilities.

You can combine page layouts and field-level security to make the lowest possible permission setting. For example, a hidden field (field-level permission) will never be displayed regardless of page layout. Likewise, a field marked as **Always requires a value in this field to save a record** will always be required on the page layout.

Page layouts allow you to create and organize sections on a page and to show or hide fields within sections.

> Hidden fields may still be accessible elsewhere in the application. Use field-level security to restrict all possible means of accessing a field.

Creating and modifying a page layout

To create or modify a page layout, navigate to **Your Name | Setup | App Setup | Customize**. Select the appropriate object and click on **Page Layouts**. In the **Page Layouts** page, you can either click on the **New** button or choose the existing page layout to modify and click on **Edit**, as shown in the following screenshot:

Account Page Layout

This page allows you to create different page layouts to display Account data.
After creating page layouts, click the Page Layout Assignment button to control which page layou

Account Page Layouts   [New] [Page Layout Assignment]

Action	Page Layout Name	Created By
Edit	Del	Account (Marketing) Layout	Paul Goodey, 19/12/2009 13:01
Edit	Del	Account (Sales) Layout	Paul Goodey, 19/12/2009 13:01
Edit	Del	Account (Support) Layout	Paul Goodey, 19/12/2009 13:01
Edit	Del	Account Layout	Paul Goodey, 19/12/2009 13:01

When clicking on the **New** button, you can optionally choose an existing layout to copy.

> **Creating a page layout based on an existing page layout**
>
> In the enhanced page-layout editor, select an existing page layout from the list of page layouts, and then click on **Save As** to create a copy of the layout.
>
> In the original page-layout editor, select an existing page layout from the list of page layouts, and then click on the **Clone** button.

Enter a name for the new page layout and finally, click on **Save**.

You can set different page layouts for profiles and different page layouts for record types.

Record types

Record types are a feature of Salesforce CRM that allow you to provide different sets of object picklists, different page layouts, and custom business processes to specific users, based on their profile. Record types can be used in various ways, for example:

- Create record types for opportunities to differentiate your internal sales deals from your field sales deals and show different fields and picklist values
- Create record types for leads to display different page layouts for your tele-sales leads versus your internal sales prospecting functions

Creating a record type

The record type called Master is always set for every object and contains all the picklist and process options. It is not, however, listed under the record types list and it can be assigned as a record type for a profile, provided it is only assigned as a record type for that profile.

Since each record type is assigned to one page-layout type per profile, the numbers of page assignments can easily increase. This means that if you have two custom record types for an account and five profiles, you will have 15 page assignments (5*2 for each custom record type, and five for the Master record type).

Selectable record types are assigned per profile and field-level security is configured separately for each record type. Consider the following when creating a record type:

- Which record types are associated with the current profile?
- If more than one record type is associated with the current profile, prompt the user for record-type selection
- If only one, select that record type without prompting (this would be set as default)
- Based upon record type and profile, assign the appropriate page layout
- Based upon record type, assign the appropriate process and picklist values

By associating different record types to different page layouts, fields, and picklist values, you can formulate a set of object-specific processes. In Salesforce CRM, the following are available:

- The `Lead` process using the `Lead` object, which is governed by the `Status` field (which is configured to be open, closed, and so on)

- The `Sales` process, which uses the `Opportunity` object and the `Stage` field (set to be won, lost, and so on), plus the `Amount` and `Probability` fields

- The `Support` process, which uses the `Case` object and is controlled by the `Case Status` field (which may be set to open, closed, and so on)

- The `Solutions` process, which uses the `Solution` object and the fields `Status` (which are set to be draft, deployed, and so on)

For example, your sales team creates an opportunity that represents a sales deal. Your sales support team then up sells on this deal. You can then create two sales processes with two different record types and two different page layouts: **Sales** and **Support**.

You would want to create a lookup relationship from opportunity to opportunity, and only require or display this relationship for the support team profile.

You would also be able to configure the sharing rules so that they could not modify each other's opportunities. This is covered in detail in *Chapter 4, Data Management*.

Related lists

Related lists display on the lower portion of the object detail page to display the related record details. Related lists show the object records that are associated with that record.

From a related list, you can:

- Click on the object record name to view detailed information
- Click on **Edit** or **Del** to edit or delete the object record
- Click on **New** to create a new object record that is associated with the record you are viewing

To define if an object can be related to another type of record, you would use either a master-detail or a lookup relationship.

Here, we show how editing a page layout for the account object enables the arrangement and configuration of any related list:

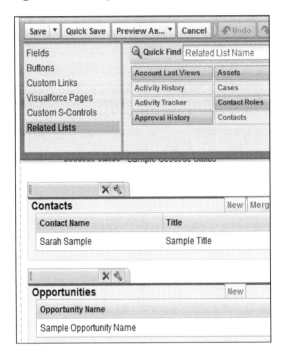

The following screenshot shows the results of changing the related lists in the page-layout editor screen when navigating to the **Account** detail page:

List views

When you click on a tab, the **Accounts tab** for instance, you will be shown the **My Accounts** field in that view. This is termed as a list view and can be seen as shown in the following screenshot:

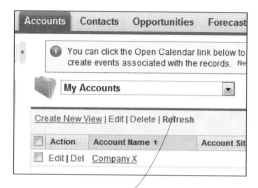

Other list views can be selected from the picklist:

You can modify existing views and define which columns and buttons (including standard and custom buttons) are to be displayed. You can click on **New** to create new views:

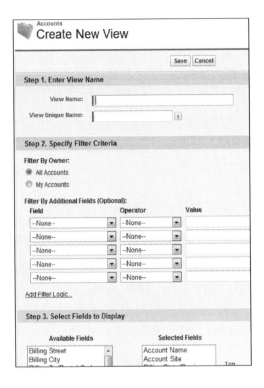

The following points apply to list views:

- Every object in Salesforce CRM that is associated with a tab automatically has at least one list view. If there is no tab set up for the object then there would be no corresponding list view.

- List views can be modified by assigning filter criteria to control which records are returned for the affected object.

- List views can be set up to be seen and accessed only by you, or you can set it to be accessed by certain roles and groups of individuals.

- List view has a print feature that can be used by you and your users. To print from a list view, click on the printable view button located at the top-right corner of the page, as shown next:

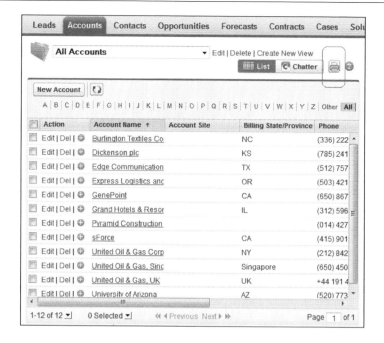

 Printable list views need to be enabled organization-wide for the print feature to be available. See user interface settings in *Chapter 1, Getting Started with the Salesforce CRM Application – Organization Administration*.

Force.com Quick Access Menu

Whenever you want to view or configure object or app-related setup information, use the Force.com Quick Access Menu to navigate directly to the relevant customization option.

The Force.com Quick Access Menu is available from object list view pages and record detail pages, and provides shortcuts to the configuration features within Salesforce CRM.

The menu can be accessed by clicking on the arrow located on the right margin of the screen, as shown in the following screenshot:

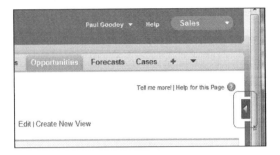

You can then use the links to navigate directly to the desired setup page or you can remove the menu by clicking on **Turn off menu** (this will remove the option from all list views and record pages), as shown in the following screenshot:

You can restore the menu by navigating to **Your Name** | **Setup** | **My Personal Information** | **Personal Information**. Now, click on **Edit** on the user detail page, select **Force.com Quick Access Menu**, and then finally click on **Save**.

Summary

In this chapter, we described the ways in which the data structure and user-interface features can be configured within Salesforce CRM.

We looked at how object and records information can be accessed. We also looked at the mechanisms for managing the methods that users use to view this information using views and page layouts.

We were shown how these record structures and user interfaces are controlled by the profile and the wider picture for the way configuration of these concepts are applied for users.

We discussed some techniques to help govern the way the configuration and creation of fields can be carried out and some common pitfalls to avoid.

In the next chapter, we will look in detail at the mechanisms for controlling access to data records and the features that provide data management and record sharing.

4
Data Management

In the previous chapters, we have looked at how Salesforce controls access to information using the user profile mechanism. We have seen how the appropriate object level permissions, such as create, read, update, and delete have to be set on the user's profile to allow the user corresponding permissions to the records of that object type.

In this chapter, we look at Organization-wide sharing defaults, roles, and other sharing settings which complement and extend the assigning of access permissions to users within the Salesforce CRM application.

This chapter also looks in detail at some of the mechanisms for controlling record updates and features available to govern and control the quality of data entered into the application.

Finally, we look at some of the data utilities that are available for importing and exporting data to and from the system.

Data access security model

There are several flexible options for you to control how records are accessed within your organization.

In the previous chapter, we looked at the broadest way that you can control data by setting properties for the objects that a user can view, edit, and create through the configuration and assignment of profiles.

We also looked at the creating of fields and field-level security which is set at profile level and is applied to records at the data storage database level. Returning to the diagram, we will now look at the security mechanism and security model shown at the top-right corner of the following diagram:

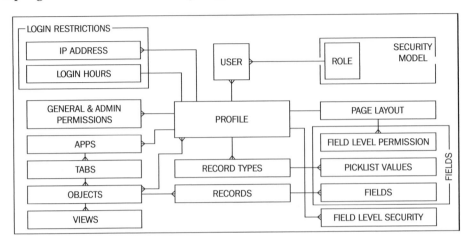

To specify and set the individual records that a user can view and edit, we now look at other mechanisms that can be applied, which are setting your Organization-wide defaults, defining a role hierarchy, and creating sharing rules.

The following diagram shows how, with the addition of each extra feature shown, the widening up of the access to records is provided:

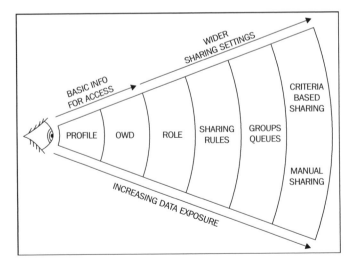

Organization-wide sharing defaults (OWD)

Organization-wide sharing settings are used to define the default sharing settings for an organization. For most objects, Organization-wide sharing settings can be set to **Private, Public Read Only**, or **Public Read/Write**.

Organization-wide sharing default settings, often referred to in Salesforce CRM as OWDs, specify the default level of access to records and can be set separately for most of the objects in Salesforce such as accounts, contacts, and activities.

As shown in the preceding diagram along with the user's profile, the OWD defines the baseline level of access to data records that users do not own. The diagram represents the visibility or data access which is increasing as the other features are incorporated to provide wider sharing settings.

To customize your OWD settings, navigate to **Your Name | Setup | Administration Setup | Security Controls | Sharing Settings**. Now click on **Edit** in the Organization-wide defaults area and then for each object, select the default access you want as shown in the following screenshot:

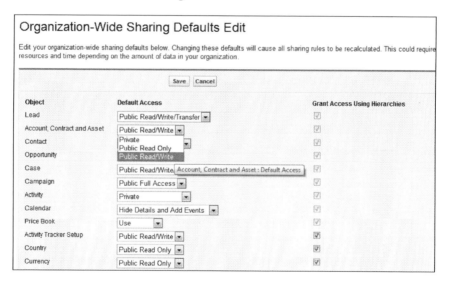

OWD access level actions

The Organization-wide sharing default (OWD) access levels allow the following actions to be applied to object records:

Access Level	Action
Public Full Access (Option for setting the **Campaign** object only)	Change ownership of record
	Search records
	Report on records
	Add related records
	Edit details of record
	Delete record
Read/Write/Transfer (Option for setting the **Lead** and **Case** objects only)	Change ownership of record
	Search records
	Report on records
	Add related records
	Edit details of record
Read/Write	Search records
	Report on records
	Add related records
	Edit details of record
Read Only	Search records
	Report on records
	Add related records
Private	No searching
	No reporting

Public Full Access (Campaigns only)

Access levels for the **Campaign** OWDs can be set to **Private**, **Public Read Only**, **Public Read/Write**, or **Public Full Access**. When **Campaign** is set to **Public Full Access**, all users can view, edit, transfer, delete, and report on all **Campaign** records.

For example, in the scenario where John is the owner of a **Campaign**, all other users in the application can view, edit, transfer, or delete that **Campaign**.

 This option is available only for **Campaign**.

Public Read/Write/Transfer (Cases or Leads only)

Access levels for **Case** or **Lead** OWDs can be set to **Private**, **Public Read Only**, **Public Read/Write**, or **Public Read/Write/Transfer**. When **Case** or **Lead** are set to **Public Read/Write/Transfer**, all users can view, edit, transfer, and report on all **Case** or **Lead** records.

For example, if Lucy is the owner of WidgetX case number 101, all other users can view, edit, transfer ownership, and report on that case. But only Lucy can delete or change the sharing on case 101.

 This option is available only for **Case** or **Lead**.

Public Read/Write

All users can view, edit, and report on all records.

For example, if Mike is the owner of the **Account** record Emerald Inc., all other users can view, edit, and report on the Emerald Inc. account. However, only Mike has the ability to delete the Emerald Inc. account record or alter the sharing settings.

Public Read Only

All users can view and report on records but they cannot edit them. Here, only the record owner and users above that user's role in the role hierarchy can edit the records.

For example, Nicole is the owner of the **Account** record EuroCorp Inc. and Nicole works in the International Sales department, reporting to Julia, who is the VP of International Sales. In this scenario, both Nicole and Julia have full read/write access to EuroCorp Inc.

Now, say Mike also works in International Sales; however, with the **Public Read Only** setting he can view and report on the EuroCorp Inc. account record, but cannot edit or delete it.

Private

Only the record owner and users above that role in the hierarchy can view, edit, and report on those records.

For example, if Mike is the owner of an **Account** record, and he is assigned to the role of International Sales, reporting to Julia, who is the VP of International Sales, then Julia can also view, edit, and report on Mike's accounts.

No Access, View Only, or Use (Price Book only)

Access levels for the **Price Book** OWDs can be set to either, **No Access**, **View Only**, or **Use**. **Use** is the default access level and allows all users to access the **Price Book** information as well as using the **Price Book** configuration for opportunities with products. **View Only** allows users to access **Price Book** information but not to use that **Price Book** detail in opportunities with products. **No Access** restricts users from accessing information for **Price Books** and **Prices**.

[This option is available only for **Price Books**.]

Granting access using hierarchies

By default, Salesforce uses hierarchies, such as the role or territory hierarchy, to automatically grant record access to users above the record owner in the hierarchy.

This automatic granting of access to users' data to other users higher up in the Salesforce CRM hierarchy can be disabled for custom objects using the **Grant Access Using Hierarchies** checkbox. When this checkbox is not selected, only the record owner and users granted access by the Organization-wide defaults gain access to the records.

Here we see the options available for setting some sample custom objects where, for the custom object **Country**, we have set the default access to **Public Read Only** and the **Grant Access Using Hierarchies** setting is checked as shown in the following screenshot:

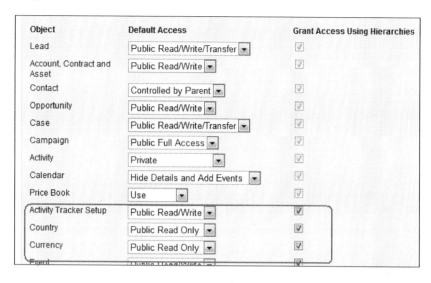

Controlled by Parent

When **Controlled by Parent** is set on an object a user can perform an action (such as view, edit, or delete) on the record based on whether they can perform that same action on the parent record associated with it. For example, if a **Contact** record is associated with the WidgetX account using **Controlled by Parent**, then a user can only edit that contact if they can also edit the WidgetX account record.

> **Tasks** and **Events** are by default set to **Private** (via the **Activity** setting as shown in the preceding screenshot). To allow users to update each other's activities (for example, to permit a user to set a task that they do not own to completed), you will need to set the **Activity** setting to **Controlled by Parent** and ensure that the object that is related to the activity is also accessible to that user.

When a custom object is on the detail side of a master-detail relationship with a standard object, its Organization-wide default is automatically set to **Controlled by Parent** and it is not editable, as shown in the following screenshot for the custom objects **Account Last View** and **Activity Tracker**:

Default Sharing Settings		
Organization-Wide Defaults	Edit	Organization-Wide Defaults Help ?
Object	**Default Access**	**Grant Access Using Hierarchies**
Lead	Public Read/Write/Transfer	✓
Account, Contract and Asset	Public Read/Write	✓
Contact	Controlled by Parent	✓
Opportunity	Public Read/Write	✓
Case	Public Read/Write/Transfer	✓
Campaign	Public Full Access	✓
Activity	Private	✓
Calendar	Hide Details and Add Events	✓
Price Book	Use	✓
Account Last View	Controlled by Parent	
Activity Tracker	Controlled by Parent	
Activity Tracker Setup	Public Read/Write	✓

 Although **Grant Access Using Hierarchies** can be deselected to prevent users that are higher in the role or territory hierarchy having automatic access, users with the **View All** and **Modify All** object permissions and the **View All Data** and **Modify All Data** profile permissions can still access records they do not own.

Organization-wide defaults need to be defined separately for any custom objects that are created in the Salesforce CRM application.

For some standard objects, you cannot actually change the Organization-wide sharing default setting.

For example, the Organization-wide default for the **Solution** object in Salesforce is preset to **Public Read/Write** which cannot be changed.

You can use Organization-wide defaults to set the default level of record access for the following standard objects where the default Organization-wide sharing settings are:

Object	Default Access
Accounts	Public Read/Write
Activities	Private
Assets	Public Read/Write
Calendar	Hide Details and Add Events
Campaigns	Public Full Access
Cases	Public Read/Write/Transfer
Contacts	Controlled by Parent
Contracts	Public Read/Write
Custom Objects	Public Read/Write
Leads	Public Read/Write/Transfer
Opportunities	Public Read Only
Price Books	Use
Service	Contracts Private

Granting users additional access

Where the Organization-wide default setting for an object is **Private** or **Public Read Only**, you can grant users additional access to records with the use of permission sets, role hierarchies, and sharing rules.

Sharing rules and permission sets can only be used to grant additional access and cannot be used to restrict access to records from what was originally specified with the Organization-wide default.

Permission sets

Permission sets allow you to further control access to the system for the users in your organization. They can be considered as a method to fine-tune the permissions for selected individuals and enable access in a similar way to the setting up of profiles.

While an individual user can have only one profile, you can assign multiple permissions and permission sets to users. For example, you can create a permission called **Convert Leads** that provides the facility for converting and **Transfer of Leads** and assign it to a user who has a profile that does not provide **Lead Conversion**. You can also create a permission called **Access Widget** which is associated to a custom object called **Widget** that is set in the Organization-wide defaults as **Private**. Here, you can assign it to a user who has a profile that does not include the ability to access **Widgets** through their profile settings.

It is a two-step process to set up permission sets for users which includes:

1. Creating the permission set from the **Permission Set edit** page.
2. Assigning the user to the permission set from the **User edit** page.

Creating the permission set from the Permission Set edit page

To view and manage your organization's permission set, navigate to **Your Name | Setup | Administration Setup | Manage Users | Permission Sets**. For a new permission set, click on the **New** button, and complete the sections **permission set information** and **Select the type of users who will use this permission set**. Now edit the **Object Permissions** and **Field Permissions** and choose the required object.

The following screenshot shows the creation of a permission set that allows users to **Access the Widgets** object (which is set to **Private** in the Organization-wide default access model).

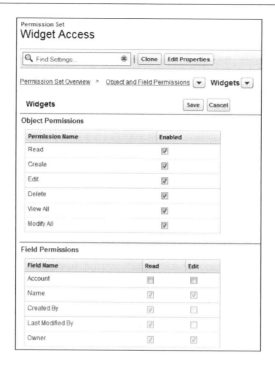

Assigning the user to the permission set from the User edit page

To view and manage which of your user's are assigned to permission sets, navigate to **Your Name** | **Setup** | **Administration Setup** | **Manage Users** | **Users**. Now choose a user by clicking on their **Username**. Click on **Permission Set Assignments** and then **Edit Assignment** to view and select from the list of available permissions. The following screenshot shows the resulting section:

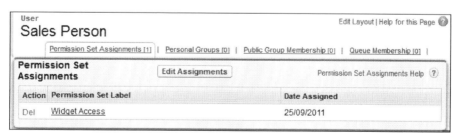

 You can create up to 1,000 permission sets for your organization.

You can group multiple permissions into a permission set to create specific profile-like permissions without actually having to create or clone complete profiles which are often unnecessary and time-consuming.

Role hierarchy

Once the Organization-wide defaults have been established, you can use a role hierarchy to ensure that managers can view and edit the same records as their line reports (or subordinates). Users at any given role level are always able to view, edit, and report on all data owned by or shared with users below them in the hierarchy, unless the OWD settings specify ignoring the hierarchies.

To view and manage your organization's role hierarchy, navigate to **Your Name | Setup | Administration Setup | Manage Users | Roles as shown in the following screenshot:**

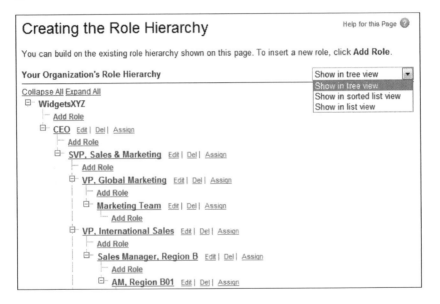

Here you can choose to view the hierarchy in one of the following options:

Show in tree view

This view displays a visual representation of the parent-child relationships between your roles. Click on **Expand All** to see all roles or **Collapse All** to see only top-level roles. To expand or collapse an individual role node, you may click on the plus [+] or minus [-] icon as shown in the preceding screenshot.

Show in sorted list view

This view displays the roles as a list that you can sort alphabetically by role name, parent role (**Reports to**), or **Report Display Name**. If your organization has a large number of roles, this view provides a far easier way to navigate the hierarchy.

To show a filtered list of roles, select a predefined list from the **View** drop-down list, or click on **Create New View** to define your own custom view of roles. To edit or delete any view you have created, select it from the **View** drop-down list and click on the **Edit** link. Once in the **Edit View** page you can click on the **Delete** button to delete the list view as shown in the following screenshot:

Show in list view

This view displays the roles as an indented list of roles and their child nodes, grouped alphabetically by the name of the top-level role as follows:

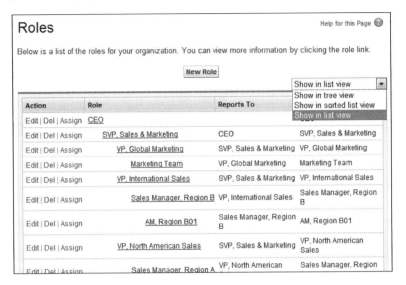

 The columns are not sortable and this view is not available for role hierarchies with more than 1,000 roles.

To create a role, click on **New Role** or **Add Role**, depending whether your view of roles is using the list view or tree view, and enter the role fields as needed.

 You can create up to 500 roles for your organization.

To edit a role, click on **Edit** next to a role name, then update the role fields as needed. You can delete a role, by clicking on **Del** next to the role name.

To assign other users to a role, click on **Assign** next to the role name and to view detailed information about a role, click on the role name.

 If your organization uses territory management, forecasts are based on the territory hierarchy instead of the role hierarchy.

Role hierarchies do not need to represent your company's organization chart and instead, each role in the hierarchy should be considered as a level of data access that your users or groups in Salesforce require.

Depending on your sharing settings, roles can control the level of visibility that users have into your organization's data. Users at a particular role level can view, edit, and report on all data that is owned by or has been shared with users below them in the hierarchy. This is assuming your organization's sharing mechanism for that object type does not specify otherwise.

Specifically, in the Organization-wide defaults related list, if the **Grant Access Using Hierarchies** option is disabled for a custom object, say, then only the record owner and users granted access by the organization-wide defaults can access that custom object's records.

Although, it is possible to create a user record without a role, users would need to be assigned to a role, so that their records will appear in opportunity reports, forecast roll-ups, and any other display based on roles.

When an account owner is not assigned a role, the sharing access for related contacts is **Read/Write**, provided the Organization-wide default for contacts is not **Controlled by Parent**. Sharing access on related opportunities and cases is **No Access**.

Users that are to have access to all records in Salesforce CRM should be set at the top-most position of the role hierarchy.

When you change a user's role, any relevant sharing rules are re-evaluated to add or remove access to records as necessary.

It is not necessary to create individual roles for each and every job title within your company. Instead, aim to define a hierarchy of roles that will help to control the access of information entered by users in lower level roles.

To view detailed information about a role, navigate to **Your Name | Setup | Administration Setup | Manage Users | Roles**, and click on the role name as shown in the following screenshot:

To view the **Role Detail** page for a parent or sibling role, click the Role Name in the hierarchy or siblings list.

To edit the role details, click on **Edit**.

To remove the role from the hierarchy, click on **Delete**.

Within the **Users** in **Role** related list you have the following options:

- Assign a user to the role by clicking on **Assign Users to Role**
- Add a user to your organization by clicking on **New User**
- Modify user information by clicking on **Edit** next to a user's name
- View a user's details by clicking on the user's **Full Name**, **Alias**, or **Username**

When you edit roles, sharing rules are usually automatically re-evaluated to add or remove access to records as required. If these changes result in too many records changing at once, a message appears warning that the sharing rules will not be automatically re-evaluated, and that you have to manually recalculate them (as shown further). Sharing rules should be used when a user or group of users need access to records not already granted to them with either the role hierarchy setup or the organization-wide default settings.

When you modify which users are in a role, any sharing rules are also re-evaluated to add or remove access as necessary.

Organization-wide defaults and sharing rules

A user's level of access to records will never be more restrictive with the use of sharing rules than the options chosen in the Organization-wide defaults. The Organization-wide defaults are a minimum level of access for all users.

Sharing rules

With sharing rules, you are in effect setting automatic extensions to your organization-wide sharing settings for particular sets of users. As shown in the funnel diagram at the beginning of this chapter, this can be considered as opening up visibility and access to records for those users.

Sharing rules can never be stricter than your organization-wide default settings and allow wider data access for the included users or groups of users.

Sharing rules apply to:

- All new and existing records owned by the specified role or group members
- Both active and inactive users

Sharing rules extend the access specified by Organization-wide defaults and the role hierarchy. To define sharing rules, navigate to **Your Name | Setup | Administration Setup | Security Controls | Sharing Settings**. Now scroll down to the lower part of the page to reveal the **Sharing Rules** sections.

The following screenshot shows the **Sharing Rules** page where there are sections to set the sharing rules for the various standard objects within the application, such as **Lead**, **Account**, and **Contact**, as well as any custom objects in your organization:

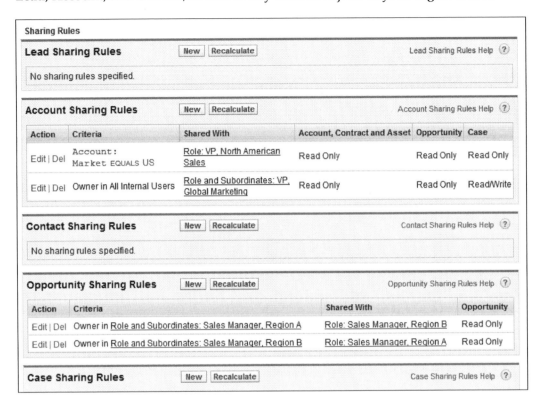

Within the **Sharing Rules** setup section, the following object sharing rules can be applied:

Account sharing rules

These rules are based on the account owner or other criteria, including account record types or field values, and set the default sharing access for accounts and their associated **Contract**, **Asset**, **Opportunity**, **Case**, and (optionally) **Contact** records.

Account territory sharing rules

These rules are based on territory assignment and set the default sharing access for **Account** and their associated **Case**, **Contact**, **Contract**, and **Opportunity** records.

Campaign sharing rules

These rules are based on **Campaign** owner and set the default sharing access for the individual **Campaign** records.

Case sharing rules

These rules are based on the **Case** owner or other criteria, including case record types or field values and set the default sharing access for the individual case and associated account records.

Contact sharing rules

These rules are based on the **Contact** owner or other criteria, including contact record types or field values and set the default sharing access for the individual contact and associated account records.

Lead sharing rules

These rules are based on the **Lead** owner and set the default sharing access for the individual lead records.

Opportunity sharing rules

These rules are based on the **Opportunity** owner or other criteria, including opportunity record types or field values and set the default sharing access for the individual opportunity and their associated account records.

Custom object sharing rules

These rules are based on the custom object record owner or other criteria, including custom object record types or field values and set default sharing access for individual custom object records.

Groups

Groups allow you to simplify the setting up of Organization-wide default sharing access via a sharing rule for sets of users or for individual users to selectively share their records with other users.

Public groups

Public groups are sets of users that only administrators are permitted to create and edit. However, when created, public groups can be used by everyone in the organization.

Public groups may contain individual users, users in a particular role or territory, users in a specified role along with all the users below that role in the role hierarchy or other public groups.

Personal groups

Personal groups are sets of users that everyone can create and edit for their personal use.

Personal groups may contain individual users, public groups, the users in a particular role or territory, or the users in a particular role along with all the users below that role or in the hierarchy.

Effects of adding or modifying sharing rules

When you add a new sharing rule, the access levels for the sharing rule are calculated and you are provided with a warning confirmation dialog message, as shown in the following screenshot, indicating that this operation could take a significant time:

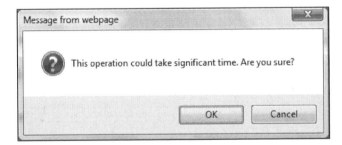

The effects of changing or deleting sharing rules, as well as the transferring of records between users, cause re-evaluation of appropriate record access for the impacted users.

 If these changes affect too many records at once, a message appears warning that the sharing rules will not be automatically re-evaluated, and you must manually recalculate them.

The following list outlines what changes can be done to **Sharing Rules** and the consequence of applying these changes:

- When you change the access levels for a sharing rule, all existing records are automatically updated to reflect the new access levels

- When you delete a sharing rule, the sharing access created by that rule is automatically removed

- When you transfer records from one user to another, the sharing rules are re-evaluated to add or remove access to the transferred records as necessary

- When you modify which users are in a group or role, any sharing rules are re-evaluated to add or remove access to these users as necessary

- Users higher in the role hierarchy are automatically granted the same access that users below them in the hierarchy have from a sharing rule

When you edit groups, roles, and territories, sharing rules are usually automatically re-evaluated to add or remove access as needed.

Manually recalculating sharing rules can be performed at any time.

To manually recalculate sharing rules, navigate to **Your Name | Setup | Administration Setup | Security Controls | Sharing Settings**. Now scroll down to the lower part of the page to reveal the **Sharing Rules** sections and in the **Sharing Rules** related list for the object you want, click on **Recalculate** as shown in the following screenshot:

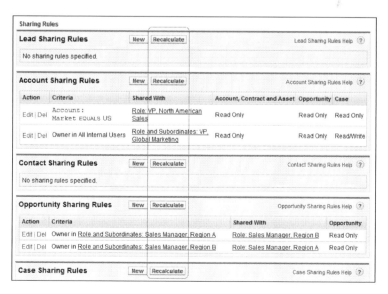

Criteria-based sharing

Criteria-based sharing rules are used to control which users have access to records based on specified field values on the records. For example, the account object has a custom picklist field named **Market**. You can create a criteria-based sharing rule that shares all accounts in which the **Market** field is set to **US** with, say, a **North American Sales** team in your organization as shown in the following screenshot:

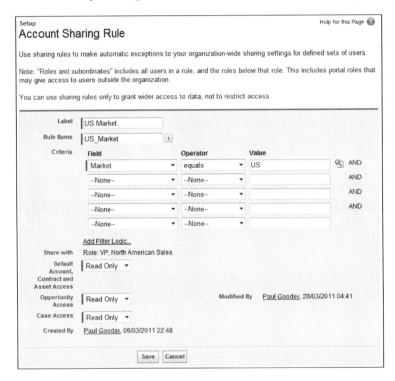

Although criteria-based sharing rules are based on values in the records and not the record owners, a role or territory hierarchy still allows users higher in the hierarchy to access the records.

You can create criteria-based sharing rules for **Account**, **Opportunity**, **Case**, **Contact**, and **Custom object**.

For example, a custom object has been created for **Newsletter**. You can create a criteria-based sharing rule that shares all newsletters in which the name is set to **International** with the **International Sales** team in your organization as follows:

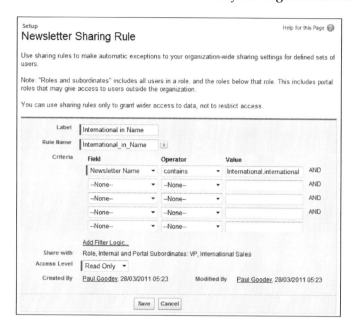

Text and textarea fields must be specified exactly as they are case sensitive. For example, a criteria-based sharing rule that specifies **International** in a text field would not share records with "international" in the field.

Criteria-based sharing rule with text fields

To create a criteria-based sharing rule that matches with several cases of a word, enter each value separated by a comma. For example International, international and use the Contains operator.

There is a restriction on the type of field that can be used for sharing as part of the Criteria-based sharing. Along with record types, the following list of fields can be set as criteria for sharing:

Auto Number, Checkbox, Date, Date/Time, E-mail, Number, Percent, Phone, Picklist, Text, Text Area, URL, and **Lookup Relationship** (to either **User** or **Queue**).

Up to 50 criteria-based sharing rules can be created per object.

Manual sharing rules

Users can manually share certain types of records with other users within the Salesforce CRM application. Some objects that are shared automatically include access to all other associated records. For example, if a user shares one of their account records, then the granted user will also have access to all the opportunities and cases connected to that account.

Manual sharing rules are generally used either on a one-off basis to share a record or whenever there is a difficulty trying to determine a consistent set of users, groups, and the associated rules that would be involved as a part of an Organization-wide sharing setting. To be able to grant sharing access for a record, the user must either be the record owner, a system administrator, a user in a role above the owner in the hierarchy, or any user that has been granted full access or the Organization-wide settings for that object must allow access through hierarchies.

Users grant access simply by clicking on the **Sharing** button found on the **Record Detail** page as shown in the following screenshot:

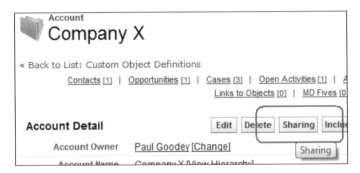

 The **Sharing** button does not appear if the object's Organization-wide sharing defaults are set to **Public Read/Write**.

Queues

Queues allow groups of users to manage shared records.

A queue is a location where records can be routed to await processing by a group member. The records remain in the queue until a user accepts them for processing or they are transferred to another queue.

When creating a new queue you must specify the set of objects that are stored. Permitted objects for queues are leads, cases, service contracts, and custom objects. You must also specify the set of users that are allowed to retrieve records from the queue.

Records can be added to a queue either manually or through an automatic case or lead assignment rules.

Once records are added to a queue they remain there until they are either assigned to a user or retrieved by one of the queue members. Here, any queue member or any user located above a queue member in the role hierarchy can take ownership of records in a queue.

Sharing access diagram

Many security options work together to determine whether users can view or edit a record. First, Salesforce checks whether the user's profile has object level permission to access that object. Then, Salesforce checks whether the user's profile has any administrative permissions, such as **View All Data** or **Modify All Data**. Finally, Salesforce will check the ownership of the record. Here, the Organization-wide defaults, role-level access, and any sharing rules will be checked to see if there are any rules that give the user access to that record.

The following flow diagram shows how users are affected by the different security options associated with record ownership and sharing models and rules that can be set:

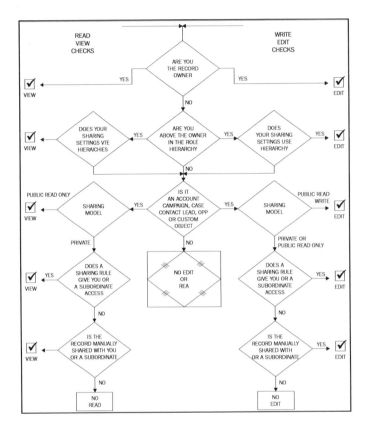

 As part of the check to determine whether a user can view a record, their profile (or permission set) must be set with the view permission for the relevant object and to determine whether a user can edit a record, and their profile (or permission set) must be set with the edit permission for the relevant object.

Data validation

In the previous chapter, we looked at how we can set the required field and auto number field properties on custom fields to help improve the quality and maintain the data integrity of records in the system.

Salesforce also provides other data validation mechanisms such as:

- Data validation rules
- Dependent picklists

Data validation rules

Data validation rules can be applied to both custom and standard fields and are used to verify that the data entered in a record meets the criteria you have specified before the record can be saved.

Validation rules contain a formula or expression that evaluates the data in one or more fields and returns a value of either true or false.

The logic that is used for validation rules is to seek an error condition, upon which a preconfigured error message is shown to the user whenever the formula or expression returns a value of `true`.

When validation rules are defined for a field or set of fields, the following actions are fired when the user creates a new record or edits an existing record and then clicks on the **Save** button:

1. Salesforce executes the validation rules and only if all data is valid, is the record then saved.
2. For any invalid data, Salesforce displays the associated error message without saving the record.

You can specify the error message to display when a record fires the validation rule and also where to display it. For example, your error message can be **The close date must occur after today's date**. You can choose to display it near a field or at the top of the page. Like all other Salesforce error messages, validation rule errors are displayed in red text and are preceded by the word **Error**.

Validation rules apply to all new and updated records for an object.

If your organization has multiple page layouts for the object on which you create a validation rule, you should verify that the validation rule operates as expected on each layout. Also if you have any data integrations that affect that object, then you should also verify that the validation rule operates as intended.

 Even if the fields referenced in the validation rule are not visible on the page layout, the validation rules still apply and will result in an error message if the rule fails.

To begin using validation rules, navigate to **Your Name** | **Setup** | **App Setup** | **Customize**.

For standard objects go to the appropriate activity, standard object, or user's link from the menu, and click on **Validation Rules**.

For custom objects, navigate to **Your Name** | **Setup** | **App Setup** | **Create** | **Objects**. Now go to the custom object.

 Validation rules are listed in the **Validation Rules** related list.

As shown, to begin adding a new validation rule, click on the **New** button in the **Validation Rules** section as shown in the following screenshot:

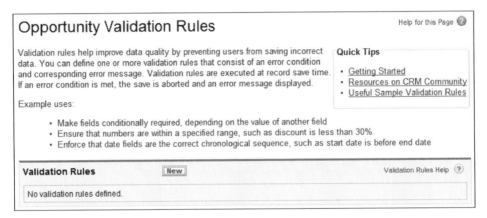

Now enter the properties of your validation rule that should include the properties detailed in the following sections:

Field description section

Add a **Rule Name** which is a unique identifier of up to 80 characters with no spaces or special characters such as extended characters.

The **Active** checkbox which is used to set that the rule is enabled.

Fill in the **Description** field which is an optional 255 character or less textbox that you can set to describe the purpose of the validation rule.

Error condition formula section

The formula that is entered here forms the expression used to validate the field.

Error message section

The **Error Message** field is the text to be displayed to the user when a record update fails the validation rule.

The **Error Location** is used to determine where on the page the error is displayed to the user. Options available are either:

- **Top of Page**
- **Field**

The **Top of Page** option sets the error message to be displayed at the top of the page. To display the error next to a field, choose the **Field** option and then select the appropriate field.

If the error location is a field, the validation rule is also listed on the **Detail** page of that field.

If the error location is set to a field that is later deleted or a field that is read only or not visible on the page layout, Salesforce automatically changes the error location to **Top of Page**.

You can click on **Check Syntax** to check your formula for errors and finally click on **Save** to finish or **Save & New** to create additional validation rules.

As an example, the following shows an opportunity validation rule to ensure that users cannot enter a date in the past into the **Close Date** field:

The formula would be: CloseDate < TODAY()

If the error location is set to a field that is later deleted or a field that is read only or not visible on the page layout, Salesforce automatically changes the error location to **Top of Page**.

An example error message for this validation rule is **Close Date Must Be a Future Date**.

Dependent picklists

Dependent picklists help to make data more accurate and consistent by applying filters.

A dependent field works in conjunction with a controlling field to filter its values. The value chosen in the controlling field affects the values in the dependent field.

In the following screenshot we see the field **Speaker Status** being controlled by the field **Speaker Event Status**:

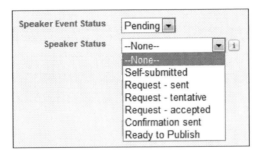

Dependent and controlling picklists

Dependent and controlling picklists work in conjunction where the value chosen in the controlling picklist dynamically changes the values that are available in the dependent picklist.

Both controlling and dependent picklists are indicated on the edit pages by an icon. By hovering the mouse over these icons, users can see the name of the controlling or dependent picklist.

To define a dependent picklist, navigate to the field's area of the appropriate object.

For standard objects, navigate to **Your Name | Setup | App Setup | Customize**. Now select the appropriate object from the **Customize** menu and click on **Fields**.

For custom objects, navigate to **Your Name | Setup | App Setup | Create | Objects**. Now select one of the custom objects in the list.

For custom task and event fields, navigate to **Your Name | Setup | App Setup | Customize | Activities | Activity Custom Fields**.

Now click on the **Field Dependencies in the Custom Fields & Relationships** section as shown in the following screenshot:

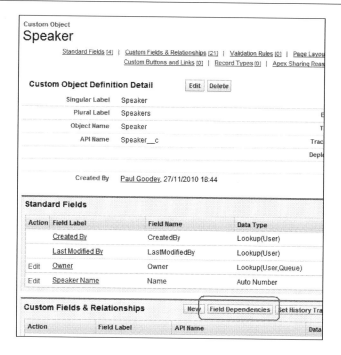

Now click on **New** and then choose a **Controlling Field** and a **Dependent Field** as follows:

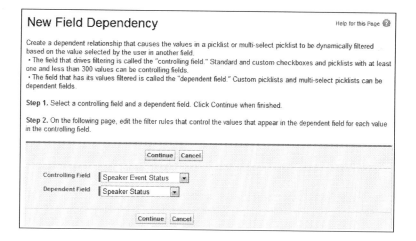

Click on **Continue** to display the next screen where you are presented with the field dependency matrix to specify the dependent picklist values that are available when a user selects each controlling field value.

The field dependency matrix lets you specify the dependent picklist values that are available when a user selects each controlling field value. The top row of the matrix shows the controlling field values, while the columns show the dependent field values.

Using this matrix, you can include or exclude values. Included values are available in the dependent picklist when a value in the controlling field is selected and excluded fields are not available.

Here you can include or exclude values by performing the following steps:

1. Double-click values to include them. Included values are then indicated with a highlight. (Double-clicking again any highlighted values will then be excluded).

2. To work with more than one value you should use the *Shift* key and click on each value to select the required range of values as shown in the following screenshot:

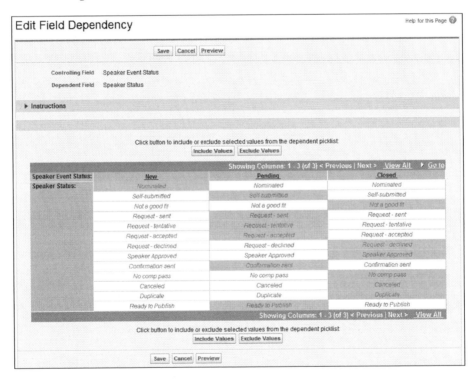

3. After selecting the values, click on **Include Values** to make the values available, or click on **Exclude Values** to remove them from the list of available values.

You can also use the *Ctrl* key and then click on the individual values to select multiple values. Again, clicking on **Include Values** makes the values available, or clicking on **Exclude Values** removes them from the list of available values. By clicking a column header you can select all the values in that column as follows:

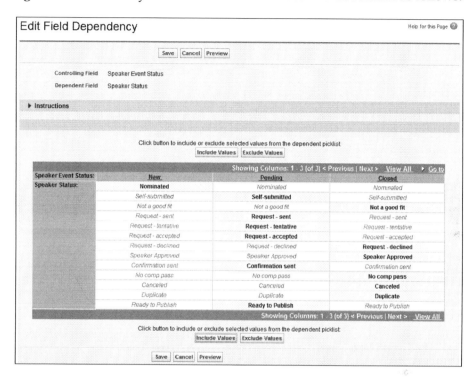

To change the values in your view, you can:

- Click on **View All** to view all available values at once.
- Click on **Go To** and choose a controlling value to view all the dependent values in that column.
- Click on **Previous** or **Next** to view the values in columns that are on the previous or next page.
- Click on **View sets of 5** to view five columns at a time.

Now, optionally, click on **Preview** to test your selections and then click on **Save**.

Dependent picklist considerations

The following are the dependent picklists considerations:

Controlling fields

- Checkbox fields can be controlling fields
- Multi-select picklists cannot be controlling fields
- There are maximum number of 300 values allowed in a controlling field

Dependent fields

- Multi-select picklists can be dependent picklists
- Checkboxes cannot be dependent fields

Standard picklist fields

Standard picklist fields cannot be defined as a dependent list. They may only be set up as a controlling field.

Default values

You can set default values for controlling fields but not for dependent picklists.

Converting fields

When converting existing fields to dependent picklists or controlling fields, this can be done without affecting the existing values in records. Only for changes going forward are the dependency rules applied to the updates to existing records or new records.

Field-level security

Field-level security settings for a controlling field and dependent picklist are completely independent. Therefore, you must manually hide a controlling field whenever its related dependent picklist is hidden.

Page layouts

For best practice and improved user visibility, make sure the dependent picklist is lower on the page layout than its controlling field.

If a dependent picklist is required and no values are available for it based on the controlling field value, users can save the record without entering a value. In this scenario, the record is saved with no value for that field.

Make sure controlling fields are added to any page layouts that contain their associated dependent picklists. If the controlling field is not on the same page layout, the dependent picklist shows no available values.

Record types

The values in controlling fields are determined by the pre-selected record type and the values in dependent picklists are determined by both the record type and the selected controlling field value.

The values available in dependent picklists are, therefore, an intersection of the pre-selected record type and subsequent controlling field selection.

Importing data

The import wizards do not consider field dependencies. Therefore, any value can be imported into a dependent picklist field regardless of the value imported for a controlling field.

Importing and exporting data

Salesforce provides data utilities that are available for the importing and exporting of data to and from Salesforce.

Import wizard

The Salesforce import wizard is an easy-to-use user interface, multi-step wizard for importing new **Account, Contact, Lead, Custom Object,** or **Solution** records into Salesforce.

The wizard can also be used for **Account, Contact, Lead, Custom Object,** or **Solution** updates based on a matching identifier.

 Contact and **Lead** can be updated by matching the e-mail address and **Custom Object** or **Solution** may be updated based on custom object names, solution titles, Salesforce Id, or an external ID.

A **comma separated value (CSV)** file format is required when using the import wizard where import wizard imports are limited to 50,000 records per session.

Account and **Contact** import wizards have a built-in de-duplicating functionality. **Account** can be matched using the account name and account site. For contacts, de-duplicating matching can be carried out using first name, last name, or e-mail address.

Data Loader

The Data Loader is a client application from Salesforce for bulk import or export of data.

When importing data, the Data Loader loads data from comma separated values (CSV) files or from a database connection and exporting of data is done using CSV files.

Data Loader and import wizards compared

With the Data Loader, you can perform operations such as insert, delete, update, extract, or upsert. You can move data into or out of any Salesforce object. There is less validation when adding data.

The import wizards have fewer options and are more limited as they only support **Account**, **Contact**, **Lead**, **Solution**, and **Custom object**. They have built-in de-duplication logic.

Use the Data Loader when:

- You need to load 50,000 or more records where the maximum is 5 million records.
- You need to load into an object that is not yet supported by web-based import wizards.
- You want to schedule regular data loads, such as nightly imports.
- You want to save mappings for later use.
- You want to export your data for backup purposes.

Use web-based import wizards when:

- You are loading fewer than 50,000 records.
- The object you need to import is an **Account, Contact, Lead, Solution**, and **Custom object.**
- You want to prevent duplicates by uploading records according to account name and site, contact e-mail address, or lead e-mail address.

If you're logging in from an IP that's not in the trusted range, you must add a security token as described in the earlier chapter.

Best practice for mass data updating

When carrying out any kind of mass data update or deletion in Salesforce CRM you should of course ensure that the data to be changed is correct but you should also consider applying the following best practices:

 Back up your data

Back up your data before performing a mass update or delete it by either requesting a data export or exporting your own report of the data.

Always include both the **Date/Time Stamp** and **Created by Alias** criteria in your mass delete to ensure that you are only deleting your imports and no one else's data.

Weekly export

Your organization can sign up to receive backup files of your data. You can export all of your organization's data into a set of comma separated values (CSV) files.

 The weekly export service can only be enabled by sending a request to Salesforce customer support.

With the data export feature, you can generate backup files manually once every six days or schedule them to generate automatically at weekly or monthly intervals.

When the export is ready, you will receive an e-mail with a link; navigate to the link provided.

To schedule a weekly export, navigate to **Your Name | Setup | Administration Setup | Data Management | Data Export and Export Now** or **Schedule Export**.

The **Export Now** option prepares your files for export immediately. This option is only available if a week has passed since your last export. The **Schedule Export** option allows you to schedule the export process for weekly or monthly intervals.

Field sets

Field sets combine the power of Visualforce to create custom user interface pages with what has always been a defining trait of the Force.com platform, the ability for administrators to customize the application using config over code.

A field set is a grouping of fields. For example, you could have an account search Visualforce page that uses a field set to control which account fields are returned in the search results. When a field set is added to a Visualforce page, developers can loop over its fields and display them. The same Visualforce page can therefore be used to present a different set of information, depending on which fields you wish to render.

Field sets enable you to customize the fields that appear on a custom Visualforce page using a simple drag-and-drop interface to add, remove, or rearrange fields from the field set, without altering the Visualforce page as shown in the following screenshot:

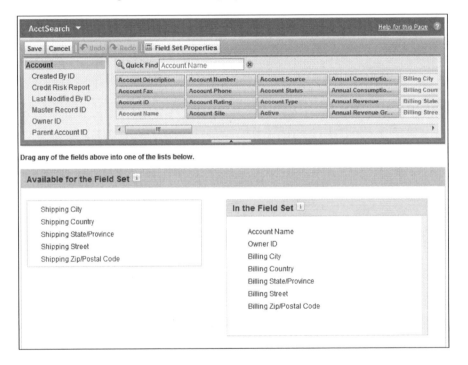

Where a field is included in the **Available for the Field Set** section, it exists in the field set, but it will not be rendered on the Visualforce page. You can display the field by moving it from the **Available for the Field Set** column to the **In the Field Set** column.

Where a field is marked as **In the Field Set**, the field will be rendered on the Visualforce page. You can remove the field from the page by removing it from the **In the Field Set** column.

Folders

Folders are used for organizing e-mail templates, docs, reports, and dashboards. Folder access is specified as read or read/write which is explicitly set for the folder and there is no rolling up of user permission to access using the role hierarchy. Only one type of media can be stored per folder; it is not possible to mix the types of files that are stored.

Recycle Bin

The **Recycle Bin** can be accessed from the **Home** tab by clicking on the link in the sidebar as shown in the following screenshot:

The **Recycle Bin** is where deleted data is stored where it can be accessed for 15 days after which the data becomes hard deleted and is no longer recoverable.

Clicking on **Recycle Bin** allows you to view both your deleted items plus your organization's deleted items as shown in the following screenshot:

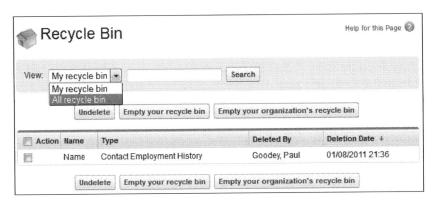

You can use the **Empty your recycle bin** button to permanently remove deleted items prior to the 15-day expiration.

 Records in the **Recycle Bin** do not count against your organization's storage limits.

To calculate the number of records that your **Recycle Bin** can store, Salesforce uses the following formula: 25 multiplied by the number of Megabytes (MB) in your storage.

For example, if your organization has 1 GB which equates to 1000 MB (a 1000 MB storage unit is used here and not 1028 MB); then your limit is 25 multiplied by 1000 MB which equals 25,000 records.

When your organization reaches the **Recycle Bin** limit, the Salesforce CRM application automatically removes the oldest records (if they have been in the **Recycle Bin** for at least two hours).

Data storage utilization

Salesforce CRM has two categories of storage namely data, which is used to store records (for example, **Opportunity**, **Account**, or **Custom object** data records) and file storage, which is used for storing file attachments (for example, presentations, spreadsheets, images, or Adobe PDFs, and so on).

Salesforce CRM (Enterprise Edition) provides 1 GB for data storage and 1 GB for file storage. In total, this 2 GB storage amount (1 GB for data plus 1 GB for files) is the minimum total storage allocated for a Salesforce CRM organization. However, the storage amount increases as more active users are added since there is also a 20 MB per user storage factor.

As an example, an organization with 500 active users sees the storage amount for data, say, increase to 10 GB. This is calculated as 500 (users) multiplied by 20 MB which equals 10,000 MB or 10 GB.

To view your organization's used data space and used file space, navigate to **Your Name | Setup | Administration Setup | Data Management | Storage Usage** as follows:

Storage Usage

Your organization's storage usage is listed below.

Storage Type	Limit	Used	Percent Used
Data Storage	20.0 MB	460 KB	2%
File Storage	20.0 MB	86 KB	0%

Current Data Storage Usage

Record Type	Record Count	Storage	Percent
Opportunities	45	90 KB	20%
Contacts	38	76 KB	17%
Accounts	32	64 KB	14%
Cases	28	56 KB	12%
Leads	22	44 KB	10%
Campaigns	5	40 KB	9%
Events	10	20 KB	4%
Solutions	10	20 KB	4%

Current File Storage Usage

Record Type	Record Count	Storage	Percent
Documents	1	86 KB	100%

Top Users by Data Storage Usage

User	Storage	Percent
Paul Goodey	394 KB	86%
Trevor Howard	40 KB	9%

Top Users by File Storage Usage

User	Storage	Percent

You can view the limits and used amounts for data and file storage, the amounts in use per record type, and the current file storage usage. You can also view the top users of data and file storage. To see exactly what is being stored by the listed users, you can click that user's name.

Summary

In this chapter, we described the ways in which permissions for accessing data records in Salesforce are controlled by object and profile permissions along with Organization-wide sharing defaults.

We looked at how the access to records could be further widened through the use of **Permission Sets**, **Sharing Rules**, criteria-based sharing, and also manual sharing. The mechanisms that are available to help manage the quality and integrity of data were covered where we looked at data validation rules and dependent picklist fields. We also learned about importing and exporting data using the import wizards for smaller fragments of data and the Data Loader for larger fragments of data.

In the next chapter, we will be covering Data Analytics, where we will look to see how we can report on the data in Salesforce. Included in the next chapter is the setting up of reports, dashboards, custom reports, and use of the Report Builder.

5
Data Analytics with Reports and Dashboards

In the previous chapter, we looked at how, through the use of various sharing rules, we can control the access to records in Salesforce CRM. Various mechanisms that help to manage the quality and integrity of data were also described, along with an overview of the facilities for importing and exporting data using import tools.

In this chapter, we will continue to look at the subject of data, but from the viewpoint of reporting, where we will describe the analytics building blocks within Salesforce CRM.

These analytics tools allow you and your users to customize and manage the reporting and visual representation of data. For example, the sales team can produce reports that show the sales pipeline, the marketing team can report on the progress of campaigns, and you can create reports that display the number of active users in your Salesforce organization.

The features available to report data are described in detail and include details on how to create, customize, and export purpose-built report data.

Reports can also be used to improve the quality of data. You can, for example, create a report that lists all, accounts with missing annual-revenue fields.

We will also look in detail at how these analytic elements can be used to provide sophisticated dashboard charting and graphics.

Salesforce CRM analytics consist of the basic mechanisms of reports, dashboards, and folders:

- **Reports**: Reports are the key building block for analytics in Salesforce CRM, where a resulting set of records are displayed in rows and columns to match the specified criteria. Report results may be further filtered and grouped, and may also be displayed as graphical summaries.

- **Dashboards**: Dashboards are visual components generated from data in reports. These components can include the following five types: charts, gauges, tables, metrics, and Visualforce pages.

- **Folders**: Folders are used to store the reports and dashboards and can either be set to read-only or read/write. To configure which of your users have access to a folder, you can set it to be either accessible by all users, hidden from all users, or accessible only by certain users. When restricting to certain users, the options exist to restrict by **Public Groups**, **Roles**, and **Roles and Subordinates**.

Reports

Within Salesforce CRM, reports are accessed from the **Reports** tab (as shown in the next screenshot). There are a large variety of predefined reports that are automatically provided when your organization is first set up by Salesforce. These predefined reports are known as standard reports, and are located in pre-prepared report folders known as standard report folders. For example, standard reports provide information about accounts and contacts; details about opportunities, forecasts, products, and sales pipelines; information about your organization's leads; details about forecast reports for customizable forecasting, and so on.

In this section on reports, we will outline the available standard reports and describe some of the key reports for system administrators in particular.

The predefined reports are suitable for existing objects and fields. They would not be suitable for reporting on any new objects that you have created. For this, we will look at how to extend the existing reports and how to create completely new types of reports, known in Salesforce CRM as custom report types.

When building reports from either standard or custom report types, Salesforce provides a full-featured drag-and-drop editor to simplify the setup and layout of reports.

We will first look at how to use report folders, which can help organize and control access to reports by your users within Salesforce CRM. When we click on the **Reports** tab, the **Reports and Dashboards** home page presents the following features:

- **New Report** and **New Dashboard** buttons.

- **Folder** search box that allows users to search for specific report and dashboard folders.

- **Create New Report Folder** and **Create New Dashboard Folder** selections.

- **Report** search box that allows users to search for specific reports and dashboards.

- **Reports and Dashboards Folders** section with different icons to show whether the folder is a report or dashboard.

- **Main Reports and Dashboards List View** section. This allows filtering of **Recent Reports** tabs, displays appropriate reports, and allows the creation of new reports.

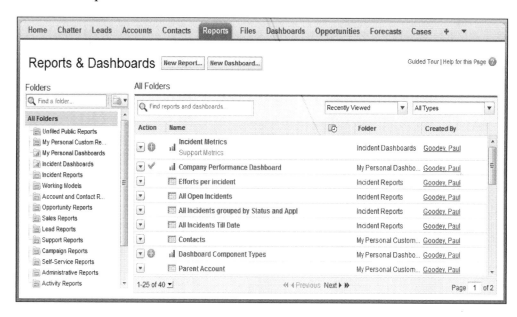

Report and Dashboard Folders

The **Report and Dashboard Folders** section allows you and your users to select the reports and dashboards that are stored in that specific folder.

In Salesforce CRM, you cannot save reports to the standard report folders. You can save reports only to the **My Personal Custom Reports** folder, the **Unfiled Public Reports** folder, or any custom report folder where you have the appropriate read/write access.

 Standard reports may not be deleted or removed, but the folder can be hidden.

Using the create folder icon and associated options allows you to create new report and dashboard folders for custom reports and dashboards, as shown in the following screenshot:

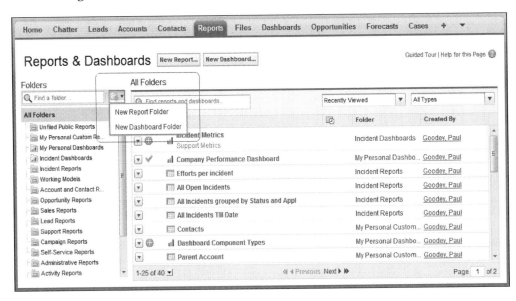

The option to create new folders is not available to all users.

 The user permission required to access the **Create New Folder** option is **Manage Public Reports**.

It is good practice to create new folders to help manage the structure of reports of your organization.

 You cannot mix standard and custom reports in the same folder.

Unlike many IT systems, creating reports in Salesforce CRM is very simple; users can themselves create reports. Since it is so easy for users to create reports, without careful control and an organized approach to report creation, it is easy for the number of reports to rapidly increase and become difficult to manage. You should, for example, create report folders that only certain users have access to. This could be restricted to certain departments or geographic regions. For example, reports could be restricted to `Global Marketing` or to the `North American Sales Team`.

To create new report folders, click on the **Create New Folder** link, where the following options are presented:

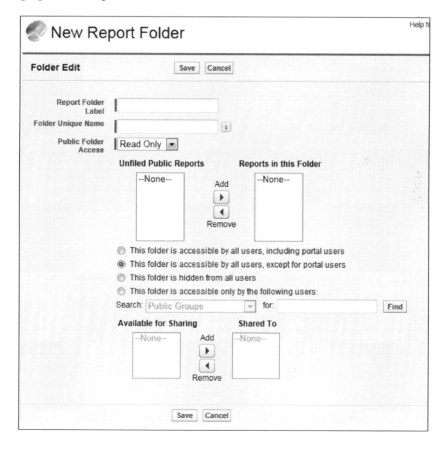

Here, you provide the name of the report folder and decide whether the public folder access is set to be read-only or read/write. You can optionally move reports from the **Unfiled Public Reports** folder. You must specify the accessibility to users—you can select either accessible by all users, hidden from all users, or accessible by certain users. These options are in the following: **Public Groups**, **Roles**, **Roles and Subordinates**.

> Only users with the **Manage Public Reports** user permission are able to delete reports from the report folders. This is true even if the user has read/write access and has created the report themselves.

Creating reports

The basic steps for creating new reports are as follows:

1. From the **Reports** tab, click on the **New Report...** button.

2. Select the report type for the report and click on the **Create** button.

3. Customize your report, then save or run it.

Best practices for reports

- Establish a report naming convention. For example, `A01 NA April Sales`, `B02 INT April Sales`, and so on—this can make it easier to refer to reports using the coding scheme (there is an upper limit of 40 characters).

- Use the **Description** field to describe exactly what the report is intended for (there is an upper limit of 255 characters).

- Consider creating reports that are only needed for dashboards in separate report folders called something like `Dashboard Reports Sales`, for example.

- Have regular "Spring Cleans" where you delete unwanted reports. You can also create temporary reports that are hidden from all users and save these reports there while you figure out if they are required.

Selecting the appropriate report type is one of the most important steps in creating a report. Report types set the rules for which records can be shown in reports. They allow predefined sets of records and fields to be available within a report based on the relationship between a primary object and any related objects.

In the Salesforce CRM application, there are standard report types, and you, as system administrator, can set up custom report types.

Terminology check

`Custom Report Type` is different from `Custom Report` in Salesforce CRM. When users create a new report using the **New Report** button on the **Reports** home page, this is sometimes known as a custom report. `Custom Report Type` is a report template that only system administrators can create. It provides a custom set of associated objects and fields to produce predefined report templates from which any user's custom report can be created.

Standard report types

Salesforce provides a large range of predefined standard report types along with standard report folders accessible from the **Reports** tab, as shown in the following table:

Standard report type	Standard report folder	Description
	`Unfiled Public Reports`	Shared custom reports created by system administrators, but not moved into a custom report folder
	`My Personal Custom Reports`	Customized reports that users have saved by clicking on **Save As** or **Save** within a report
`Account & Contacts`	`Account and Contact Reports`	Information about accounts and contacts
`Activities`	`Activity Reports`	Information about calendar events and tasks
`Administrative Reports`	`Administrative Reports`	Information about your Salesforce users, documents, and reports
`Call Center Reports`	`Call Center Reports`	Information about phone calls that were handled with Salesforce CRM Call Center
`Campaigns`	`Campaign Reports`	Information about marketing campaigns
`Salesforce CRM Content`	`Content Reports`	Information about Salesforce CRM Content
`Forecasts`	`Forecast Reports`	Details about forecast reports for customizable forecasting
`Leads`	`Lead Reports`	Information about leads

Standard report type	Standard report folder	Description
Opportunities	Opportunity and Forecast Reports	Details about opportunities, forecasts, products, and sales pipelines
Price Books, Products, and Assets	Products and Asset Reports	Information about products, price of books, and assets

The selection for standard reports in Salesforce CRM is shown as follows:

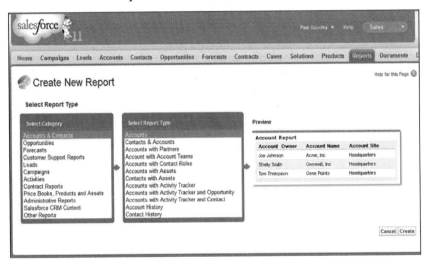

 By default, the standard report folders are set to read-only and are accessible by all users.

Administrative reports

One of the most useful standard reports for system administrators are the administrator reports, which can be found in the Administrative Reports folder, and can be used to analyze your Salesforce users' documents, reports, and login locations. For example, you can run reports on the active Salesforce users and see who has been logging in. The following administrative reports are available:

Report	Description
All Active Users report	Lists the active users in your organization and when they last logged in
Users Logged in This Week report	Lists all of the users who have logged in to Salesforce in the past seven days
Documents report	Lists the documents within each document folder
New Login Locations	List of users, IP addresses, and login dates

Creating a custom report to list your organization's reports

You can create a custom report that lists the reports within your organization and the last time each report was used. Choose **Administrative Reports** and then select **Reports** as the report type.

Custom report types

In addition to the standard report types, you can also create custom report types. Custom report types extend the types of reports from which all users in your organization can create or update custom reports.

Creating custom report types

Custom report types are set up using the following steps:

1. Define a custom report type by name, description, primary object, development status, and the category of report to store it.

2. Choose the related objects for the custom report type.

3. Specify the layout for the resulting standard and custom fields that a report can display when created using the custom report type.

4. Create a report from the `Custom Report Type` template to verify that all of the objects and field definitions are correct.

Once you have created a custom report type, you can later update or delete it as required.

When a `Custom Report Type` template is deleted, any reports that have been created from it are also deleted. Furthermore, any dashboard components that have been created from a report that was created from a deleted `Custom Report Type` template will show an error message whenever viewed.

Defining custom report types

To navigate to the **Custom Report Types** page, navigate to **Your Name | Setup | (App Setup) | Create | Report Types**. Now click on **New Custom Report Type**:

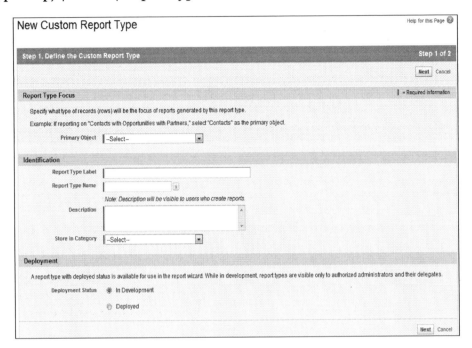

Step 1 – Defining the Custom Report Type template

From the **Primary Object** drop-down list, select the primary object from which you want to build your custom report type.

The primary object you choose determines the views available to users creating or running reports from your custom report type. For example, if you select accounts as the primary object for your custom report type, then users can view their report results by **All Accounts** or **My Accounts** from the report builder's **Show** drop-down list.

If you select opportunities, then when users create reports based on that report type, they can view their report results by **My opportunities**, **My team's opportunities**, or by **All opportunities**, as shown next:

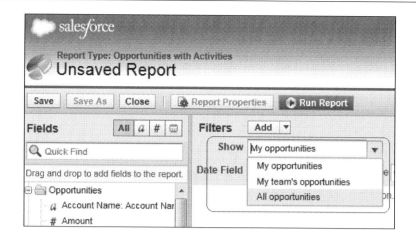

 When a `Custom Report Type` template is saved, the primary object associated with it cannot be changed. So, if you later want to change the primary object, you have to define a new custom report type.

Now enter the **Report Type Label** and the **Report Type Name** fields, and enter a description for the custom report type. The description will be visible to users who create reports and is used to help explain the purpose for the `Custom Report Type` template.

 The **Report Type Label** field can be up to 50 characters long and the description can be up to 255 characters.

Select the category to store the custom report type in. Then, select a development status. Here, you can select **In Development** while you are first creating the custom report type to hide it from users while you are defining it. This will hide the `Custom Report Type` template and prevent users from creating and running reports from the report type. Choose **Deployed** when you are finished defining it and want to let users create and run reports using that `Custom Report Type` template.

Now click on **Next** and then choose the object relationships that a report can display when run from a custom report type.

Step 2 – Defining report records set

After the initial definition for the `Custom Report Type` template, the object relationships can be selected for it. These object relationships determine the objects and fields available for display on reports. Using diagrams, they help to understand the object relationships formed within `Custom Report Type`, which will display the data fields whenever reports are created from the `Custom Report Type` template:

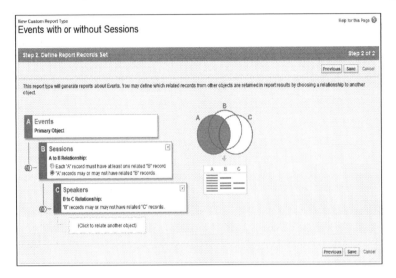

In this `Custom Report Type` example called **Events with or without Sessions**, we have object relationships for a custom primary object, `Event`, which has relationships with `Sessions` and `Speakers`.

To add an object that is associated with another object to the report type, click on the rectangle section, **(Click to relate another object)**. Then, select the object from the picklist.

The objects available for you to choose from are based on the primary object's relationships to other objects.

For example, our custom object, `Event`, is set as the primary object for the `Custom Report Type` template—so only standard and custom objects associated with `Events` can be chosen, such as `Sessions`. This also applies to additional objects added to the `Custom Report Type` template. In our example with `Events` selected as the primary object and `Sessions` selected as the secondary object, only the objects associated with `Sessions` can be selected as the third object on the `Custom Report Type` template, which is our custom object `Speakers`.

Although up to four object levels can be set up for Custom Report Type templates, some of the object combinations may not be able to reach that limit. For example, if you add contacts as the primary object, opportunities as the secondary object, and activities as the third object, then you cannot add any additional objects because activities do not have any child object relationships.

Within the diagram, there is the option of setting the first relationship to the primary object with either **"A" records may or may not have related "B" records** or **Each "A" record must have at least one related "B" record**.

The following paragraph describes the effects of selecting may or may not options:

All subsequent objects automatically include the may-or-may-not association on the custom report type. For example, if accounts are the primary objects and opportunities are the secondary objects, and you choose that accounts may or may not have opportunities, then any third and fourth level objects included on the Custom Report Type template default to may-or-may-not associations.

Blank fields display on report results for object B when object A does not have object B. For example, if a user runs a report on accounts with or without opportunities, then opportunity fields display as blank for accounts without opportunities.

Edit layout

After clicking on **Save**, the Custom Report Type definition and the object relationships are set:

Now the layout can be edited to specify which standard and custom fields a report can display when created or run from the template.

Clicking on **Preview Layout** shows which fields will display on the **Select Columns** page of a report based on this report type.

To start configuring the layout, select fields from the right-hand box and drag them to a section on the left, as shown next:

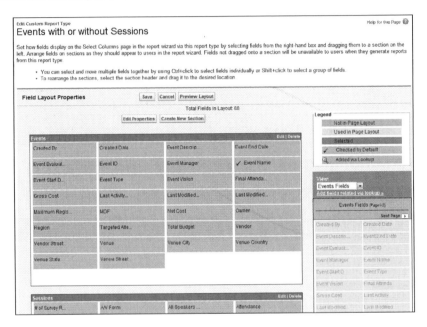

You can view a specific object's fields by selecting an object from the **View** drop-down list and arrange fields within sections as they should appear to users.

Fields not dragged onto a section will not be visible to users when they create reports using this report type.

 You can add up to 1000 fields to each `Custom Report Type` template.

To rename or set which fields are selected by default for users, select one or more fields and click on **Edit Properties**, as shown in the following screenshot:

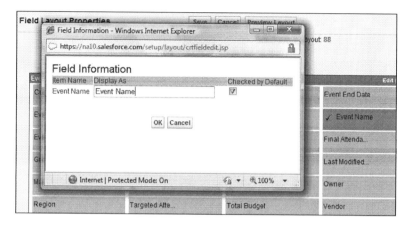

Click on the **Checked by Default** checkbox next to the field you want selected by default.

Change the text in the **Display As** field next to the field you want to rename. To rename the sections, click on **Edit** next to an existing section or create a new section by clicking on **Create New Section**. Now click on **Save**.

Running reports

The **Reports** tab presents the report's home page, on which users can search for reports and select or create a folder for reports:

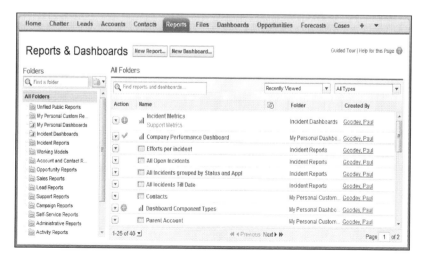

The list of folders (represented by the folder icon) displays all the report folders that the user has permission to access. Within this section, you can view, edit, and manage all of your organization's public report folders. By clicking on the **Reorder Folders** option, you can change the order in which folders appear on the sub-tab.

The section on the right displays the selected report folder and allows users to click on the **Actions** drop-down, which appears as the first column. Here, the options are **Edit**, **Delete**, and **Export**.

Choosing the **Delete** option will remove the report for all users and move it to the Recycle Bin. Here, you are prompted with a warning before the deletion is carried out.

Before doing so, you would need to check that the report is no longer required, as it will be removed for all users—you would be able to recover it from the Recycle Bin for 30 days (if necessary) though.

 You cannot delete reports that are being used by dashboards. To delete these reports, you must first delete the calling dashboard component.

All users can click on **Export** to export a report directly to an Excel spreadsheet or CSV (comma separated values) file.

Printing and exporting reports

To print a report, users can perform the following steps:

1. Click on the **Printable View** button to open (or save) the report as a printed view, as shown in the following screenshot:

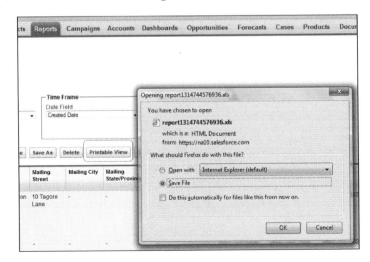

2. Click on the print icon.

To export a report, users can perform the following steps:

1. Click on **Export Details**.

2. Set the appropriate file encoding option for the language. The default option is **ISO-8859-1 (General US & Western European, ISO-LATIN-1)**:

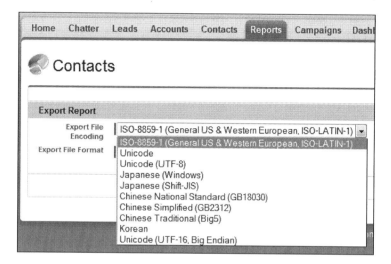

3. Set the **Export File Format** field to either **Excel** or **CSV** (comma delimited).

4. Click on **Export**.

In the browser's **File Download** dialog, users can then choose where to save the file to on their local or network disk.

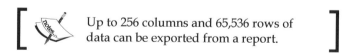

Up to 256 columns and 65,536 rows of data can be exported from a report.

Report considerations

There are various issues to consider when running reports, whether in Salesforce CRM or on any other information system. There are typical limits to the volume of data that can be processed, or restrictions to the type of changes that can be made to existing reports. Both the method of controlling the amount of data that is returned in Salesforce and the effects of changing aspects of existing reports are described next.

Running large reports

If your report returns more than 2,000 records, only the first 2,000 records are displayed. To see a complete view of your report results, click on **Export Details**.

 Reports that take longer than 10 minutes to complete will be cancelled by the Salesforce system.

Report timeout warning

The report timeout warning analyzes reports that are invoked from the **Run Reports** page. The standard timeout for reports is 10 minutes. If the report is identified to be highly complex and is likely to time out, a warning is displayed.

The report timeout warning analyzes reports that are activated manually and ignores reports run via dashboards or scheduled reports.

 You can have the timeout period for reports extended from the default 10 minutes by sending a request to Salesforce customer support.

If your organization has extended the limit to say 20 minutes, the report timeout warning might be less likely to appear. However, bear in mind that highly complex reports may still time out in the future.

 Salesforce recommends that you follow the steps outlined in their online help section, **Tips for Improving Report Performance**, to simplify the report.

You can disable the report timeout warning by navigating to **Your Name | Setup | (App Setup) | Customize | Reports & Dashboards | User Interface Settings**. Uncheck the **Enable Report Timeout Warning** checkbox and then click on **Save**.

Exporting reports to the background

Exporting reports to the background enables you to run reports in the background so that you can continue working in Salesforce without waiting for report results to be displayed. Exporting reports to the background is very useful when creating large reports that would otherwise time out due to the volume of resulting report data.

When the report has finished running and the results are ready for viewing, an e-mail notification is sent by Salesforce. The e-mail contains a link that, when clicked, enables the viewing of the report information. From this page, you can then download the report results in CSV (comma separated values) format.

 The feature for exporting reports to the background can only be enabled by sending a request to Salesforce customer support.

User verification test

For security purposes, user verification can be set up to require users to be tested before exporting data from the Salesforce CRM application. This text data-entry test prevents automated programs from attempting to access the data from within Salesforce. This feature is available on request from Salesforce customer support.

To pass the test, users must type the two words displayed into a textbox field and submit. Note that the words entered into the textbox field must be separated by a space.

Salesforce uses CAPTCHA technology provided by reCaptcha for the user verification testing.

CAPTCHA is an acronym that stands for **Completely Automated Public Turing Test To Tell Computers and Humans Apart**. It is a computer data-entry verification that ensures the entry is being carried out by a person. The verification requests the user to complete a small test, which the computer creates first, and then checks the result. Because only humans are able to solve the test, whenever the correct solution is returned, the computer accepts that it is a request by a person and not from an automated computer program.

Report builder

The report builder in Salesforce CRM is a visual editor to enable the creation and modification of reports. The report builder interface uses drag-and-drop functionality to configure reports, and the interface consists of the following three sections, known as panes:

- The **Fields** pane
- The **Filters** pane
- The **Preview** pane

The following screenshot shows the report builder page, which is presented as a full-screen window in order to maximize the display of the **Fields**, **Filters**, and **Preview** panes:

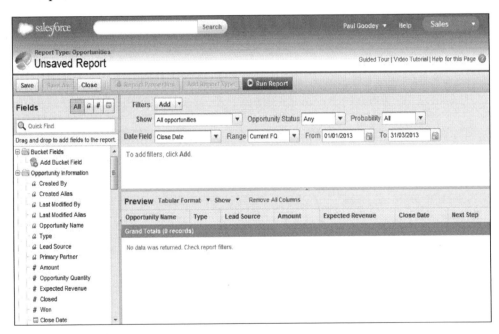

To exit the report builder editor page, click on the **Close** button located in the top-left corner of the page, where you will be prompted to save any unsaved changes.

 You can also click on the Salesforce.com logo in the top-left corner of the page. However, you will not be prompted to save any changes.

Looking at each of the panes in detail, we now start with the **Fields** pane.

The Fields pane

The **Fields** pane is shown on the left-hand side of the report builder page and, as the name suggests, lists all the accessible fields in the selected report type. The list of fields is organized by the sections that were set in the page layout of the associated report type. Here, fields can easily be identified by using the **Quick Find** search box at the top of the pane. You can also limit the number of fields shown by using the field type filters. In this pane, the fields can be dragged into the **Preview** pane to add them to the report. Additional calculated fields can be created just for the specific report. These are known as custom summary formulas and buckets.

The Filters pane

To limit the number of rows of data results that are returned when you run a report, you can either limit your report results by clicking on the **Hide Details** button at the top of the report or you can add custom filters. To restore the full set of returned data, click on the **Show Details** button.

For tabular reports (only), you can set the maximum number of records to be displayed by clicking on **Add Row Limit** in the report builder accessed from the **Add** button in the **Filters** pane.

The **Filters** pane is displayed in the top-right part of the report builder page, and is used to configure the view, the time period, and also any custom filters to limit the data that is actually displayed as part of the report.

Within the **Filters** pane, you click on the **Add** box to add report filters, as shown here:

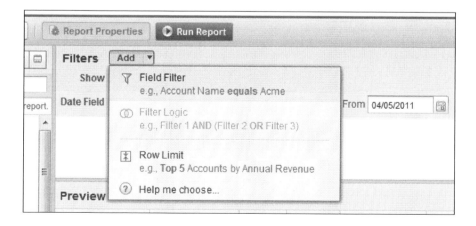

Report filters set the criteria for the data in a report according to the following:

Report filter	Description	Notes
Field Filter	**Field Filter** allows you to set the field, the operator, and the value.	For example, **Account Name** equals Acme.
Filter Logic	**Filter Logic** adds Boolean conditions to control how field filters are evaluated.	For example, **Filter 1** AND (**Filter 2** OR **Filter 3**).
		You must add at least one field filter before applying filter logic.
Row Limit	With a **Row Limit**, you set the maximum number of rows to be displayed; choose a field to sort by and the sort order.	Only available for Tabular reports.
		Tabular reports that have a limited row count can be used in dashboards.

The Preview pane

The **Preview** pane is where the report can be customized. You and your users can add, rearrange, and remove columns, summary fields, formulas, and field groupings. When you enter the report builder for the first time, the **Preview** pane shows an initial result to provide a starting point from which the crafting and fine-tuning of the report results can be done. In the **Preview** pane, you can also set the required report format, which can be either, **Tabular**, **Summary**, or **Matrix**.

The preview shows only a limited number of result records. You need to actually run the report in order to see all the results.

You can drag-and-drop report columns to change the order in which they are displayed. By clicking on the data-column header, you can sort your report using that column. Sorting can also be performed by clicking on the column menu and then choosing either the **Sort Ascending** or the **Sort Descending** option from the drop-down list.

[Sort is disabled when **Show Details** has not been selected.]

If a field has been added to the preview pane and is not required, it can be removed by grabbing its column header and dragging it back to the **Fields** pane. You can also click on the column menu and choose **Remove Column**, or click on **Remove All Columns** to clear the **Preview** pane of all the fields.

While **Show Details** is disabled, you can only add summary fields.

Setting the Date Range option to All Time

When first creating a report involving dates, the date range may not initially be set appropriately. So, there will no obvious results returned. By setting the date range to **All Time**, you will most likely see some data returned, which can be useful as a quick check to see whether the report is working as intended.

Report formats

The following four report formats are available in Salesforce CRM: **Tabular**, **Summary**, **Matrix**, and **Joined**. The features and benefits of each format are outlined next.

The Tabular report format

Tabular reports are the easiest and quickest way to report data. They can be linked to a spreadsheet, where they comprise a set of records listed in rows and fields (ordered in columns). Tabular reports are most suited for creating lists of records or a list with a single grand total as they cannot be used to group data.

Tabular reports cannot be used in dashboards unless the number of rows that are returned are limited.

The Summary report format

Summary reports are similar to tabular reports except that they allow the grouping of rows of data. They can be used for reports to show subtotals based on the value of a field. Summary reports with no groupings are simply displayed as tabular reports.

Summary reports can be used as the source report for dashboard components.

The Matrix report format

Matrix reports are similar to summary reports, but they also allow the grouping and summarizing of data by both rows and columns and can be used for comparing related totals.

Matrix reports are useful for summarizing large amounts of data to compare values in several different fields or for analyzing data by date or by product, person, region, and so on.

 Matrix reports can be used as the source report for dashboard components.

The Joined report format

Joined reports are reports that can store and group multiple reports together and allow you to build a single report that contains data from multiple report types.

A joined report can have up to five report blocks that can be added from either standard or custom report types, but can only be included if they share a common object relationship. For example, if you have a joined report that contains the Opportunities report type, you can then add the Contacts report type since both Opportunity and Contact objects have a relationship with the Accounts object.

For joined reports with multiple report types, any field that is shared by all report types is known as a common field. Common fields appear in the **Common Fields** area in the **Fields** pane and can be used to group together the separate report blocks.

 Joined reports can be used as the source report for dashboard components if the joined report includes a report chart by configuring the dashboard component with the **Use chart as defined in the source report** setting.

The following features are not available in joined reports: **Bucket** fields, **Cross** filters, and **The Rows to Display** filters.

Groupings

Groupings can be added to summary, matrix, and joined reports to group together sections of report data. For example, you might want to group accounts by the number of employees that the account has.

To add a summary field, follow the steps as shown:

1. Drag a field from within the **Fields** pane.

2. Drag the field into the grouping section of the **Preview** pane.

3. Wait for the loading dialog to complete.

4. Observe what the field is showing on the grouping section:

This would produce a report showing the grouped sections, as shown in the following screenshot:

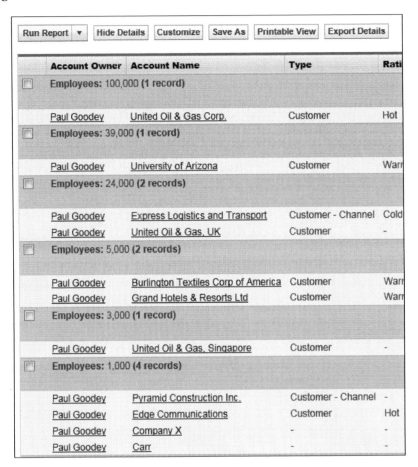

Summary reports can have up to three grouping levels.

Matrix reports can have two row and two column groupings. You cannot use the same field for both the row and the column groupings.

Joined reports can have up to three grouping levels.

Summary fields

A summary field is the SUM, AVERAGE, MIN, or MAX for a number or a currency field. Summary fields are displayed at all grouping levels, including the grand total level for reports that have been created using the summary and matrix report formats.

To add a summary field, click on a column drop-down menu section (shown in the following screenshot) for a field in the report and choose **Summarize this Field**. You can also use this method to add a grouping by choosing **Group by this Field**, as shown here:

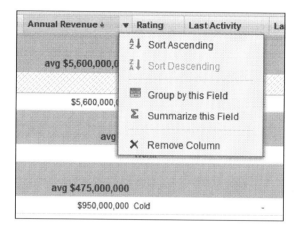

Clicking on the **Summarize this Field** button gives you the following options:

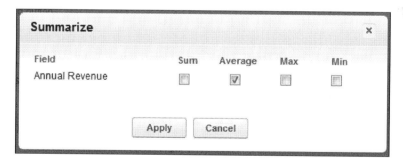

This would produce a report result, as shown in the following screenshot:

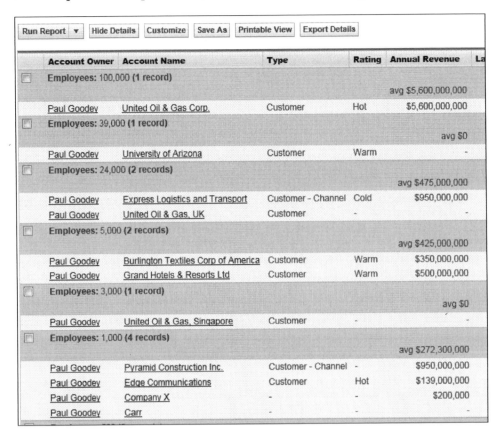

Conditional highlighting

Conditional highlighting is a very powerful way to show at a glance whether the values in reports are within acceptable limits. By setting up conditional highlighting, you can specify different colors for different ranges of values in your reports. It is relatively easy to set up and it offers great visual benefits, and yet it is a feature that seems to be underused by users within Salesforce CRM.

To enable conditional highlighting, your report must contain at least one summary field or custom summary formula.

To set up conditional highlighting, click on **Show** and then on **Conditional Highlighting**, as shown from within the **Preview** pane on the report builder page:

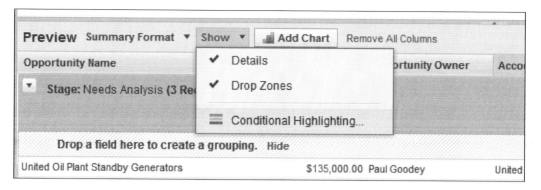

You then have the option to set colors according to whether the value falls below a low breakpoint threshold, above a high breakpoint threshold, or a value that sits between these range of values. The following table helps clarify the thresholds and the colors that would be seen, given the settings shown in the following screenshot:

The color to show data that are below the `Low Breakpoint` value.	The threshold value between the `Low Color` and the `Mid Color` values. In this example: 60,000	The color to show data that are between the `Low Breakpoint` and `High Breakpoint` values.	The threshold value between the `Mid Color` and the `High Color` values. In this example: 95,000	The color to show data that are above the `High Breakpoint` value.
In this example: Red	Values that are exactly the same as the `Low Breakpoint` value are shown as `Mid Color`.	In this example: Amber	Values that are exactly the same as the `High Breakpoint` value are shown as `High Color`.	In this example: Green

The settings are shown in the following screenshot:

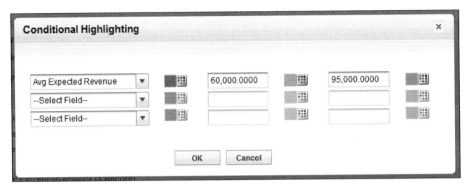

When running the report, the result appears as shown in the following screenshot:

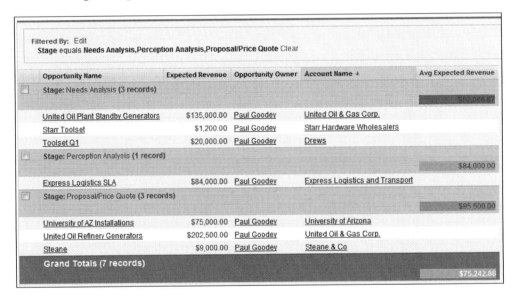

Custom summary formulas

Custom summary formulas allow you to calculate values based on the numeric fields available in the report type. This means you do not have to create custom formula fields for calculated results if they are only relevant in reports.

Formulas must be 3,900 characters or less. Up to five formulas can be created per report. Fields available for custom summary formulas are **Number**, **Percent**, and **Currency**. To add a new formula to a summary or matrix report, navigate to the **Fields** pane, where at the top, you will see the formulas folder icon. By double-clicking on the **Add Formula** option, you can define it and then click on **OK**. After you have defined a new formula on the report, it automatically gets added to the preview pane as a column for summary reports and as a summary field for matrix reports. The following screenshot shows the formula called **Avg Expected Revenue** the top-left section of the **Fields** pane and how it automatically appears in the preview pane as a column (on the far right) for the example summary report:

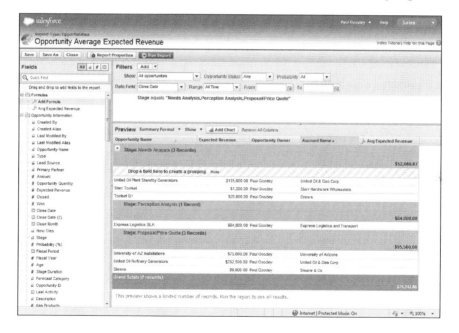

To define a formula field, follow these steps:

1. Click on **Add Formula** in the **Fields** pane:

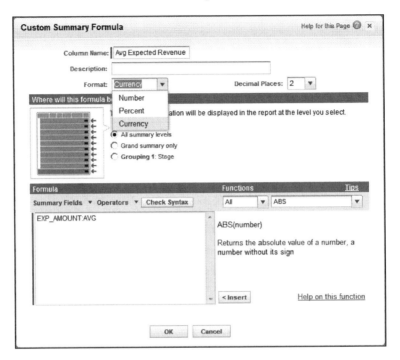

2. Enter a column name for the formula. This will be displayed within the report.
3. Optionally, enter a description.
4. Select the data type from the **Format** picklist.
5. Select the number of decimal places from the **Decimal Places** picklist.
6. Set the option, where this formula is to be displayed.
7. The formula calculation will be displayed in the report at the level that is selected.
8. Build the formula by selecting one of the fields listed in the **Summary Fields** picklist and then select the summary type:

Summary type	Description
Sum	The sum of data in a field or grouping of fields
Largest Value	The largest value of data in a field or grouping of fields
Smallest Value	The smallest value of data in a field or grouping of fields
Average	The average of data in a field or grouping of fields

9. Click on **Operators** to add operators to the formula. Select the function category, choose the function you want to use in your formula, and click on **Insert**.

10. Click on **Check Syntax** to check that the formula contains no errors and then click on **OK**.

Hiding details when building new reports

Often when building new reports, you will not necessarily know just how many records are actually going to be returned. This can be the reason for the report in the first place. You may also be experimenting with the report format to see which data are being returned. In these cases, you should set the **Hide Details** option to prevent the detailed data being returned and show just the "skeleton" of the report—this shows the number of rows that will be returned. Limiting rows on a tabular report allows you to use it as a source report for dashboard table and chart components. However, if you change the report format, the **Row Limit** setting is automatically removed.

Bucket fields

Bucket fields allow you to categorize values based on fields available in the report type. This means you do not have to create custom formula fields for categories or segmentation of values if they are only relevant in reports. For example, sales managers can bucket or group opportunities by size based on amount, support managers can age cases based on days opened, and sales reps can group accounts into strategic accounts.

Fields available as Bucket fields are **Number**, **Percent**, **Currency**, **Picklist**, and text fields.

Changing the report format

Sometimes it is necessary to change the report format for the existing reports. The effects of changing the report format are as follows:

Report format change	Effects of the change
Change from `Tabular` to either `Summary` or `Matrix`	The `Rows to Display` filter is not applicable for `Summary` or `Matrix` reports, and is therefore removed.
Change from `Summary`, `Matrix`, or `Joined` to `Tabular` reports	Groupings are not applicable for `Tabular` reports and are removed from the report. The fields used for grouping are removed and not converted to columns in the tabular report.
Change from `Summary` report to `Matrix` report	The `Summary` first grouping is used as the first `Matrix` row grouping. The second summary grouping is used as the first column grouping. The third summary grouping is used as the second row grouping. Note: When using the report wizard, the third summary grouping is automatically removed.
Change from `Matrix` report to `Summary` report	The `Matrix` first row grouping becomes the first summary grouping. The second row grouping becomes the third summary grouping. The first column grouping becomes the second summary grouping. The `Matrix` second column grouping is removed. Note: When using the report wizard, both the second row grouping and second column grouping are removed.
Change from `Tabular`, `Summary`, or `Matrix` to `Joined`	The `Matrix` first row grouping becomes the first summary grouping. The second row grouping becomes the third summary grouping. The first column grouping becomes the second summary grouping. The `Matrix` second column grouping is removed. Note: When using the report wizard, both the second row grouping and second column grouping are removed.

Dashboards

Dashboards are visual information snapshots that are generated from the data in associated reports and are presented as graphical elements. These graphical elements are known as dashboard components, of which there are the following five types: charts, gauges, tables, metrics, and Visualforce pages.

Dashboards can have up to 20 components, and you can control users' access to dashboards by storing them in folders with appropriate permissions, where folders can be public, hidden, or restricted to groups or roles.

Dashboards can be further configured to run with the concept of a **running user**, which means that the named user's security settings determine which data to display. Here, all dashboard viewers see data according to the security settings of that user who has been set as the running user, irrespective of the dashboard viewer's own personal security settings.

A more flexible and dynamic approach, however, allows you to set the running user to be the logged-in user, so that each user is presented with the dashboard according to their own data access level. This is known as **dynamic dashboards**.

Dashboard component types

In Salesforce CRM, the following dashboard component types (shown in the following screenshot) can be set up for display in dashboards:

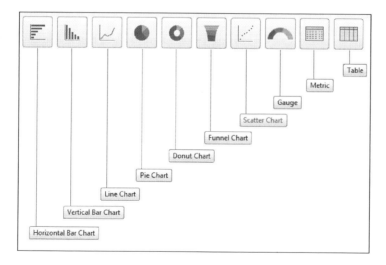

Chart

Chart component types may be used to show data graphically, where the following variety of chart types can be selected: horizontal and vertical bar charts, line charts, pie, donut, funnel, and scatter charts.

Gauge

Gauge component types may be used to show a single value that is to be shown as a part of a range of custom set values. Here, the ranges that can be set can represent say, low, medium, and high values, and the value from the report is plotted accordingly.

Metric

Metric component types may be used to show a single value to display.

Table

Table component types may be used to show a set of report data in column form.

Visualforce page

In addition to the standard types, Visualforce page component types may be used to create a custom component type and present information in a way not available in the standard dashboard component types.

Creating dashboards

Before creating dashboards, you need to have pre-prepared source reports containing the data you wish to display.

 These source reports must be stored in folders that your intended dashboard viewers have access to or they will not be able to view the information.

To create a dashboard, click on the **Reports** tab. This then presents the common reports and dashboards main page with the heading **Reports & Dashboards**. On this page, click on the **New Dashboard...** button, as shown in the following screenshot:

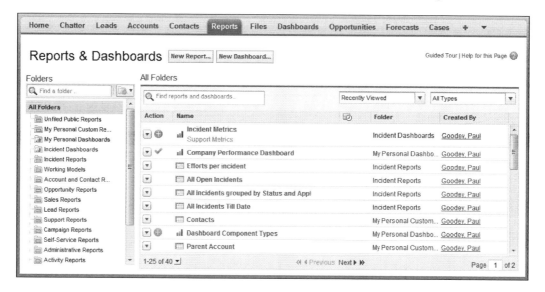

Dynamic dashboards

A dynamic dashboard runs using the security settings of the user viewing the dashboard. Each user sees the dashboard according to his or her own access level. This approach helps you to share one common set of dashboard components to users with different levels of access. A single dynamic dashboard can display a standard set of metrics across all levels of your organization.

> Salesforce CRM limits permit organizations to have up to five dynamic dashboards for Enterprise Edition and up to ten for Unlimited Edition.

Setting up dynamic dashboards

Before setting up dynamic dashboards, you should create folders that are accessible to all dashboard viewers in which to store dynamic dashboards and corresponding component source reports.

To create dynamic dashboards, follow the steps given here:

1. From the **Dashboards** tab, create a new dashboard by following the steps discussed earlier in this chapter.

2. Click on the drop-down arrow button to the right of the **View dashboard as field** option.

3. Select the **Run as logged-in user** option

4. Optionally, check the **Let authorized users change running user** checkbox to enable those with permission to change the running user on the dashboard view page.

5. Click on **OK**.

6. Finally, click on **Save** on the main dashboard.

Customizing dashboards

The Salesforce dashboard builder is a drag-and-drop interface for creating and modifying dashboards. To customize an existing dashboard, display it and then click on **Edit**. The dashboard builder main page presents options to set the properties for the dashboard and also to change how the dashboard is viewed by selecting the appropriate running user option.

Clicking on **Dashboard Properties** allows you to set the title, a unique name, and the dashboard folder:

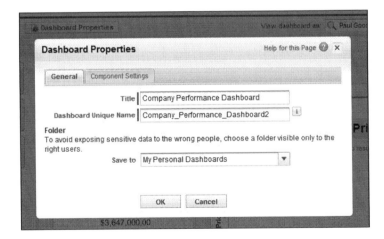

Setting the running user

To view or set the running user for the dashboard, select from the **View dashboard as:** option located on the top right of the page:

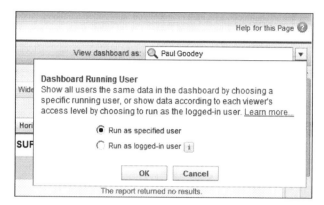

You can add a description to the dashboard by clicking on the text **Click to enter a dashboard description** at the top of the dashboard.

 Changes are lost if you close or navigate away from the dashboard builder without saving it first.

Column-level controls

Within the main dashboard's editing page, you are able to add the specific dashboard components:

- Click on **+** to add a new column. Dashboards can have up to three columns.
- Click on **x** on a column to delete it. Before removing a column, move the dashboard components to another column if you want them to remain visible.

 Dashboards must have at least two columns.

- To set the width for the column, you can select either, **Narrow**, **Medium**, or **Wide** in the column width drop-down list, as shown next:

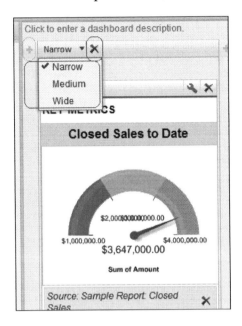

 If the component is a pie or donut chart with **Show Values** or **Show Percentages** enabled and **Legend Position** set to **Right**, the dashboard column width must be **Wide** for the values and percentages to be shown on the dashboard.

Component-level controls

You can add components by dragging a component type onto a column and then dropping a data source (which is a source report) or a Visualforce page onto it.

You can also drop the data source first and then drop a component type onto it. To change the type or source after you have created it, you can drop a different one onto the component. Each component must have a type and a data source.

 Each folder can display up to 200 data sources. However, if there are more than 200, you can use the **Quick Find** option or set filters to reduce the displayed list.

The following screenshot shows the drag-and-drop feature using a report from the **Data Sources** tab:

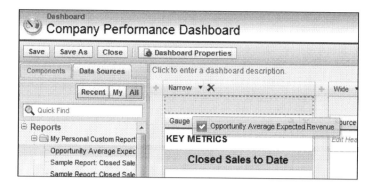

To drag-and-drop a line chart from the **Components** tab, you simply select, hold, and drag the icon onto the source, as shown here:

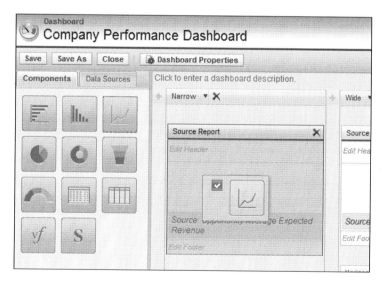

The following is the result:

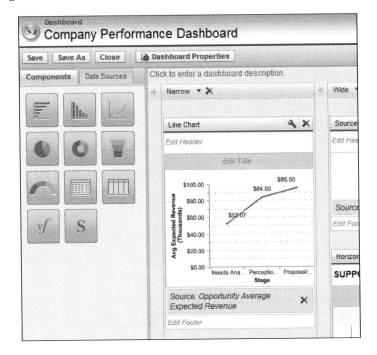

Again, using the drag-and-drop feature, it is possible to rearrange components. Start by grabbing components by the header bar and then dragging them to the right-side location on the dashboard.

As shown in the preceding screenshot, you can edit or delete the dashboard component and also edit the header, title, and footer.

Here you can also delete the data source associated with the dashboard component.

> Dashboard Metric components that are positioned above and below each other in a dashboard column are presented together as a single component.

Setting dashboard properties

To set dashboard properties, follow these steps:

1. Edit a dashboard and click on **Dashboard Properties**.
2. Enter a title for the dashboard.
3. Select a folder to store the dashboard.
4. Under **Component Settings**, select the title color and size, text color, and background fade. If you don't want a gradient, choose the same color for both **Starting Color** and **Ending Color**.
5. Click on **Save**.

Deleting dashboards

Deleting a dashboard also deletes the components within it, although the custom reports used by the components are not deleted. Deleted dashboards are moved to the Recycle Bin.

To delete a dashboard, follow these steps:

1. Click on the **Dashboards** tab.
2. Click on **Go To Dashboards List**.
3. Choose the folder where the dashboard is stored.
4. Click on **Del** next to the name of the dashboard.

Printing dashboards

Dashboards can be printed using the web browser's print option. Set the paper orientation to print in landscape format so that it is wide enough for all three columns of dashboard components.

Some dashboards may not print as expected due to browser issues. Here, you can try resizing the dashboard columns and removing the browser-imposed headers and footers. Also, setting the paper orientation to print in landscape format can help ensure that the printed output is wide enough for all three columns that contain the dashboard components.

Summary

In this chapter, we looked at data analytics, where it was shown how data can be reported and presented within Salesforce CRM. We looked at setting up reports, dashboards, custom reports, and how to use the report builder.

In the next chapter, we will look at the methods for automating business tasks and activities to align them with business rules. The mechanisms that are available to help manage business processes will also be covered in detail, where we will look at the way approvals can be configured.

6
Implementing Business Processes in Salesforce CRM

In the previous chapter, we looked at data analytics, where we covered reports and dashboards.

In this chapter, we will cover in detail how, with the use of the workflow rules and approval process features within the Salesforce CRM application, you can automate and streamline the key business processes for your organization.

This chapter will focus on how you can configure actions for workflow rules and approval processes to automate, improve quality, and generate high-value processes within your organization.

The topics covered are:

- Workflow rules
- Approval process
- Workflow actions
- Workflow queue
- Approval wizard
- Process visualizer
- Visual Workflow

Workflow rules and approval processes

The workflow rules and approval process features within the Salesforce CRM application allow you to automate and streamline the key business processes for your organization.

Workflow rules can be used to capture key business processes and events to generate automated actions. They allow you to configure various types of actions to fire based on the field or fields of the record, meeting predefined conditions. In essence, a workflow rule sets workflow actions into motion when its predefined conditions are met. You can configure workflow actions to execute immediately whenever a record meets the conditions specified in the workflow rule, or you can set time-dependent features that execute the workflow actions on a specific day.

Approval processes are a structured set of steps used to facilitate formal sign-off on data records. They can range from simple, single steps to complex, sophisticated routing to provide automated processing that your organization can use to approve records in Salesforce CRM. Along with the steps that must be taken, the approval process also specifies who must approve these steps. Approval steps can either be specified for all records included in the process or restricted to records that have certain attributes. Approval processes also specify the actions that are to be taken when a record is first submitted, approved, rejected, or recalled.

Workflow rules and approval processes provide benefits such as improving the quality and consistency of data, increasing data integrity, improving efficiency and productivity, lowering costs, and reducing risks.

Workflow rules and approval processes allow you to automate the following types of actions: e-mail alerts, tasks, field updates, and outbound messages.

E-mail alerts can be sent to one or more recipients. For example, e-mail alert actions can be used to automatically send an account owner an e-mail whenever updates are made to one of their accounts by another user.

Tasks can be assigned to users or record owners. For example, task actions can be used to automatically assign follow-up tasks to a marketing executive whenever a new lead is entered in the system.

Field updates can be used to modify the value of a field on a record. For example, a field update action can be used to automatically update an opportunity field called "Next Step" when it reaches a certain sales stage.

Outbound messages can be used to send a secure configurable API message (in XML format) to a designated listener. For example, outbound messages can be used to automatically invoke a new account creation process. This could be, say, whenever a new account is entered in the Salesforce CRM application by triggering an outbound API message to an external financial system.

Workflow rules in Salesforce CRM can be combined to help manage an entire process. For example, when a lead is entered through your website using the Web to lead (covered later), workflow rules can be used to automatically send a responding e-mail to the lead contact and also to someone within your organization. Here, a workflow rule can be set to create a task for one of your salespersons to telephone the lead contact along with a reminder e-mail alert to be sent after a specified number of days after the lead record has been entered.

If the salesperson changes the lead status, then a date field could be updated automatically with the date that the lead was contacted.

Up until now, we have looked at the similarity of workflow rules and approval processes. However, there are some key differences. Workflow rules consist of a single step and a single action, whereas approval processes consist of multiple steps and different actions that can be taken based upon whether the record is approved or rejected. Workflow rules trigger automatically and the rules when triggered are not visible to the user. Approval processes, on the other hand, contain multiple steps each requiring a specific "I approve or reject" user action by the specified approver(s).

In practice, the first step in creating workflow rules and approval processes is to define and map out the process and for each step in the process, detail the objects, the criteria, the users, and the actions required.

Workflow and approval actions

Workflow and approval actions consist of e-mail alerts, tasks, field updates, and outbound messages that can be triggered either by a workflow rule or by an approval process.

- **E-mail alert**: An e-mail alert is an action that can be generated by both workflow and approval actions using an e-mail template that is sent to specified recipients which can be either Salesforce CRM application users or external e-mail recipients.

- **Field update**: A field update is an action that can be activated by use of both workflow and approval actions that specifies the field for update and the new value for it. The field's update action depends on the data type of the field, where you can choose to apply a specific value, clear the field, or calculate a value according to a criteria or a derived formula that you can a specify.

- **Task**: Tasks are workflow and approval actions that are triggered by workflow rules or approval processes, and they allow the assignment of tasks to a user that you can specify. You would also specify the **Subject, Status, Priority**, and **Due Date** of the task. Tasks appear on the user's calendar, and can be accessed by the **My Tasks** section of the **Home** tab or on the specific day for the task within the **Day View** section on the user's calendar. Tasks can be assigned on their own, but you can also combine them with an e-mail alert to inform the user.

- **Outbound message**: An outbound message in Salesforce CRM is an action that can be activated by both workflows and approvals that sends information to a web URL endpoint all of which you specify. The outbound message contains the data in specified fields in what is known as a SOAP message to the endpoint. As this requires development of a receiving web-service, this action is not covered in this book.

Configuring e-mail alerts for workflow rules and approval processes

To configure e-mail alerts, follow the path **Your Name | Setup | (App Setup) | Create | Workflow & Approvals | Email Alerts**, and then click on the **New Email Alert** button.

Within the **Email Alert Edit** page, the following settings are presented:

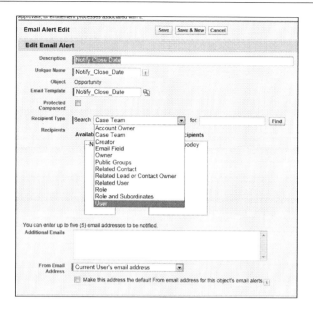

To set the details for the e-mail alert, carry out the following steps:

1. Enter a description for the e-mail alert.

2. Enter a unique name for the e-mail alert.

 The unique name for the e-mail alert is required and used by the API and managed packages. The name is auto-populated when you enter the preceding field called **Description**. There are restrictions for permitted characters whereby the unique name must begin with a letter and use only alphanumeric characters and underscores. Also, the unique name cannot end with an underscore nor have two consecutive underscores.

3. Choose an e-mail template.

 The **Protected Component** checkbox is used to mark the alert as protected. This option can be ignored as it is a setting used by developers who are building applications with the "managed release" package functionality. If you install a managed package, there are restrictions on what can be edited by non-developers. This is discussed later in the book.

Now select who should receive this e-mail alert from the available options:

Recipients	Description
Account Owner	If the **Account Owner** is selected, then the e-mail alert is sent to the user in Salesforce CRM who is set as the account owner of either the account record or the account that is related to the record. Since this option requires an account relationship to be present, it is only valid on accounts, opportunities, contacts, and custom objects that are children of the account object.
Account Team	Choose from the list of users that are assigned to a particular account team role. Note that e-mail alerts are only sent when the rule is associated with the account object or any of its direct child objects.
Case Team	Choose from the list of users assigned to a particular case team role.
Creator	This is the user listed as the record creator and is the user who is set in the **Created By** field.
Customer Portal User	Choose from the list of users that are associated with a Customer Portal.
Email Field	An e-mail address field on the selected object, such as the **Email** field on contact records or a custom e-mail field.
Owner	The record owner.
Partner User	Choose from the list of users that are associated with a partner portal.
Portal Role	Choose from the list of users that are assigned to a particular portal role.
Portal Role and Subordinates	Choose from the list of users assigned to a particular portal role, plus all users in roles below that role.
Public Groups	Choose from the list of users in a particular public group.
Related Contact	An associated contact on the record. For example, you may have created a custom contact on the opportunity object called "Key Decision Maker".
Related Lead or Contact Owner	This is a related user lookup to the owner fields set on either the lead or contact record that is associated to the record. As an example, for opportunities, this field could be set to a contact role field linking to a contact.
Related User	A **Related User** is a user lookup field that is associated to the record. As an example, this field may be set to the **Last Modified By** field.
Role	Choose from the list of users assigned a particular role.
Role and Internal Subordinates	Choose from the list of users in a particular role, plus all users in roles below that role, excluding partner portal and Customer Portal users.

Recipients	Description
Role and Subordinates	Choose from the list of users in a particular role, plus all users in roles below that role.
User	Choose from the list of available users in Salesforce CRM.
Sales Team	After having set up sales teams, this option allows you to choose from the list of users associated to a sales team.

Select the recipients who should receive this e-mail alert in the **Available Recipients** list and click on **Add**.

 If you change the object after selecting the recipients, the **Selected Recipients** list will be automatically cleared.

Optionally, enter to and from e-mail addresses, and then finally click on **Save**.

Here you can do the following:

- Enter up to five additional recipient e-mail addresses (which may or may not be users in Salesforce)
- Set the **From Email Address** to either the current user's e-mail address or to the default workflow user's e-mail address
- Finally, to begin using the e-mail alert, associate it with either a workflow rule or an approval process

 Set the From Email Address

Setting the **From Email Address** also allows you to use a standard global e-mail address for your organization, such as `Customer_Services@WidgetXYZ.com`, instead of the default **From** field, which is the e-mail address of the user who updates the record. Only verified, organization-wide e-mail addresses will appear in the **From Email Address** picklist options.

There is a daily limit of 1,000 e-mail alerts per standard Salesforce license for workflows and approvals.

There is also an overall daily limit of 2,000,000 e-mail alerts for your entire organization and when the daily limits are reached, a warning e-mail is sent out by the Salesforce CRM application to the default workflow user where one is set. If there is no default workflow user set, then the warning e-mail goes out to a system administrator.

Organization-wide e-mail addresses

By setting up organization-wide e-mail addresses, your users can share a set of common e-mail aliases. Here, you can define a list of organization-wide e-mail addresses for each user profile.

When sending e-mails from Salesforce, users with these profiles can then choose a different **From** address than the e-mail address that they have defined on their user record, and any e-mail responses are then returned to the organization-wide address.

To set up the list of organization-wide e-mail addresses, follow the path **Your Name | Setup | (Administration Setup) | Email Administration | Organization-Wide Email Addresses**.

From **Organization-Wide Email Addresses**, you can set the display name, the e-mail address, and the profiles that are permitted to use that address as shown in the following screenshot:

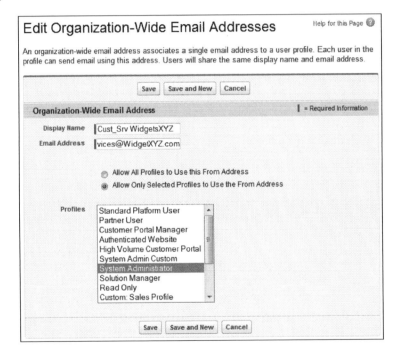

When the organization-wide e-mail address is saved or changed, Salesforce will send an e-mail to the address specified in the e-mail address field to verify that the e-mail address is valid, as shown next:

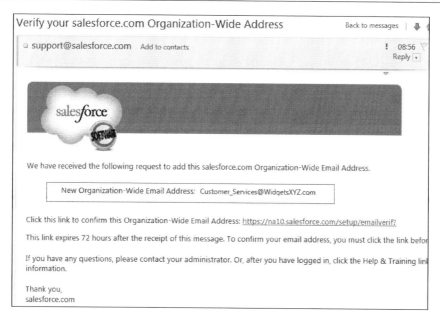

Now, the verified organization-wide e-mail addresses will appear in the **From Email Address** picklist options when configuring e-mail alerts, as shown next:

Configuring tasks for workflow rules and approval processes

To configure tasks, follow the path **Your Name | Setup | (App Setup) | Create | Workflow & Approvals | Tasks,** and then click on the **New Task** button.

From the **Step 1: Select object** page, select the type of object type for the record from the select object picklist and click on **Next**.

 When creating tasks for custom objects, only custom objects that have been set with activities are available for selection in the picklist.

Within the **Step 2: Configure Task** page, the following settings are presented:

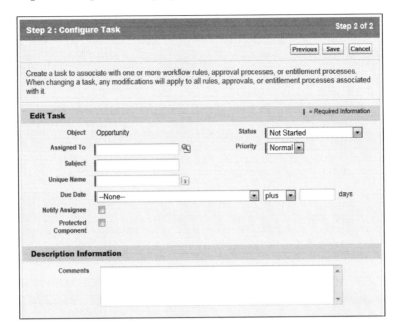

To set the details for the task, carry out the following:

1. You must select an individual or individuals in which to set the required **Assigned To** field. Here, the options when you click on the lookup dialog for the **Assigned To** setting allows for the selection of either **User**, **Role**, or **Record Owner**.

> If the assignee of a workflow task is a role, and that particular role has multiple users, the record owner is then assigned the task. This is done regardless of the type of role that the record owner has, which can cause some confusion.
>
> This is because tasks cannot be assigned to more than one user, and hence best practice dictates that you do not assign tasks to roles even though the option exists

2. Enter a subject and a unique name for the task.

The unique name for the task is required and used by the API and any managed packages. The name is auto-populated when you move from the preceding field called **Subject**. There are restrictions for permitted characters whereby the unique name must begin with a letter and use only alphanumeric characters and underscores. Also, the unique name cannot end with an underscore nor have two consecutive underscores.

3. Choose a due date, status, and priority where due dates appear in the time zone of the assignee.

4. Set the **Notify Assignee** checkbox to also send an e-mail notification when the task is assigned.

 The **Protected Component** checkbox is used to mark the alert as protected. This is used by developers who are building managed package applications for the AppExchange Marketplace (the AppExchange will be covered in a later chapter).

5. Optionally, enter any comments for the description information that is included with the task and then click on **Save**.

6. Finally, to set the task into action, associate it with the required workflow rule or approval process.

 When the task is assigned, it will include a **Created By** field that contains the name of the person who saved the record that triggered the rule to assign the task.

Configuring field updates for workflow rules and approval processes

To configure field updates, follow the path **Your Name** | **Setup** | **(App Setup)** | **Create** | **Workflow & Approvals** | **Field Updates**, and then click on the **New Field Update** button.

Within the **Field Update Edit** page, perform the following:

1. Enter a name and a unique name for the field update.

Both the name and a unique name for the field update are required. The unique name is used by the API and managed packages. The name is auto-populated when you exit the preceding **Name** field. There are restrictions for permitted characters in that the unique name must begin with a letter and use only alphanumeric characters and underscores. Also, the unique name cannot end with an underscore or have two consecutive underscores.

2. Now, optionally enter a description for the field to update and then choose the object type to present the field to be updated as shown here for the **Opportunity** object:

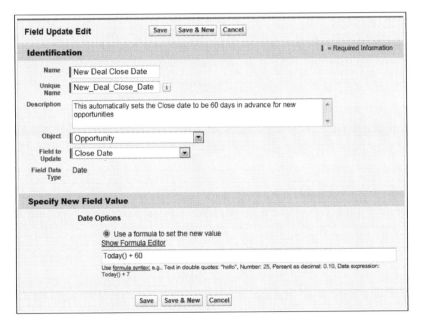

Upon choosing the object and field to update, a new section called **Specify New Field Value** appears where you can set the logic of the desired field update. Here, the available options depend on the type of field you are updating, with the following scenarios:

Checkboxes

For checkboxes, choose **True** to select the checkbox and **False** to deselect it as shown:

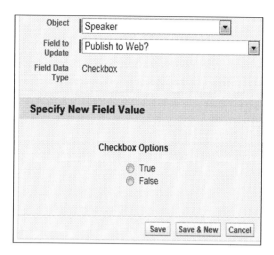

This is useful for automating the setting of status flags for records whenever a certain business process is complete. In the previous example, the field update of the field **Publish to Web?** allows the automatic setting of the checkbox option to **True**, say, so that the record can be published.

Record owners

For record owners, choose the user to whom the record should be assigned as shown in the following screenshot:

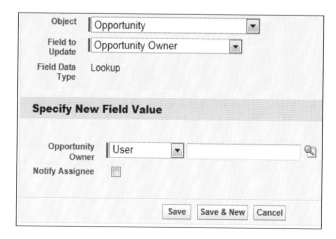

This is useful for automating the changing of the record owner for records whenever a certain business process is complete. For example, you could automate the field update of the record owner from, say, a marketing executive to an account manager if a lead matches certain criteria.

Select Notify Assignee

Selecting **Notify Assignee** allows the automatic sending of an e-mail to the new record owner whenever the field's update fires.

Picklists

For picklist fields, you can either select a specific value from the picklist or you can select the value above or below the current value as shown in the following screenshot. The above or below selection is based on the sorting order that is set in the picklist field definition:

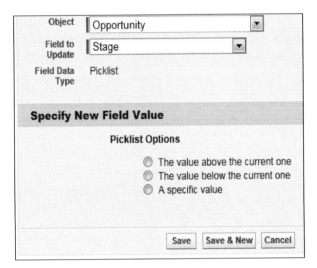

Other data types

For all other data types, you can set the following **Text Options** as shown here:

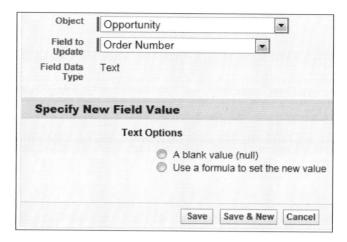

Follow these steps to finish the field update configuration:

1. Choose **A blank value (null)**, if you want to remove any existing value and leave the field blank.

 This option is not available for required fields, checkboxes, and some other types of fields.

2. Choose **Use a formula to set the new value** to calculate the value based on the formula logic.
3. Now click on **Save** to complete the configuration of the field update.
4. Finally, to set the field update into action, associate it with the required workflow rule or approval process.

Configuring outbound message notifications for workflow rules and approval processes

An outbound message in Salesforce CRM is an action that can be activated by both workflows and approvals that sends information to a web URL endpoint that you specify.

The outbound message contains the data using the specified fields in what is known as a SOAP message to the endpoint URL. Once the endpoint receives the message data, it consumes the information from the message and processes it.

 Simple Object Access Protocol (SOAP) is an industry-standard protocol that defines a uniform way of passing data encoded in the XML format. **Extensible Markup Language (XML)** is an industry-standard markup language that enables the sharing and transportation of structured data.

As this requires the development of a receiving web-service endpoint, setting up this action is beyond the scope of this book.

Configuring workflow rules

You can configure your organization's workflow by creating workflow rules. Each workflow rule consists of:

- Criteria that cause the Salesforce CRM application to trigger the workflow rule
- Immediate actions that execute when a record matches the criteria
- Time-dependent actions that the Salesforce CRM application processes when a record matches the criteria and executes according to the specified time triggers

The following table is an overview of the key aspects of configuring workflow rules in Salesforce CRM:

Rules		Actions		Users
Object	Criteria	E-mail alerts	Immediate	People
			Time-dependent	
		Tasks	Immediate	
			Time-dependent	
		Field updates	Immediate	System
			Time-dependent	
		Outbound messages	Immediate	
			Time-dependent	
Example workflow rule				
Opportunity	Whenever an opportunity record is updated	E-mail Alert	Immediate	Account Owner

Create workflow actions ahead of workflow rules

Create actions and any associated e-mail templates before starting to configure workflow rules.

The following outlines the steps required to create a workflow rule:

1. Create the workflow rule and select the object.
2. Configure the settings and criteria for the workflow rule.
3. Specify the workflow actions.
4. Activate the workflow rule.

To create a workflow rule, follow the path **Your Name | Setup | (App Setup) | Create | Workflow & Approvals | Workflow Rules**.

The **Workflow Rules** detail page shows a list of the current workflow rules along with various properties such as the associated object and whether the rule is active. On this page, you can create views to help filter and manage the list of rules as the numbers increase. The following screen shows the list of all the workflow rules in our organization using the **All Workflow Rules** view:

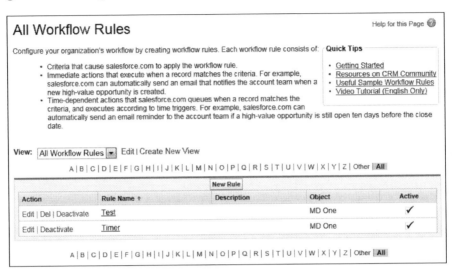

From the workflow rules list page, you can click on the **New Rule** button and then select an object (either a custom or standard object) on which you want to apply your new workflow rule. In the **Step 1: Select object** screen shown as follows, the standard object **Opportunity** has been selected:

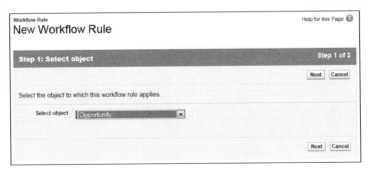

Now, click on **Next** to navigate and display the **Step 2: Configure Workflow Rule** page to allow the rule settings and criteria to be specified, as shown in the following screenshot:

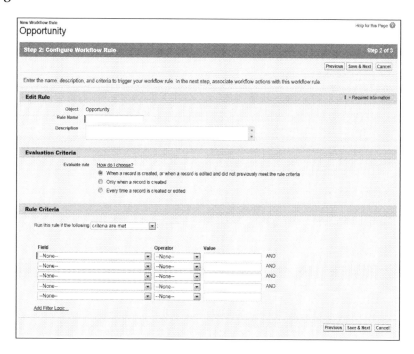

Configuring rule settings and criteria

In the **Edit Rule** section, you must enter a rule name and, optionally, you may enter a description for the rule.

Evaluation Criteria

In the **Evaluation Criteria** section, you choose the appropriate criteria that causes the Salesforce CRM application to trigger the workflow rule.

The criteria can be selected from the following three options:

- **When a record is created, or when a record is edited, and did not previously meet the rule criteria**: Choose this option to include new records and updates to existing records.

 The rule is not re-triggered on record updates that do not affect the specified rule criteria.

For example, if the updating of an opportunity record's probability to 90 percent causes the rule to run, with this option, the rule will only get triggered again if the probability changes and then changes back to 90 percent, regardless of how many times the record is itself updated.

- **Only when a record is created**: Choose this option to ignore any subsequent updates to existing records, as the rule will only ever run once: when the record is inserted.

- **Every time a record is created or edited**: Choose this option to include new record inserts and updates to existing records. These actions cause repeated triggering of the rule as long as the record meets the criteria.

 You cannot add time-dependent actions to a rule if you choose the **Every time a record is created or edited** option.

Rule Criteria

In the **Rule Criteria** section, there are two ways of formulating the logic that is used to trigger the workflow rule. They are as follows:

- Run this rule if the following criteria are met
- Run this rule if the following formula evaluates to true

Run this rule if the following criteria are met

This option is displayed by default and allows you to select the filter criteria that a record must meet to trigger the rule.

As an example, the filter has been set to:

- **Opportunity: Close Date equals NEXT 7 DAYS AND**
- **Opportunity: Closed not equal to True**

These criteria would allow us to construct a workflow rule that could be used to notify a salesperson that they have an open opportunity with a close date that will be reached within a week:

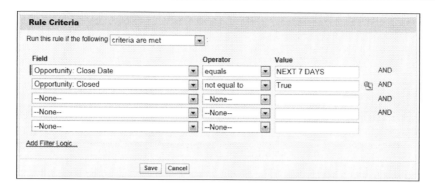

Clicking on the **Add Filter Logic...** link presents additional options for adding rows and advanced filter conditions, as shown in the following screenshot:

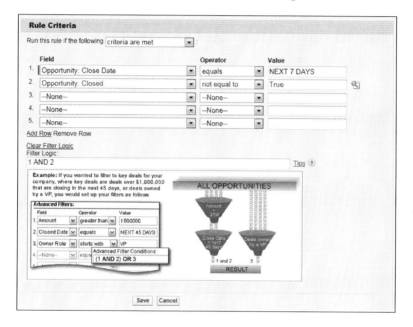

The **Add Row** link allows you to add more criteria options where up to a maximum of 25 can be added.

The **Filter Logic** section allows you to use Boolean expressions to set the criteria. These expressions are known as **Advanced Filters**.

For example, **(1 AND 2)** results in an expression that requires both of the first two filter lines to be valid.

Run this rule if the following formula evaluates to true

This option allows you to enter a formula that returns a value of "True" or "False". The Salesforce CRM application triggers the rule if the formula returns "True".

Workflow formulas can be used to capture complicated logic as shown next for the following use case example:

Whenever an opportunity is set as lost where the sales stage was previously **"Negotiation/Review"** and the amount is greater than $50,000, send an e-mail or task to be sent to Sales Management for follow-up:

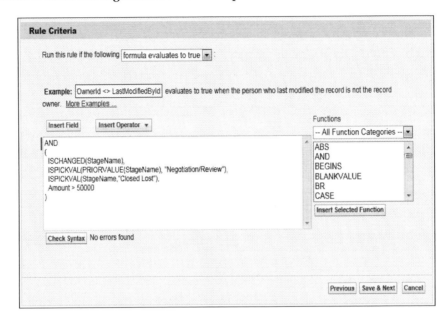

 Some functions are not available in workflow rule formulas; you cannot create a formula in which a custom object references fields on a parent object.

In addition to the functions that are shown on the right-hand side of the **Rule Criteria** section, you can also use merge fields for directly related objects in workflow rule formulas. The rule **Formula evaluates to true** can be useful wherever it is needed to trigger some actions if the value of a particular field is being changed. As for all formula merge fields that allow you to reference fields on related objects across multiple relationships, the field name is prefixed by the name of the relationship. For standard relationships, the name of the relationship is the master object. For example, you can reference the account name merge field from an opportunity using `Account.Name`.

Check Syntax

Click on the **Check Syntax** button to validate that the formula contains no error before progressing beyond this page.

Now click on **Save & Next** to proceed to the **Step 3: Specify Workflow Actions** page, which allows you to configure the workflow actions.

Specifying the workflow actions

The **Specify Workflow Actions** page allows you to add both immediate and time-dependent actions to the workflow rule, as shown in the following screenshot:

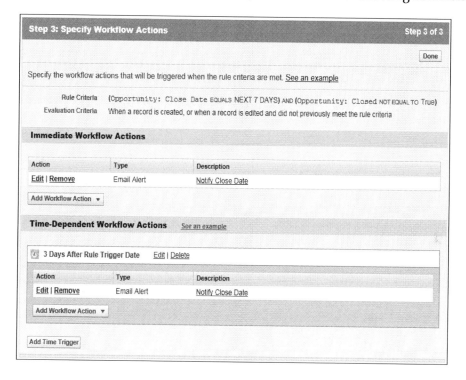

Immediate workflow actions

Immediate actions trigger as soon as the evaluation criteria are met. As shown in the preceding example, the Salesforce CRM application can immediately send an e-mail to the salesperson if an opportunity is created or edited and is still open seven days before the specified close date.

Time-dependent workflow actions

Time-dependent actions specify when Salesforce CRM is to execute the workflow action. As shown in the preceding example, the Salesforce CRM application can automatically send an e-mail reminder to the salesperson three days later if an opportunity is created or edited and is still open seven days before the specified close date.

Time-dependent actions and time triggers are complex features with several considerations

Workflow rules that have time-dependent actions should be specified with a default workflow user to ensure they fire for future actions. This is in case the user who activated the workflow later leaves the organization and is set as an inactive user.

Adding immediate workflow actions

To add an immediate workflow action, click on the **Add Workflow Action** drop-down selection in the **Immediate Workflow Actions** section and choose either **New Task**, **New Email Alert**, **New Field Update**, **New Outbound Message**, or **Select Existing Action** to select an existing action to associate with the rule:

- **New Task** to create a task to associate with the rule
- **New Email** to create an e-mail alert to associate with the rule
- **New Field Update** to define a field update to associate with the rule
- **New Outbound Message** to define an outbound message to associate with the rule
- **Existing Action** to select an existing action to associate with the rule

Adding time-dependent workflow actions

To add a time-dependent workflow action, click on **Add Time Trigger** in the **Time-Dependent Workflow Actions** section. Then, specify the number of days or hours before or after a date relevant to the record, such as the date the record was created or modified or even for an opportunity close date as shown in the following screenshot:

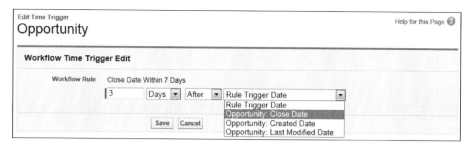

The **Add Time Trigger** button is unavailable if either:

- The rule criteria is set to **Every time a record is created or edited**
- The rule is already active (here, you must temporarily deactivate it in order to apply the action)
- The rule is deactivated, but has pending actions in the workflow queue

Additional, immediate, or time-dependent actions can now be configured, and then finally click on the **Done** button in the top-right corner of the screen.

Activating the workflow rule

The Salesforce CRM application will not trigger a workflow rule until you have manually activated it.

To activate a workflow rule, click on **Activate** on the workflow rule detail page. Click on **Deactivate** to stop a rule from triggering (or if you want to edit the time-dependent actions and time triggers associated with the rule):

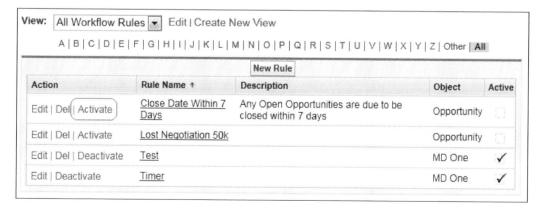

Workflow rule considerations

Consider the following when configuring workflow rules:

- You can deactivate a workflow rule at any time. However, if you deactivate a rule that has pending actions, Salesforce.com completes those actions as long as the record that triggered the rule is not updated.

- You cannot add time-dependent workflow actions to active workflow rules. You must deactivate the workflow rule first, add the time-dependent workflow action, and then re-activate the rule.

- Workflow rules on custom objects are automatically deleted if the custom object is deleted.

- You cannot create e-mail alerts for workflow rules on activity records.

- Creating new records or updating existing records can trigger more than one rule.

- Time-dependent field updates can retrigger the re-evaluation of workflow rules.

- The order in which actions are executed is not guaranteed. Field update actions are executed first, followed by other actions.

> For custom objects, you can create workflow actions where a change to a detail record updates a field on the related master record.
>
> On standard objects, workflow rules can only perform field updates on the object associated with the rule.

For example, in a custom publishing application, you may create a workflow rule that sets the status of a book (the master object) to **In Process - Editor** when a chapter (the detail object) is being reviewed by the editor.

Cross-object field updates only work for custom-to-custom master-detail relationships, and they are displayed in the following way:

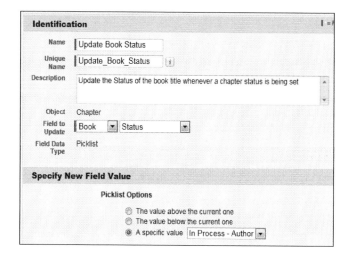

If you require cross-object actions for standard objects such as updating a field on each Opportunity Product record when a certain field on the Opportunity changes, or further complex updating such as automatic record creation or deletion actions, you would need to develop Apex triggers instead of workflow rules.

Monitoring the workflow queue

You can use the time-based workflow queue to monitor any outstanding workflow rule that has time-dependent actions. Here you can view pending actions and cancel them if necessary.

To access the **Time-based Workflow** queue, follow the path **Your Name | Setup | (Administration Setup) | Monitoring | Time-Based Workflow**, where the following page is presented:

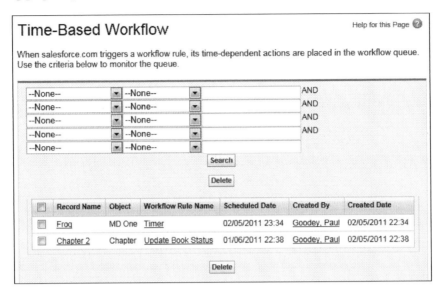

Click on **Search** to view all the pending actions for any active time-based workflow rules, or set the filter criteria and click on **Search** to view only the pending actions that match the criteria. Set the checkbox for any listed workflow rule(s) that you wish to cancel and then click on **Delete** to terminate the selected queued workflow rule(s).

Approval process

An approval process in Salesforce CRM is an automated mechanism that you can set up to process the approval of records within your organization.

Working with approval processes involves the creation of a structured set of steps to enable the sign-off of specified records that must be approved along with specifying which users must be set to approve it at each of the steps. Here, each step can apply to all the records within the process or specified records that have certain field values. The building of approval processes also requires the setting of the required actions to be taken after the record is either, first submitted, approved, rejected, or recalled for approval.

Approval processes are similar to workflow rules in the sense that they can invoke the same key actions; however, there are significant differences between workflow rules and approval processes, such as:

- Workflow rules are activated when a record is saved, whereas approval processes are triggered by explicitly clicking on the **Submit for Approval** button.

- Workflow rules consist of a single step and a single action. Approval processes consist of multiple steps where a different action is taken based upon whether the record is approved or rejected.

- Workflows can be modified or deleted. In approvals, some attributes cannot be modified, and approval processes must be deactivated before outstanding approvals can be deleted.

- Approval processes result in the approval history being automatically tracked, which is not applied to workflow rules.

- When an approval is initiated, the record is "locked down" and cannot be changed by someone other than the approver or system administrator until the record has completed the approval process.

Approval processes require a good understanding of your business rules and processes in order to be successfully implemented.

They must, therefore, be implemented correctly so that records are "locked down" only when necessary to avoid hindering Salesforce users that are attempting to update records.

Approval processes can, however, be a powerful mechanism to control an internal process that must be completed as part of a business process.

Example uses for approval processes are obtaining management sign-off before quotes or contracts are sent to customers or prospects for certain deals, or getting authorization before users are set up in the Salesforce CRM application itself. In this example, the user activation request could be approved by the sales management and individuals from other departments, such as finance, before the user license is obtained and the user record created.

In the same way as workflow actions, approval actions consist of e-mail alerts, tasks, field updates, and outbound messages that can be triggered by the approval process.

The following outlines the work items necessary to configure approval processes:

- Provide the name of the process
- Specify the entry criteria for the records
- Specify who is going to approve
- Specify the e-mail template
- Determine the fields to be displayed on the approver page
- Specify who is going to send the approval mail

Approval process checklist

It is useful to carefully plan Salesforce CRM approval processes to help ensure a successful and smooth implementation. The following checklist specifies the required information and prerequisites needed before starting to configure your approval process:

- Determine the steps and how many levels your process has. It is often useful to map out the process using a charting tool such as Microsoft Visio.
- Decide if users can approve requests by e-mail and set up this feature accordingly.
- Create an approval request e-mail template.
- Determine the approval request sender.
- Determine the assigned approver.
- Determine the delegated approver, if necessary.
- Decide if your approval process needs a filter.
- Design initial submission actions.
- Determine if users can edit records that are awaiting approval.
- Decide if records should be auto-approved or rejected.
- Determine the actions when an approval request is approved or rejected.

Configuring approval processes

To create an approval process, follow these steps:

1. Launch the approval process wizard.
2. Specify **Name**, **Unique Name**, and **Description**.
3. Specify **Criteria** for **Entering Process**.

4. Specify **Approver Field** and **Record Editability**.

5. Select **Email Notification Template**.

6. Configure **Approval Request Page Layout**.

7. Specify **Initial Submitters**.

8. Activate the approval process.

Choosing an approval process wizard

When you click on the **Create New Approval Process** button to start creating an approval process, you are presented with the following two options in which to build the process: **Use Jump Start Wizard** or **Use Standard Setup Wizard**. The following sections outline the differences between these two mechanisms.

Jump Start Wizard

Jump Start Wizard is provided as a quick way to create simple approval processes that have a single step. To simplify the settings, the Salesforce CRM application automatically determines some default options for you with this option.

Standard Setup Wizard

Standard Setup Wizard enables the creation of complex approval processes, and is used where multiple processing steps are required. This option provides the mechanisms to define your process and then uses a setup wizard to define each step within that process.

To create an approval process, follow the path **Your Name | Setup | (App Setup) | Create | Workflow & Approvals | Approval Processes**.

Choose the object for the new approval process, click on it, and then select **Use Standard Setup Wizard** as shown next, where we have selected **Opportunity**:

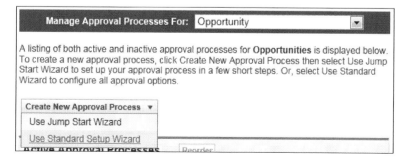

To set the details for the approval process, carry out the following in the **Step 1. Enter Name and Description** page (where this is step 1 of 6):

- Enter a **Process Name**, a **Unique Name**, and optionally a **Description**, and then click on **Next**

To specify the entry criteria, which is an optional step in the **Step 2. Specify Entry Criteria** page and is used to determine the records that enter the approval process, you can either choose from the formula logic or you can select certain fields, operators, and values to specify when the desired criteria are met. This is shown in the following screenshot, which is presented as step 2 of 6:

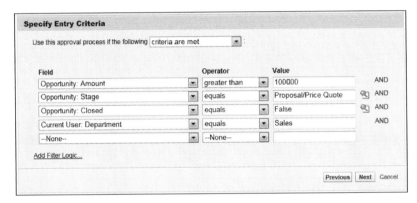

In **Step 2. Specify Entry Criteria**, either enter the filter criteria for records that are to be included by this approval process or leave all the filters blank to have all records submitted within the approval process.

Restrict the approval process for specific users

If only specific users are involved in this approval process, you can specify it here. For example, if only the sales team is to submit opportunity reviews, enter the following filter criteria: **Current User: Department Equals Sales**.

As shown in the preceding screenshot, in the fourth entry criteria row where **Field** is **Current User: Department**, **Operator** is **equals** and **Value** is **Sales**.

Click on **Next** to set the **Specify Approver Field and Record Editability** options.

In this step (step 3 of 6), you would specify who the users are for the approval steps in Salesforce CRM. Here, a user field can be used to automatically route approval requests, and this field can be the **Manager** field on an individual's user record or you can create a custom hierarchical (User to User) field on the User object.

In **Step 3. Specify Approver Field and Record Editability Properties**, using the **Next Automated Approver Determined By** picklist, select a user field if you want the Salesforce CRM application to automatically assign approval requests to an approver based on the value in the user field. For example, you may want to automatically send approval requests to a user's manager as specified in the user's **Manager** field, as shown next:

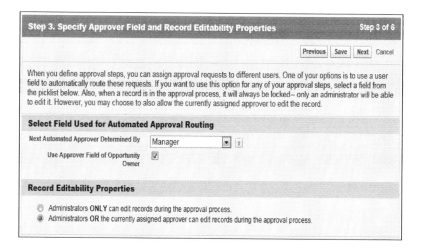

To allow users to manually choose another user that will approve any approval requests, leave the **Next Automated Approver Determined By** field blank:

- By selecting the **Use Approver Field of Record Owner** checkbox, you can set the approval process to use the standard **Manager** field or a custom field on the record owner's user record instead of the submitting user's record.

> If you set the **Use Approver Field of Record Owner** checkbox (applying the manager of the record owner instead of the manager of the submitting user), it is applied to all subsequent steps.

- Select the appropriate **Record Editability Properties** and click on **Next**.

> When a record is in the approval process, it is always locked, and only you as system administrator can edit it. However, you can specify that the currently-assigned approver can also edit the record.

- When an approval process assigns an approval request to a user, Salesforce. com automatically sends the user an approval request e-mail. This e-mail contains a web link that the user can click on to access the approval page within the Salesforce CRM application, which lets the user approve or reject the request and also to enter comments.

Enable e-mail approval response

By enabling e-mail approval response, the user can alternatively reply to the e-mail by typing approve, approved, yes, reject, rejected, or no in the first line of the e-mail body, and then add comments in the second line. This option makes it easy to approve or reject approval requests, and is especially useful for users who access approval requests using a mobile device.

- In **Step 4. Select Email Notification Template,** you can choose a custom e-mail template to be used when notifying an approver that an approval request has been assigned to them, as shown next for the example **Approval Request** template. Alternatively, by leaving this field blank, a simple default e-mail template is used:

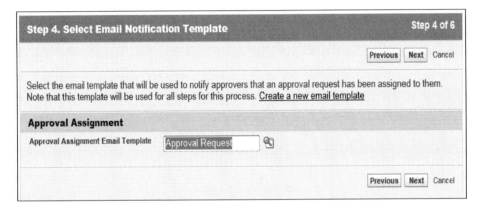

If e-mail approval response is enabled and the user does not respond correctly, perhaps by misspelling the word approve or typing it on the wrong line, the Salesforce CRM application will not process the incorrect response made by the user.

Within the **Step 5. Select Fields to Display on Approval Page Layout** page, the option to configure the approval request page layout can be carried out as shown in the following example:

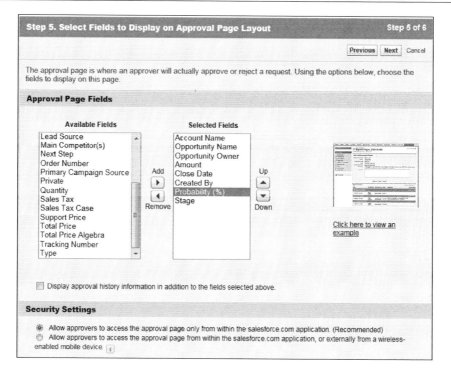

The approval page is where an approver approves or rejects a request, and it is on **Step 5. Select Fields to Display on Approval Page Layout** of configuring the approval process where you can carry out the following:

1. Select and sort the fields you want to display on the approval request page.

2. Select **Display approval history information** in addition to the field selected previously to include the **Approval History** related list which displays the **Date**, **Status**, **Assigned To**, **Actual Approver**, **Comments**, and **Overall Status** columns on the resulting approval request page, as shown in the following screenshot:

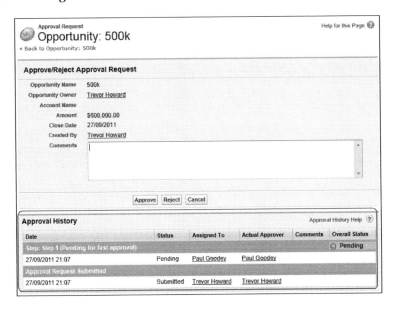

3. To specify how approvers can access an approval page, select either **Allow approvers to access the approval page only from within the application. (Recommended)   Allow approvers to access the approval page from within the salesforce.com application**, or **externally from a wireless-enabled mobile device**, and then click on **Next** (as shown previously in the step 5 screen).

4. Now specify **Initial Submitters** as shown in the following screenshot:

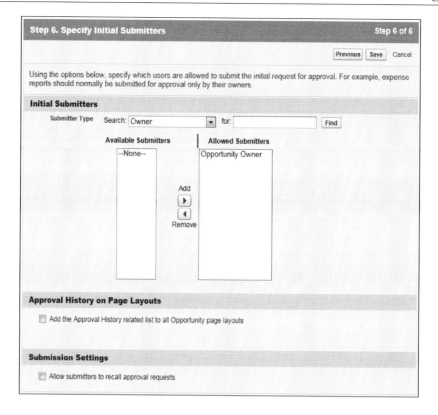

5. Specify which users are allowed to submit records for approval.

6. Optionally, select **Add the Approval History related list to all [object name] page layouts** (as shown for the Opportunity object-related approval). This will automatically update all the page layouts for this object and include a related list that allows users to view and submit approval requests.

7. Optionally, select **Allow submitters to recall approval requests** to give submitters the option to withdraw their approval requests.

When the **Allow submitters to recall approval requests** option is selected, the **Recall Approval Request** button in the **Approval History** related list is visible for the users that have submitted the record as well as you as system administrator.

When a user clicks on **Recall Approval Request**, the pending approval request for the record is withdrawn and the recall action is run.

This option is required for scenarios where changes occur to the record while waiting for approval sign-off. For example, an opportunity might be set to lost or the amount might be lowered below the approval threshold after having submitted it for approval.

Now click on **Save** then **Next**, and then finally click on the **Activate** button next to the process.

 You will be unable to activate the process until you have created at least one approval step for the approval process.

Creating approval steps

Approval steps in Salesforce CRM set the flow of the record approval process that associates the participating users at each chain of approval. For each approval step, we set "who" can approve requests for the records, "what" the record must contain to meet the criteria, and "why" the record should be allowed to be approved (in the case of a delegated approver).

In addition, the very first approval step in a process also specifies the action required whenever the record fails to reach that step. Later steps then require you to set the action to be taken whenever an approver rejects the request.

To create an approval step, follow the path **Your Name | Setup | (App Setup) | Create | Workflow & Approvals | Approval Processes** and select the name of the approval process, and then carry out the following:

- Click on the **New Approval Step** button from the **Approval Steps** related list section

 For both Enterprise and Unlimited Editions, there is a limit of 15 steps per process.

- Enter the **Name**, a **Unique Name**, and an optional **Description** for the approval step
- Enter a step number that positions the step in relation to any other step in the approval process, as shown next, and click on **Next**:

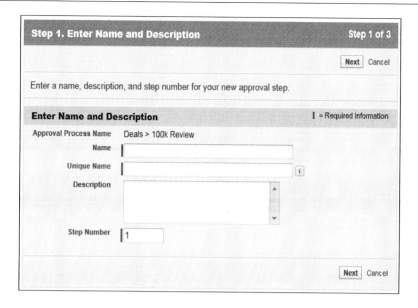

On this page, you specify that either all records should enter this step or that only records with certain attributes should enter this step, as shown in the following screenshot:

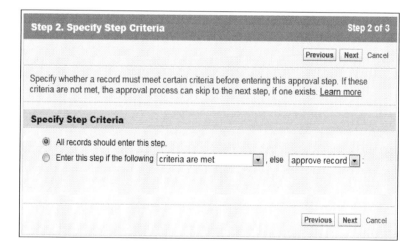

If you specified the filter criteria or entered a formula, you can choose what should happen to records that do not meet the criteria or if the formula returns "False", where the options are:

- **Approve record** to automatically approve the request and perform all final approval actions.

- **Reject record** to automatically reject the request and perform all final rejection actions. This option is only available for the first step in the approval process.

Now click on **Next** to display the page **Step 3. Select Assigned Approver** where you specify the user who should approve records that enter this step and optionally choose whether the approver's delegate is also allowed to approve these requests as shown next:

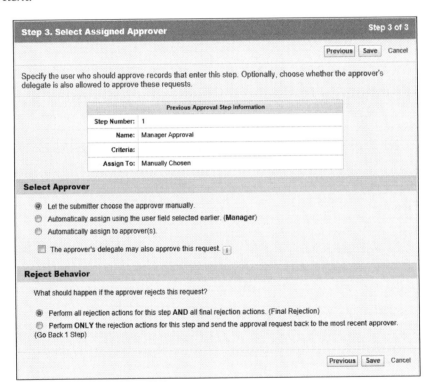

The options are:

- **Let the submitter choose the approver manually,** which prompts the user to manually select the next approver

- **Automatically assign using the user field selected earlier**, which assigns the approval request to the user in the custom field that is displayed next to this option (where this custom field was selected during the earlier configuration of the approval process, which in the preceding screenshot is Manager)

- **Automatically assign to approver(s)**, which allows you to assign the approval request to one or more users or related users as shown next:

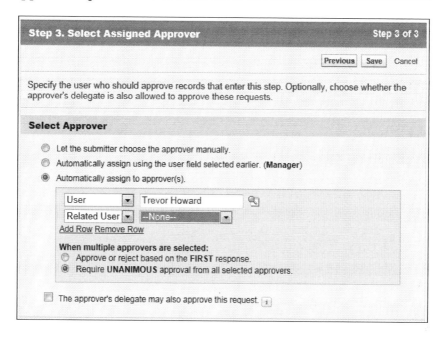

If you specify multiple approvers in the **Automatically assign to approver(s)** option, choose one of the following options:

- **Approve or reject based on the FIRST response**, whereby the first response to the approval request determines whether the record is approved or rejected.

- **Require UNANIMOUS approval from all selected approvers**, whereby the record is only approved if all of the approvers approve the request. If any of the approvers reject the request, then the approval request is rejected.

> For both Enterprise and Unlimited Editions, each approval step can have up to 25 approvers.

Also on this page, there is the option to specify that **The approver's delegate may also approve this request**, where the delegate user is set in the **Delegated Approver** field on the assigned approver's user page.

Delegated approvers cannot reassign approval requests, and they are only permitted to approve or reject approval requests.

If this is not the first step in the approval process, you must specify what will happen if the approver rejects a request in this step, as shown in the following example, where the options are:

- Perform all rejection actions for this step and all final rejection actions (Final Rejection).
- Perform only the rejection actions for this step and send the approval request back to the most recent approver (go back one step).

Now click on **Save** and specify any workflow action you want to set within this step using the following options:

- Yes, I'd like to create a new approval action for this step now
- Yes, I'd like to create a new rejection action for this step now
- No, I'll do this later. Take me to the approval process detail page to review what I've just created

Finally, click on **Go!** to complete the approval process.

Measuring and refining

Although you will need to plan for successful implementation of approval processes, it is highly likely that they will need to change over time. This could be due to a change of business processing or refinement of the process within the Salesforce CRM application.

It is therefore a good idea to create analytics to help measure and verify that the approval process is operating successfully. You could, for example, produce reports and dashboards to measure how long approvals take through the process and identify any areas of the process that are not working as expected and refine them accordingly.

Process visualizer

The process visualizer provides a read-only representation of your saved approval processes. It can be accessed by clicking on the **View Diagram** button from within the saved approval process as shown in the following screenshot:

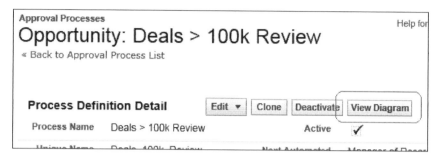

The following screen is displayed for the simple two-step approval process for reviewing opportunity deals that are greater than 100k:

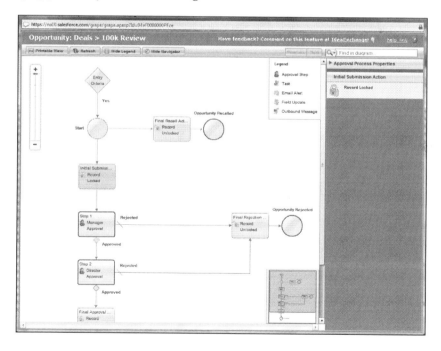

With the process visualizer, you can also print an annotated version of the approval process, where numbers appearing on the diagram correspond to details in a table that is included in the printable view.

Having the process set out diagrammatically can help in the understanding of:

- The steps necessary for a record to be approved
- The designated approvers for each step
- The criteria used to trigger the approval process
- The specific actions taken when a record is approved, rejected, recalled, or first submitted for approval

Visual Workflow

Visual Workflow allows you to build collections of screens, which are known as **flows**, to guide users through the process of collecting and updating data.

Working with flows involves the creation of a structured set of steps to enable users to complete specified business processes. These business processes could be, for example, call scripts for a customer support team, questionnaires and surveys for customers or employee interaction, or processes to handle incoming sales enquiries for your organization.

Use cases for flows are many and varied and the **Visual Workflow** options allow you to create screens that collect and display information, create and update Salesforce records, and carry out logic based on input from users all from within the drag-and-drop **Visual Workflow** user interface.

Configuring Visual Workflow

Working with Visual Workflow involves the following three concepts: flow design, flow management, and runtime. Flow design and management is carried out using the **Flow Designer**, which is part of the Salesforce CRM setup options. Once the flow has been designed and created, you can then manage it by setting properties, activating, deactivating, deleting, or running it all from within the Salesforce CRM application. Finally, users can then run activated flows, again from within Salesforce. Here, you can configure the flow to be run from a custom button, link or tab, from within a Visualforce page, or directly using the Salesforce flow URL.

Flow Designer

Visual Workflow and the Flow Designer are accessed by following the path **Your Name | Setup | (App Setup) | Create | Workflow & Approvals | Flows**.

To create and manage flows in the Cloud Flow Designer, click on **New Flow** or edit an existing flow.

The Flow Designer has a drag-and-drop user interface that lets you configure screens and define branching logic without writing any code, as shown in the following screenshot:

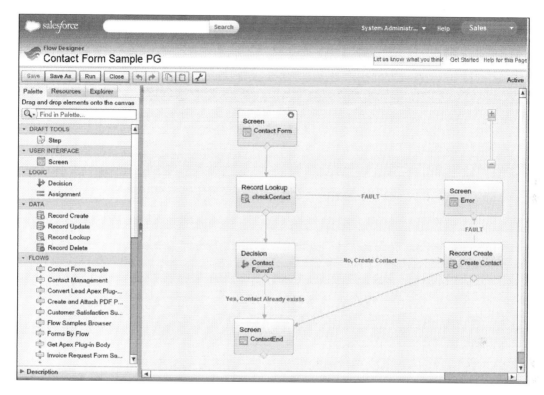

The Flow Designer user interface has the following features and functional sections:

- Buttons in the button bar section let you save, close, undo or redo, view properties of, or run the flow.

- Status indicator on the right-hand side of the bar indicates that the flow is active, saved, or whether it has any warnings or errors.

- The **Palette** tab lists all the element types available for the flow. Here you can drag-and-drop elements from the Palette onto the Canvas to configure them.

- The **Resources** tab lets you create new resources for the flow, like variables, constants, formulas, and so on. Once created, the new resources will appear in the **Explorer** tab.

- The **Explorer** tab is a library of all the elements and resources that have been created for the flow.

- The **Description** pane is used to show details for the selected item when you click on them in the **Pallet, Resources**, and **Explorer** tabs.

- Canvas is where your flow is built. Here, elements are added from the Palette then configured and connected to create the structured set of steps for the flow.

Flow Designer considerations

It is useful to have a general idea for how the flow will be built in Salesforce CRM to help ensure a successful and smooth implementation. Consider the following considerations before starting to configure your flow:

- Use a **Step** element as a placeholder if you are unsure of exactly which element you need at a given point in the flow. This allows for the iterative building of the flow allowing you to further refine it as your understanding of the process develops.

- To select multiple elements, either use the left-mouse to click and select an area around the multiple elements to highlight them or use control-click to select individual elements. You can then press the *Delete* button on your keyboard to delete them all at once.

- To view the description or details for an item in the **Palette, Resources,** or **Explorer** tab, click on the item and look at the caption in the **Description** pane.

Now, let's look at the **Palette, Resources**, and **Explorer** tabs in more detail.

The Palette tab

The **Palette** tab lists the element types available for the flow. Here, you can drag-and-drop elements from the **Palette** tab onto the main canvas. Once created, the new elements appear in the **Explorer** tab.

Elements are the key aspects of building flows. They represent an action such as collecting or displaying information from users, or querying, creating, updating, and deleting data records. Elements can be connected to create a structured set of steps consisting of screens, inputs, outputs, and branch logic through which users are guided.

Elements

The following elements are available in the Cloud Flow Designer:

- **Step**: A placeholder element you can use to quickly sketch out a flow and then convert into a Screen element

- **Screen**: A user-facing screen that can be used to collect input or display output

- **Decision**: Uses conditions to determine where to route users next in the flow

- **Assignment**: Set or change the value of variables

- **Record Create**: Create a new record and insert resource values into its fields

- **Record Update**: Update one or multiple records' fields with resource values

- **Record Lookup**: Find a record and assign its fields to variables

- **Record Delete**: Delete records that match certain criteria

- **Subflows**: Nested flow

- **Apex Plug-In**: Logic built in apex code via apex classes or Appexchange packages

Using the Step element

From within the **DRAFT TOOLS** section, the **Step** element can be used to diagram the flow of your business process. The **Step** element is simply a placeholder, and it cannot be used in an active flow. It is used instead to quickly diagram out the series of steps for the business process that is being built. Once you have each **Step** in place and you want to get the flow activated, you can hover over the **Step** and click on the **Convert Element** (double arrow icon) option. This then enables the conversion of the draft **Step** into a **Screen** element, which is the building block for every flow.

Using the Screen element

The **Screen** element can be created by using the **Convert Element** option on a **Step** element as described previously, or it can be created from within the **USER INTERFACE** section. The screen elements contain the series of windows that the user will see along with the built-in navigational buttons (for previous and next). The **Screen** element has various options for user interaction, and it is from the **Add a Field** tab on the **Edit** screen where you can select from the following sections: **INPUTS**, **CHOICES**, **MULTI-SELECT CHOICES**, or **OUTPUTS**, as shown in the following screenshot:

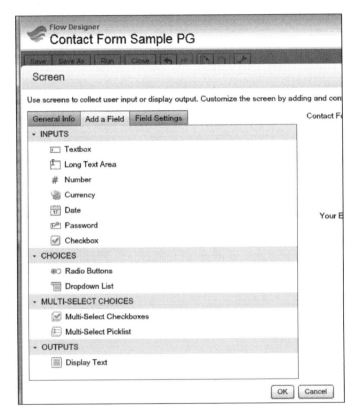

Using the Decision element

Upon having interacted with a **Screen** element, the user may then need to be directed along a specified path in the flow depending on how they responded. The **Decision** element under the **LOGIC** section allows you to configure how users move through the flow by setting up conditions for each decision outcome.

The **Decision** element is used to navigate the flow and route the user to the next screen or interaction based on their response within the previous **Screen** element. Within the **Decision** element, you can create an **Editable Outcome** for each of the responses as shown in the following screenshot:

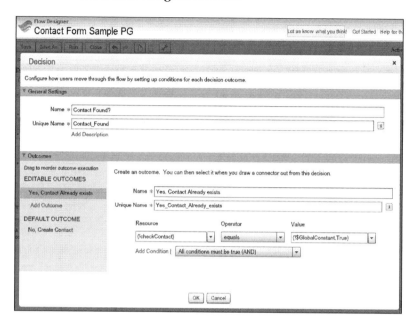

The Resources tab

The **Resources** tab lets you create new resources for the flow, such as variables, constants, formulas, and so on, as shown in the following screenshot:

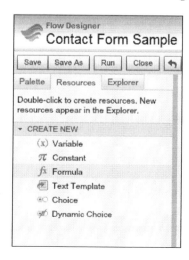

After new resources have been created or items from the **Palette** tab have been added to a flow, they appear in the **Explorer** tab.

The Explorer tab

By double-clicking on items in the **Explorer** tab, you can access the edit page for them. You can single-click on an item to view details for the item in the **Description** pane. When viewing items within the **Explorer** tab, the **Description** pane includes two subtabs:

- **Properties**: Shows you information about the element or resource you have selected, such as its label, unique name, description, and data type.

- **Usage**: Lists the elements where the selected item is used. To see where one of the listed elements is located on the canvas, hover over it and click on the magnify icon as shown in the following screenshot:

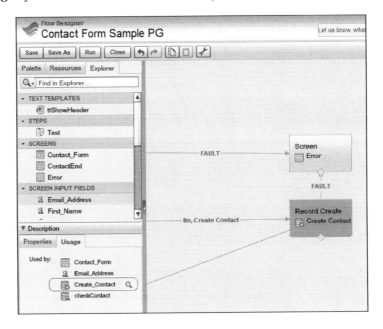

Saving a flow

After you have created a flow in the Flow Designer, the options for saving are:

- **Initial save**: When saving for the first time, a dialog box appears. Enter a flow name, unique name, and description. Once the flow has been saved, the unique name cannot be modified.

- **Quick save**: Having saved the flow, the **Save** button works as a quick-save, overwriting your previous work. Note that the **Save** button is unavailable when editing active flows. Here, you must use **Save As** to save the changes as either a new flow or a new version of the flow.

- **Save as**: Once you have saved the flow, this button is available with two options: **Save As New Flow**, which opens a dialog box where you can input new details and save as an entirely new flow, or **Save As New Version**, saves the flow as a new version of the current flow (as shown in the following screenshot). This option is useful if you are about to make changes to a flow and want to keep the old flow as a backup, just in case you need to retrieve it later:

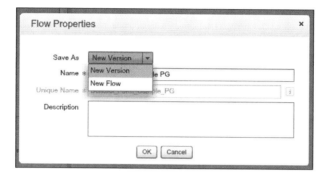

Saving a flow considerations

Consider the following when saving a flow or flow version:

- If you have the flow detail page open in one browser tab, then open a flow version in a new browser tab to edit it, after saving and closing it, you must refresh the first flow detail page before you can successfully run the flow version you just edited.

- If you have changed the flow properties and for some reason the save fails, the flow properties do not revert to the previous values.

- Each flow can have up to 50 versions.

- You can update the flow name and description when you save a new version, but not the unique name.

Flow runtime considerations

Flows can be run directly from the flow URL or from a custom Web tab, link, or button pointing to the flow URL.

Depending on how you wish to set up flows for your users, you have the following specific options:

- Add it as a custom link on a detail page
- Add it as a custom button on a detail page
- Add it as a link on the Home page
- Add it as a flow within a Visualforce page

In order to run flows, users require either one of the following permissions to be set up:

- **Run Flows** profile permission
- Force.com **Flow User** field enabled on the user detail page

Consider the following when running flows:

- Do not use the browser's back or forward buttons to navigate through a flow. This may result in inconsistent data between the flow and Salesforce.
- A single flow may have up to 50 different versions. When users run a flow, they see the active version, which may not necessarily be the latest version.

Summary

In this chapter, we looked at the automation features within the Salesforce CRM application through the use of workflow rules and approval processes. We walked through the configuration of these features and discovered how they can be used to automate and streamline the key business processes for your organization. We also looked at Visual Workflow and learned how flows can be used to build screens that guide users through the process of collecting and updating data.

We saw how workflow rules allow one or more actions to fire based on fields on the record (or its parent) meeting certain conditions. Workflow rules are a little more complex than validation rules, and take a bit more familiarity with Salesforce.com to properly execute. However, they can be implemented without any custom code or the work of a developer.

Approval processes can be a strong tool to police an internal process that must be completed prior to moving forward with the process. They also provide great visibility into the timeliness of approvals, for example, monitoring how long it takes to get expenses approved and putting measures in place to help improve your organization's processes.

Workflow automation can also improve your organization's adherence to approval processes.

By leveraging workflow automation, your users benefit from greater control over routine activities and elimination of redundant tasks. Ask your users about their recurring work and look for ways to automate it.

In the next chapter, we will look at some of the functional areas of the Salesforce CRM application where the CRM functions provide the facilities for the following:

- Sales Automation, such as opportunity and forecast management
- Marketing Automation, such as campaign and lead management
- Service and Support to include case and solution management
- Enterprise social network capabilities within Salesforce CRM using Salesforce Chatter

7
Salesforce CRM Functions

This chapter gives an overview of the functional areas within Salesforce CRM where we will look at the process from campaign to customer and beyond. Within the functional areas there are various touch points where the business teams concerned with marketing, sales, and customer service have to agree on roles and responsibilities for aspects of the business processes. We will now look at each of these core Salesforce CRM functions:

- Marketing administration
- Salesforce automation
- Customer service and support automation
- Salesforce Chatter

Functional overview of Salesforce CRM

The Salesforce CRM functions are related to each other and, as mentioned previously, have cross-over areas which can be represented as shown in the following diagram:

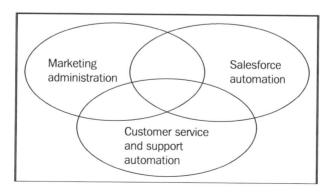

Marketing administration

Marketing administration is available in Salesforce CRM under the application suite known as the **Marketing Cloud**.

The core functionality enables organizations to manage marketing campaigns from initiation to lead development in conjunction with the sales team. The features in the marketing application can help measure the effectiveness of each campaign by analyzing the leads and opportunities generated as a result of specific marketing activities.

Salesforce automation

Salesforce automation is the core feature set within Salesforce CRM and is used to manage the sales process and activities. It enables salespeople to automate manual and repetitive tasks and provides them with information related to existing and prospective customers. In Salesforce CRM, Salesforce automation is known as the **Sales Cloud** and helps salespeople manage sales activities, leads and contact records, opportunities, quotes, and forecasts.

Customer service and support automation

Customer service and support automation within Salesforce CRM is known as the Service Cloud and allows support teams to automate and manage the requests for service and support by existing customers. Using the Service Cloud features, organizations can handle customer requests such as the return of faulty goods or repairs, complaints, or provide advice about products and services.

Associated with the functional areas, described previously, are features and mechanisms to help users and customers collaborate and share information known as enterprise social networking.

Enterprise social networking

Enterprise social network capabilities within Salesforce CRM enable organizations to connect with people and securely share business information in real time. Social networking within an enterprise serves to connect both employees and customers and enables business collaboration. In Salesforce CRM, the enterprise social network suite is known as **Salesforce Chatter**.

Salesforce CRM record life cycle

The capabilities of Salesforce CRM provides for the processing of campaigns through to customer acquisition and beyond as shown in the following diagram:

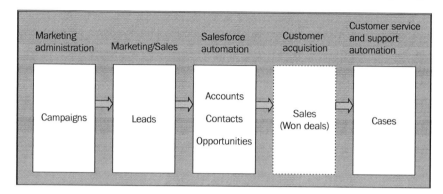

At the start of the process, it is the responsibility of the marketing team to develop suitable campaigns in order to generate leads. Campaign management is carried out using the Marketing Administration tools and has links to the lead and also any opportunities that have been influenced by the campaign.

When validated, leads are converted to accounts, contacts, and opportunities. This can be the responsibility of either the marketing or sales teams and requires a suitable sales process to have been agreed upon. In Salesforce CRM, an account is the company or organization and a contact is an individual associated with an account.

Opportunities can either be generated from lead conversion or may be entered directly by the sales team. As described earlier in this book, the structure of Salesforce requires account ownership to be established which sees inherited ownership of the opportunity. Account ownership is usually the responsibility of the sales team.

Opportunities are worked through a sales process using sales stages where the stage is advanced to the point where they are set as won/closed and become sales. Opportunity information should be logged in the organization's financial system.

Upon financial completion and acceptance of the deal (and perhaps delivery of the goods or service), the post-customer acquisition process is then enabled where the account and contact can be recognized as a customer. Here the customer relationships concerning incidents and requests are managed by escalating cases within the customer services and support automation suite.

Marketing administration

Marketing administration in Salesforce CRM provides closed-loop marketing automation from within the marketing app which can be accessed from the **App Menu** at the top-right corner of the Salesforce CRM screen.

Marketing administration enables integrated marketing functions such as campaign management, lead management, reporting and analysis, response tracking, and campaign effectiveness and it allows users from various departments to centrally access marketing activity.

By default, the marketing administration features provide some level of read-only access to all users. However, to create, edit, and delete campaigns and carry out advanced campaign and lead management functions, users must have the Marketing User License set on their user record as shown next:

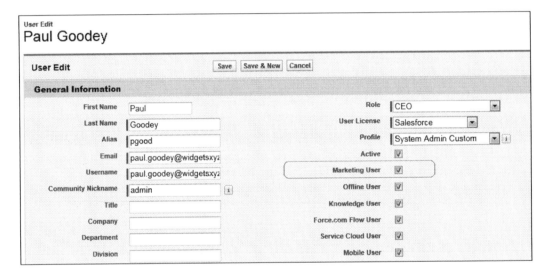

 The Marketing User License is available as standard for organizations with Enterprise or Unlimited editions and can be applied to any active user.

The following key features are available within Salesforce CRM marketing administration:

- Campaign management
- Lead management

Campaign management

With targeted marketing campaigns, companies can build market awareness, generate leads, and learn from their campaign results to fine-tune offers to various customer segments.

The campaign management feature in Salesforce CRM allows your users to manage and track outbound marketing activities. These can be direct mail, roadshow, online or print advertising, e-mail, or other types of marketing initiative.

Some CRM systems have sales and marketing features separated, requiring marketing and sales users to log on to two separate modules; however, with Salesforce CRM, a dedicated **Campaign** tab is provided to enable marketing and sales users to work together within a single system.

Within the **Campaign** tab, the marketing team can access sales information for their campaigns and the sales team can have visibility into the marketing activities that affect their accounts, contacts, and leads. Campaigns can also be organized into hierarchies for flexible analysis of related marketing initiatives.

By integrating the marketing and sales effort for campaign and lead management activities, far greater collaboration can be achieved.

Essential success criteria for campaigns can be captured and used to further develop the definition of marketing targets. This enables marketing departments to become more accountable and to better demonstrate their marketing ROI (return on investment).

The steps to consider when managing and working with campaigns in Salesforce CRM are:

- Campaign planning
- Campaign setup
- Campaign creation
- Campaign execution
- Campaign responses
- Campaign effectiveness

Campaign planning

Before starting to build and run campaigns, it is useful to have an overall plan of the goals and objectives of the campaign, such as the core processes and the type of campaign, such as mass marketing e-mails, hosting a conference, sending direct mail, and so on.

The targets for the campaign need to also be identified and whether they should be existing customers, existing leads, or new leads. With existing leads you can use lead scoring and lead status to facilitate customer segmentation. For example, a series of archived status definitions could be used, such as No Interest, Future Interest, Nurture, and so on.

Consider how you need to analyze and report on campaigns.

It is worth considering this at an early stage and look to create custom campaign fields. You can customize campaigns so that you can improve the targeting and customer segmentation and help to compare and analyze which types of campaigns are the most effective for your sales and marketing teams.

Your marketing team may also want to target new leads through the use of third-party lists. These third-party lists of suspects, prospects, or leads can be flagged in Salesforce with a specific indicator. By flagging with a different record type, or assigning to a different queue, these lead records can be kept apart from existing prospects so that any pre-qualification or de-duplicating can be done before they are available for use in campaigns.

Campaign setup

When setting up campaign management, you should identify who should have access to campaigns.

 To create, edit, and delete campaigns and configure advanced campaign setup, users must have the Marketing User license checked on their user record.

By default, all users have read access to campaigns, but to create, edit, or delete campaigns, users must have the **Create** permission on their profile as shown:

Standard Object Permissions

The permissions defined here control access at the object level. Access to individual records within that object type is controlled by the sharing model. Set access levels based on the functional requirements for the profile. For example, create different groups of permissions for individual contributors, managers, and administrators. **How do I choose?** (?)

When starting new types of campaigns, your marketing and sales teams should collaborate to agree on the customer information that is to be captured. Here you can use the standard fields for both the Campaign and Campaign Member objects or create new custom fields as appropriate.

Standard campaign fields

The following key standard fields are available on the Campaign object:

Field	Type	Description
Campaign Name	Text	This is the name of the marketing campaign. A relevant name should be chosen that is useful for both the marketing and sales teams. For example, Webinar Widgets EMEA FY12Q1.
Type	Picklist	This field is used for the type of campaign. Salesforce provides the following standard list: Conference, Webinar, Trade Show, Public Relations, Partners, Referral Program, Advertisement, Banner Ads, Direct Mail, E-mail, Telemarketing, and Other.
Status	Picklist	This field is used for the current status of a campaign. Salesforce provides the following standard list: Planned, In Progress, Completed, and Aborted.
Start Date	Date	This field is used for the date when a campaign starts.
End Date	Date	This field is used for the date when a campaign ends.
Expected Revenue	Currency	This field is used to set the amount of revenue the campaign will generate.

Field	Type	Description
Budgeted Cost	**Currency**	This field is used to set the amount of money that has been budgeted for the running of the campaign.
Actual Cost	**Currency**	This field is used to set the amount of money that the campaign actually cost to run. This field must be recorded to calculate ROI.
		Note: The ROI is calculated as the net gain using the following expression: ((Total Value Won Opportunities - Actual Cost) / Actual Cost)) * 100.
Expected Response (%)	**Percentage**	This field is used to set the expected response rate for the campaign.
Num Sent	**Number**	This field is used to set the quantity of individuals targeted in the campaign. For example, if a webinar campaign involved sending out invites to 25,000 people, then 25000 would be entered as the number sent.
Active	**Checkbox**	This field is used to set the campaign to either active or not active.
		Note: If the campaign is not active, it will not appear in reports or campaign selection picklists (found on lead, contact, opportunity edit pages, and related lists).
Description	**Text** (long-text area)	This field allows up to 32,000 characters to be entered to add detailed information for the campaign.
Total Leads	**Number**	This field is the sum of all leads linked to this campaign.
Total Contacts	**Number**	This field is the sum of all contacts linked to this campaign.
Converted Leads	**Number**	This field is the sum of all leads linked to this campaign that have been converted.
Total Responses	**Number**	This field is the sum of all Campaign Members which are linked to this campaign and have their member status set to **Responded**.
Total Value Opportunities	**Currency**	This field is the total amount of all opportunities linked to this campaign.
Total Value Won Opportunities	**Currency**	This field is the total amount of all Closed/Won opportunities linked to this campaign

The complete set of fields is shown next where the picklist values can be adapted to suit your organization. They are accessed by following the path **Your Name | Setup | (App Setup) | Customize | Campaigns | Fields**:

Campaign Fields

Help for this Page

This page allows you to specify the fields that can appear on the Campaign page. You can create up to 500 Campaign custom fields.

Note that deleting a custom field will delete any filters that use the custom field. It may also change the result of Assignment or Escalation Rules that rely on the custom field data.

Campaign Standard Fields

Campaign Standard Fields Help

Action	Field Label	Field Name	Data Type	Controlling Field
Edit	Active	IsActive	Checkbox	
Edit	Actual Cost	ActualCost	Currency(18, 0)	
Edit	Budgeted Cost	BudgetedCost	Currency(18, 0)	
Edit	Campaign Member Type	CampaignMemberRecordType	Lookup(Record Type)	
Edit	Campaign Name	Name	Text(80)	
Edit	Campaign Owner	Owner	Lookup(User)	
Edit	Converted Leads	NumberOfConvertedLeads	Number(9, 0)	
	Created By	CreatedBy	Lookup(User)	
Edit	Description	Description	Long Text Area(32000)	
Edit	End Date	EndDate	Date	
Edit	Expected Response (%)	ExpectedResponse	Percent(8, 2)	
Edit	Expected Revenue	ExpectedRevenue	Currency(18, 0)	
	Last Modified By	LastModifiedBy	Lookup(User)	
Edit	Num Sent	NumberSent	Number(18, 0)	
Edit	Num Total Opportunities	NumberOfOpportunities	Number(9, 0)	
Edit	Num Won Opportunities	NumberOfWonOpportunities	Number(9, 0)	
Edit	Parent Campaign	Parent	Lookup(Campaign)	
Edit	Start Date	StartDate	Date	
Replace | Edit	Status	Status	Picklist	
Edit	Total Actual Cost in Hierarchy	HierarchyActualCost	Currency(18, 0)	
Edit	Total Budgeted Cost in Hierarchy	HierarchyBudgetedCost	Currency(18, 0)	
Edit	Total Contacts	NumberOfContacts	Number(9, 0)	
Edit	Total Contacts in Hierarchy	HierarchyNumberOfContacts	Number(9, 0)	
Edit	Total Converted Leads in Hierarchy	HierarchyNumberOfConvertedLeads	Number(9, 0)	
Edit	Total Expected Revenue in Hierarchy	HierarchyExpectedRevenue	Currency(18, 0)	
Edit	Total Leads	NumberOfLeads	Number(9, 0)	
Edit	Total Leads in Hierarchy	HierarchyNumberOfLeads	Number(9, 0)	
Edit	Total Num Sent in Hierarchy	HierarchyNumberSent	Number(18, 0)	
Edit	Total Opportunities in Hierarchy	HierarchyNumberOfOpportunities	Number(9, 0)	
Edit	Total Responses	NumberOfResponses	Number(9, 0)	
Edit	Total Responses in Hierarchy	HierarchyNumberOfResponses	Number(9, 0)	
Edit	Total Value Opportunities	AmountAllOpportunities	Currency(18, 0)	
Edit	Total Value Opportunities in Hierarchy	HierarchyAmountAllOpportunities	Currency(18, 0)	
Edit	Total Value Won Opportunities	AmountWonOpportunities	Currency(18, 0)	
Edit	Total Value Won Opportunities in Hierarchy	HierarchyAmountWonOpportunities	Currency(18, 0)	
Edit	Total Won Opportunities in Hierarchy	HierarchyNumberOfWonOpportunities	Number(9, 0)	
Replace | Edit	Type	Type	Picklist	

Standard campaign member fields

The following key standard fields are available on the Campaign Member object:

Field	Type	Description
Campaign	**Lookup (Campaign)**	This field is the campaign name. Set using a link to the campaign record.
Contact	**Lookup (Contact)**	This field is the contact name. Set using a link to the contact record.
		Note: Either a **Contact** is set or **Lead** is set (not both).

Field	Type	Description
Lead	Lookup (Lead)	This field is the lead name. Set using a link to the lead record.
		Note: Either a **Contact** is set or **Lead** is set (not both).
Status	Picklist	This is the status of the Campaign Member as part of the linked campaign. Salesforce provides the following standard values: Planned, Sent, Received, and Responded.
		Every campaign has a specific outcome which can be captured on the member status and response fields. With well-defined member status and response values, reporting can be carried out much easier.

The complete set of fields is shown next where the picklist values can be adapted to suit your organization. They are accessed by following the path **Your Name | Setup | (App Setup) | Customize | Campaigns | Campaign Members | Fields**:

Action	Field Label	Field Name	Data Type	Controlling Field
Edit	Campaign	Campaign	Lookup(Campaign)	
Edit	City	City	Text(40)	
Edit	Company (Account)	CompanyOrAccount	Text(255)	
Edit	Contact	Contact	Lookup(Contact)	
Edit	Country	Country	Text(80)	
	Created By	CreatedBy	Lookup(User)	
	Created Date	CreatedDate	Date/Time	
Edit	Description	Description	Text(255)	
Edit	Do Not Call	DoNotCall	Checkbox	
Edit	Email	Email	Email	
Edit	Email Opt Out	HasOptedOutOfEmail	Checkbox	
Edit	Fax	Fax	Fax	
Edit	Fax Opt Out	HasOptedOutOfFax	Checkbox	
Edit	First Name	FirstName	Text(40)	
Edit	First Responded Date	FirstRespondedDate	Date	
	Last Modified By	LastModifiedBy	Lookup(User)	
	Last Modified Date	LastModifiedDate	Date/Time	
Edit	Last Name	LastName	Text(40)	
Edit	Lead	Lead	Lookup(Lead)	
Replace | Edit	Lead Source	LeadSource	Picklist	
Edit	Mobile	MobilePhone	Phone	
Edit	Phone	Phone	Phone	
Edit	Responded	HasResponded	Checkbox	
Replace | Edit	Salutation	Salutation	Picklist	
Edit	State/Province	State	Text(40)	
Replace | Edit	Status	Status	Picklist	
Edit	Street	Street	Text(255)	
Edit	Title	Title	Text(80)	
Edit	Zip/Postal Code	PostalCode	Text(20)	

Campaign Member Standard Fields

Both your marketing and sales teams should also help define and agree on any required custom fields or picklist values; for example, segmentation definitions, status, and responses.

Campaign creation

To create campaigns, users must have the **Marketing User** checkbox selected in their user record and have the **Create** permission on campaigns in their profile as shown previously.

To create a campaign, follow the steps:

1. Click on the **Campaigns** tab to view the campaign's home page or select **Campaign** from the **Create New** drop-down list in the sidebar.

2. Enter values for the fields that apply to the campaign as shown in the following screenshot:

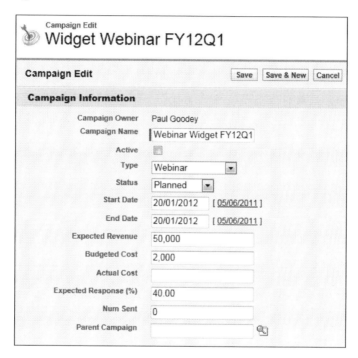

3. Now click on **Save**, or click on **Save & New** to save the campaign, and then add another.

Member status values

New campaigns have two default member status values: **Sent** and **Responded**. These are populated from the **Campaign Member Status** picklist that we looked at earlier.

Non-system administrator users can, however, overwrite the status values (for the specific campaign record only) from within the campaign detail page by clicking on the **Advanced Setup** button as shown in the following screenshot:

Here, your users can edit or replace them, or create new ones as necessary:

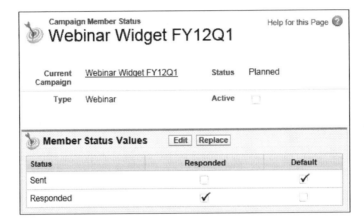

Create multiple responded values

You can have more than one **Responded** value. These are summed together to produce the calculated field **Total Responses**.

Target lists

Target lists is a marketing term used to describe the individuals or types of people that are to be included as part of the marketing campaign.

In some situations, such as with an online advertising campaign, people are not specifically set up as individual targets. Here the campaign would usually be set up in Salesforce as one without members.

If your campaign is targeting individuals, it is important to create a target list that has been segmented according to criteria that will result in the highest quality returns.

Targeting existing leads or contacts

To target existing leads or contacts, you can use the following methods in Salesforce CRM:

Method	Description
Use the **Campaign Detail** page	Click on the **Manage Members** button to add multiple campaign members
Create **Lead or Contact** reports	Click on the **Add to Campaign** button to add multiple campaign members
Use **Lead or Contact List** views	Click on the **Add to Campaign** button to add multiple campaign members
Use the **Lead or Contact Detail** pages	Click on the **Add to Campaign** button to add a single campaign member

Using the campaign detail page

To add multiple campaign members from the **Campaign Detail** page, users should select the **Manage Members** button as shown in the following screenshot:

You can add existing contacts or leads by selecting **Add Members - Search** from the **Manage Members** drop-down button on a **Campaign Detail** page.

Creating lead or contact reports

To add multiple campaign members from either lead or contact reports, carry out the following:

1. Create a custom lead or contact report.

2. In the **Select Criteria** step, enter up to three criteria to segment the report data.

For example, to target all CFOs at Electronics or Energy companies with annual revenue greater than 10 million, you would set the following:

- **Title equals CFO**

- **Industry equals Technology, Telecommunications** (using a comma to indicate an OR Boolean result)

- **Annual Revenue greater than 10,000,000**

Now you can run the report and use the **Add to Campaign** button as shown in the following screenshot:

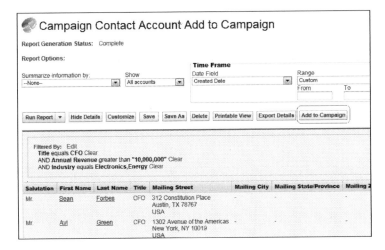

Using lead or contact list views

From within a lead or contact list view, you can click on the **Add to Campaign** button to add multiple campaign members as shown in the following screenshot:

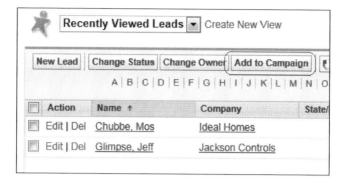

Using the lead or contact detail pages

You can use the **Add to Campaign** button within the **Lead Detail** and **Contact Detail** pages to add that record as an individual campaign member as shown in the following screenshot:

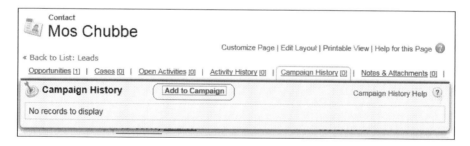

Targeting new leads or prospects

When using externally purchased lists of new prospects within Salesforce, it is advisable to flag the records with a specific third-party designation (say by record type, or custom picklist value). These records can then be pre-qualified before adding to any campaign or sales activity. Particularly important is the de-duplication of any new leads against existing records in your Salesforce database to determine which are existing customers or leads.

Salesforce does not recommend mass importing rented or purchased lists of prospects into Salesforce as these lists are usually controlled by the list vendor and may have restriction or limited use policies. Here you should simply make use of the list of names as your target list and only after the prospect has responded to your campaign should you import the lead record.

Campaign execution

Although campaign execution activities occur outside the Salesforce CRM application during the execution of either an offline or an online campaign, there are some features of the campaign activity that can be aided using the export facilities within Salesforce.

Users can use Salesforce to generate lists of accounts and individuals for mailing houses or e-mailing specialist partners to send out the mass marketing e-mails used in both online and offline events (such as trade shows, advertisements, direct mail, and so on).

There are various options available for integrating Salesforce with other solutions, including provision for mass e-mailing. Integration solutions are covered later in this book where sources include the AppExchange directory (a Salesforce.com sponsored market place for accredited products and services).

Salesforce can be used to deliver some mass e-mail, but the application is not intended for large volume mass e-mail marketing and there are limits to the quantity of e-mails that can be sent.

For each Salesforce application, a total of 1,000 e-mails can be sent per day to external e-mail addresses. Using the Enterprise Edition, the maximum number of external addresses (unique or non-unique) you can include in a mass e-mail is 500 and for the Unlimited Edition, the limit is 1000.

 The mass e-mail limits do not take unique addresses into account. For example, if you have john.smith@widgetsXYZ.com in your mass e-mail 500 times, that counts as 500 against any limit.

You can build an integrated web form to automatically capture individuals as leads in Salesforce. This is detailed later in this chapter in the *Lead Management* section under *Marketing administration*.

Campaign responses

After the campaign has been executed, your company will want to track the responses which can include:

- Website response using a form on your website where you can set up a Web-to-Lead form to create a target page with a response form. All responses appear in Salesforce as leads but can be linked to the campaign. This is covered later in this chapter.

- Mass update or offline response using the campaign member import wizards to import a list of leads or contacts and their responses. Users need the **Marketing User** profile or the **Import Leads** permission to use these wizards.

- Manual response, for example, when prospects and customers respond by phone or e-mail, users can manually record these responses on the **Campaign History** related list on the lead or **Contact Detail** page:

Campaign influence

To ensure existing opportunities are included in the results for the campaign, you can add the campaign to the **Campaign Influence** related list on the opportunity as shown next.

 The **Campaign Influence** related list is not included in the set of related lists on the Opportunity Page Layout by default so you may need to include it on your chosen Opportunity Page Layout.

By setting the **Primary Campaign Source** flag (a checkbox on the **Campaign Influence** record), the opportunity amount is included in the campaign statistics and reports:

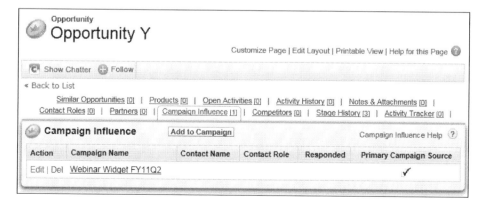

Campaign effectiveness

Campaign effectiveness can be analyzed using either the statistics on the campaign record or by running campaign reports.

Campaign statistics

The summary fields on the **Campaign Detail** page as shown next allows various statistics to be seen, such as the total number of responses, the amount of business generated from the campaign, and so on:

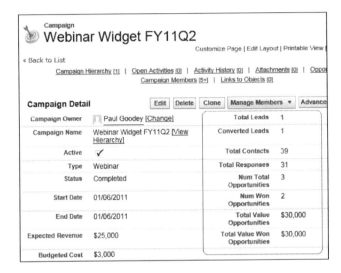

The campaign statistics are automatically recalculated every time a campaign is saved. When a lead gets converted to an opportunity, the campaign that was most recently associated to the lead will automatically pass over to the opportunity.

Campaign reports

Reports can be accessed from the **Reports** tab by selecting the **Campaign Reports** folder as shown in the following screenshot:

As an example, the **Campaign ROI Analysis Report** shows performance metrics and gives you a figure for the return on investment for the campaign as shown in the following screenshot:

ROI calculation

The ROI percentage calculation taken from the **Campaign ROI Analysis Report** uses the following equation:

((Total Value of Won Opportunities -Actual Cost) / Actual Cost)) * 100.

In the example shown, we have: ((30,000 – 2500)/2500))*100 = 1100%.

Lead management

Managing prospective customers appropriately often raises issues within companies. The status and quality of prospect data can cause obstacles when trying to automate the processing through the sales process. Prospect data often comes from various sources which, if not carefully controlled, can make them difficult to accurately process.

Without a central system and agreed approach, there can be conflicts between the marketing team, who are often unable to trace what is happening to the prospects after distributing them to sales, and the sales team who are unable to verify the quality of the data. Salesforce CRM helps bridge any gap between sales and marketing, and by using lead management mechanisms offers a way to improve the management and automation of the flow from potential customers to a closed sales deal.

Leads are prospects or potential opportunities and are accessed in Salesforce CRM from the **Leads** tab. They are sources of potential deals that usually need more qualification and may be visitors to your website who requested more information, respondents to marketing campaigns as described previously in managing campaigns, trade show visitors, and so on. Leads are stored and managed separately to account, contact, and opportunity records which are covered later in this chapter.

Standard lead fields

The following key standard fields are available on the Lead object:

Field	Type	Description
Lead Owner	**Lookup** (to lead or queue)	This field is the user or queue who owns the lead. A lead can be owned by a person or stored in a queue. Here, you can allow specified users to accept (and return) leads from a queue. This is covered in more detail later in this section.
Last Name	**Text**	This field is the last name and is a required field. The last name is copied over to the **Last Name** field on a contact record during the lead conversion process.
Company	**Text**	This field is the company name and is a required field. The company name is copied over to the company name on an account record during the lead conversion process.

Field	Type	Description
Lead Status	Picklist	This field is the status and is a required field. Salesforce provides the following standard values: **Open – Not Contacted, Working – Contacted, Closed – Converted**, and **Closed – Not Converted**. **Lead Status** is an important field used in the lead process settings as described later in this section.
Lead Source	Picklist	This field is used to set the source from which the lead appeared. Salesforce provides the following standard values: **Web, Phone Inquiry, Partner Referral, Purchased List**, and **Other**.

The complete set of fields is shown next where the picklist values can be adapted to suit your organization. They are accessed by following the path **Your Name | Setup | (App Setup) | Customize | Leads | Fields**:

Lead Standard Fields

Action	Field Label	Field Name	Data Type
	Address	Address	Address
Edit	Annual Revenue	AnnualRevenue	Currency(18, 0)
Edit	Campaign	Campaign	Lookup(Campaign)
Edit	Company	Company	Text(255)
	Created By	CreatedBy	Lookup(User)
Edit	Description	Description	Long Text Area(32000)
Edit	Do Not Call	DoNotCall	Checkbox
Edit	Email	Email	Email
Edit	Email Opt Out	HasOptedOutOfEmail	Checkbox
Edit	Fax	Fax	Fax
Edit	Fax Opt Out	HasOptedOutOfFax	Checkbox
Replace | Edit	Industry	Industry	Picklist
	Last Modified By	LastModifiedBy	Lookup(User)
Edit	Last Transfer Date	LastTransferDate	Date
Edit	Lead Owner	Owner	Lookup(User,Queue)
Replace | Edit	Lead Source	LeadSource	Picklist
Replace | Edit	Lead Status	Status	Picklist
Edit	Mobile	MobilePhone	Phone
	Name	Name	Name
Edit | Replace	Salutation	Picklist	
	First Name	Text(40)	
	Last Name	Text(80)	
Edit	No. of Employees	NumberOfEmployees	Number(8, 0)
Edit	Phone	Phone	Phone
Replace | Edit	Rating	Rating	Picklist
Edit	Title	Title	Text(80)
Edit	Website	Website	URL(255)

Lead business process

Creating a business process within the lead management function involves agreeing on and implementing the steps and field values that are to be recorded by the sales and marketing teams during the lead life cycle.

The lead processes are accessed by following the path **Your Name | Setup | (App Setup) | Leads | Lead Processes** where processes can be created or edited as shown in the following screenshot:

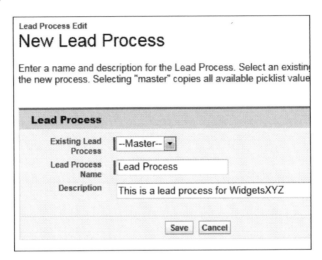

You can now assign the status values for the lead as shown in the following screenshot:

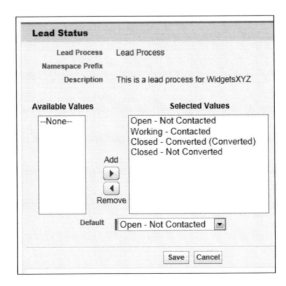

Finally, by associating the lead business process with one or more record types, this will make it available to your users (based on their profile).

Creating leads in Salesforce CRM

There are several ways of creating lead records within the Salesforce CRM application. This includes manual entry of single leads by your users, the manual entry of leads by the prospect themselves (using public facing web forms known as Web-to-Lead), or the manual importing of multiple leads within the application by you or your users.

Manually creating lead records within the application

Leads can be manually created from either the **Lead** tab by clicking on the **New** button, or from the **Create New** selection in the left-hand side bar as shown in the following screenshot:

Manually creating leads with Web-to-Lead

With the Web-to-Lead functionality in Salesforce CRM, leads can be directly entered into your Salesforce application from a public-facing website. This means prospect information can be gathered directly from the individual. This feature is used to generate HTML (HyperText Markup Language) code which can then be incorporated into the required web page.

Lead settings

To enable the Web-to-Lead feature, you must first configure the appropriate lead settings by following the path **Your Name | Setup | (App Setup) | Customize | Leads | Settings**. Now click on the **Edit** button to display the page as shown in the following screenshot:

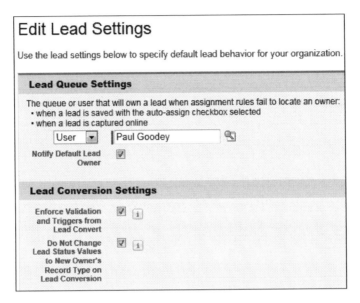

Now select a Default Lead Owner and select the **Notify Default Lead Owner** checkbox to automatically notify the default lead owner whenever a lead is assigned to them.

 The default lead owner becomes the owner of any leads that are not auto-assigned by lead assignment rules.

The Web-to-Lead settings

To enable the Web-to-Lead feature, you must first configure the Web-to-Lead settings by following the path **Your Name | Setup | (App Setup) | Customize | Leads | Web-To-Lead**. Now click on the **Edit** button to display the page as shown in the following screenshot:

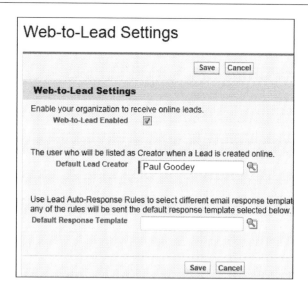

Now check the **Web-to-Lead Enabled** checkbox, select the user who will be set as the creator whenever the lead is entered from an online web form and finally, create Web-to-Lead e-mail auto-response rules to determine which e-mails to send to prospects when they submit information online. Then click on **Save**.

Generating the Web-to-Lead HTML code

To generate the Web-to-Lead HTML code, follow the path **Your Name | Setup | (App Setup) | Customize | Leads | Web-To-Lead**. Now click on the **Create Web-To-Lead Form** button to display the page as shown in the following screenshot:

Now select the fields to include in the form, and specify a URL that users will be taken to after submitting the form. Finally, click on the **Generate** button, then copy the generated HTML code and send it to the team responsible for the website in your organization.

The page style can be customized for your website, but the core form elements that have been generated within the HTML code should not be changed.

With the Web-to-Lead feature, you can capture up to 500 leads per day.

To increase the limit of 500 leads per day

This feature may be increased by sending a request to Salesforce customer support, although there may be additional costs for this increase.

Web-to-Lead auto-response rules

Auto-response rules provide a method to customize any communication that is sent back to an individual after they have filled out a web lead form. These auto-response rules can contain logic to determine which e-mail template and what content to send to leads that have been generated using Web-to-Lead.

To enable auto-response rules, follow the path **Your Name | Setup | (App Setup) | Leads | Auto-response Rules**. Then click on the **New** or **Edit** button as shown in the following screenshot:

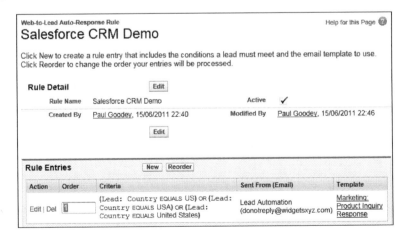

Here you first create the rule detail and name, and activate the rule. Then you add the rule entries which contain the logic and where multiple rule entries may be created. Rule entries require the following:

- An order of execution
- The criteria for when the rule is triggered
- A sent from e-mail address detail
- An e-mail template to be used to send to the respondent

 Any e-mails that are sent are included in the daily limit of 1,000 mass e-mails for an organization.

Manual importing of multiple leads

To import leads, follow the path **Your Name | Setup | (Administration Setup) | Data Management | Import Leads**. Now follow the on-screen instructions to export your data from its current source and label each column in the file with the correct field name as shown in the following screenshot:

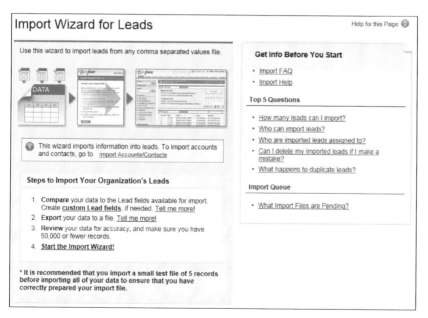

 Only users with the **Import Leads** permission on their profile (in the general user permissions section) have access to the importing leads feature, where files of up to 50,000 leads can be imported.

A lead assignment rule can automatically assign leads to users or queues based on values in lead fields. Alternatively, a **Record Owner** field in the import file can determine lead ownership for each imported lead.

Without a lead assignment rule or **Record Owner** field, imported leads are automatically assigned to the user that has carried out the import.

The **Import Queue** shows the status of the import. You will be notified by e-mail when your import is complete (this notification may take up to 24 hours).

 Marketing users with the **Marketing User** profile can also import new leads by selecting **Add Members - Import File** from the **Manage Members** drop-down button on the **Campaign Detail** page.

Lead queue

Queues can be thought of as a storage location to group leads together, usually by geographic region or business function. Leads remain in the queue until they are assigned or accepted by users. Users who have been included as part of the queue can access and accept the records by clicking on the **Accept** button as shown in the following screenshot:

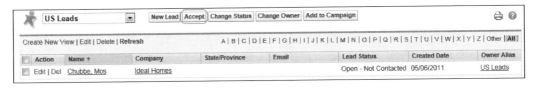

 Whenever you create a lead queue, Salesforce automatically generates a lead list view to enable users to access the records in the queue.

Creating and adding users to a lead queue

To create and provide users with access to a lead queue, follow the path **Your Name | Setup | (Administration Setup) | Manage Users | Queues | New**.

Here you can carry out the following: name the queue, select the supported object (selection being either lead or case), and assign the queue member (selection being either users, public groups, roles, or role and subordinates).

You can also set up the queue so that e-mails are sent to the queue members (using a default e-mail address for the queue) whenever a case is assigned to the queue:

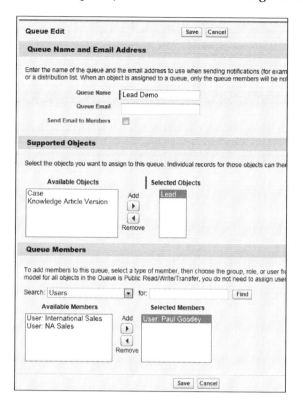

Lead assignment rules

Lead assignment rules determine how leads are automatically assigned to users or a queue. They contain rule entries which are predefined business rules that determine the lead routing.

Lead assignment rules can be accessed by following the path **Your Name | Setup | (App Setup) | Customize | Leads | Assignment Rules**.

Only one lead assignment rule can be active at any given time but each rule can have multiple criteria as shown here:

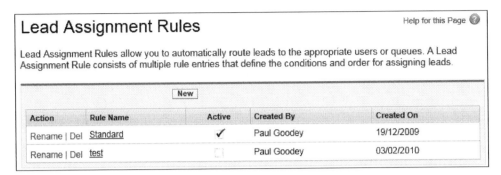

Criteria are evaluated in the order in which they appear in the list. When there are multiple rules which could be applied, you can set the priority for the criteria by setting the most specific criteria at number 1 and then adding more criteria numbers that are more generic. The following screenshot shows a simple example and use of multiple criteria rules which is used to assign leads according to a geographic flag by using the **Country** field:

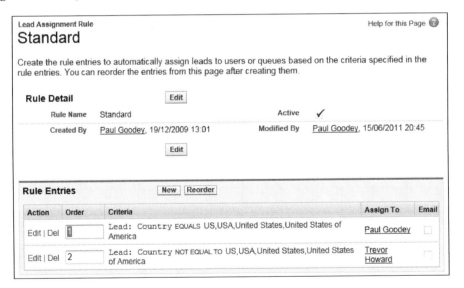

Lead conversion

Lead qualification depends on your business process and should have been developed in conjunction with both the marketing and sales team.

As part of the lead conversion routine, certain key information contained on the lead record is mapped to the Salesforce CRM objects' account, contact, and optionally the opportunity records. During lead conversion, new records are created for these objects where the account record name field will contain the **Company Name** field value from the lead, and the contact record name field will be populated from the **Name** field within the lead record.

> Any existing account or contact records are automatically checked before the lead conversion to avoid record duplication.

Opportunities that are created upon lead conversion contain default values for the required fields, where the **Close Date** defaults to the last day of the current quarter and **Sales Stage** is set to the first value in the **Stage** picklist.

> During the lead conversion, there is no opportunity amount value set on the resulting opportunity.

To convert a lead, select the lead that is to be converted either by clicking on the **Lead** tab and selecting from the list view or by searching and then clicking on **Convert** on the **Lead Detail** page as shown in the following screenshot:

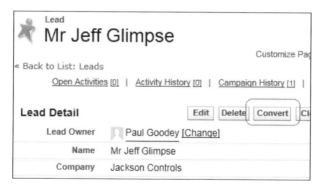

The lead conversion screen will be displayed where you can check the owner of the new records. Here you can choose to send the record owner an automated notification e-mail. You can also set the status of the converted lead and also specify that a new task is created for the record owner to act as a follow-up task, as shown in the following screenshot:

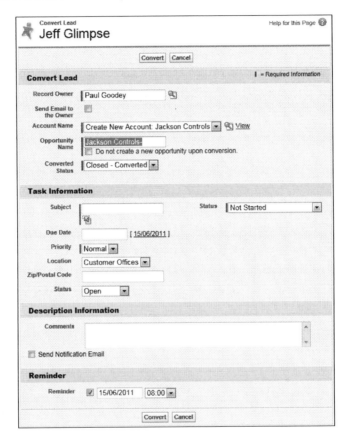

Before creating any new account or contact records, the Salesforce CRM application attempts to match existing account and contact names and the name of the lead. Where there is a match, you will have the option of selecting the existing records as shown in the following screenshot:

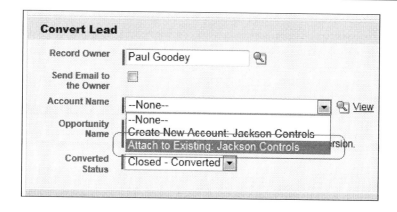

Clicking on the **Convert** button completes the lead conversion process and results in the following:

- The company name from the lead becomes the account name
- The lead name from the lead becomes the contact name
- The opportunity and contact are associated with the account
- Any campaigns related to the lead are associated with the opportunity

 Converted leads can no longer be viewed in the **Leads** tab and the only way to view the record is to create a lead report.

When customizing your report, enter a filter option of **Converted equals True** to view converted leads.

Lead conversion field mappings

There are standard field mappings between the lead and account, contact, and opportunity records that are provided by Salesforce for the lead conversion process; however, you can extend these. To extend the mappings, follow the path **Your Name | Setup | (App Setup) | Customize | Leads | Fields**. Now navigate to the **Lead Custom Fields & Relationships** section at the bottom of the page as shown in the following screenshot:

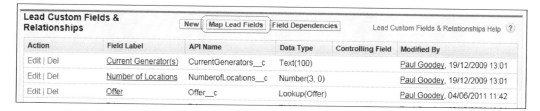

Extending the field mappings may become necessary whenever you add required custom fields on either the account, contact, or opportunity records which are to be populated from the lead records. This is done as shown in the following screenshot:

It is important to ensure the field mapping is in place whenever you have certain mandatory fields or rules for your account, contacts, or opportunities. This is because the validation logic for required custom fields and workflow or validation rules are enforced by the Salesforce application during the lead conversion process.

Salesforce automation

Salesforce automation allows the management and control of the phases required for the sales process within a Customer Relationship Management (CRM) system. Enabling and automating these phases within CRM systems helps improve the quality and also minimizes the time that sales representatives spend on each phase.

Salesforce automation in Salesforce.com is performed within the Sales App which can be accessed from the App Menu at the top-right corner of the Salesforce CRM screen.

At the core of the Sales App in Salesforce CRM are the account, contact, and opportunity management functions for tracking and recording each stage in the sales process for new and existing customers.

Accounts can be sorted by standard views or customized views, and users can add new accounts and edit existing accounts. Associated contacts and activities are also listed in the same page of the account where users can manipulate other operations, such as viewing, adding, and editing as necessary. Account views can be filtered based on time variables, such as by viewing recently modified or created accounts, new accounts this week, and so on.

Account management

In Salesforce CRM, account management is carried out using the facilities found in the **Accounts** tab and is typically where customer information is located.

Account records are used to store the company information from converted leads and can also be used for the storage of company information for partners, suppliers, and even competitors.

Accounts may be considered as "business accounts" from a **business-to-business (B2B)** perspective and are usually the company records stored within the application. However, Salesforce provides another variety of account called a Person Account which allows organizations with a **business-to-consumer (B2C)** business model to manage the relationships with individuals. The business account and Person Account record offer very similar features and fields; however, Person accounts do not have certain fields or features such as a **Reports To** field, a **Parent Account** field, or the **Account Hierarchy** feature.

> Person accounts are not enabled by default in the Salesforce CRM application and are only available by request to Salesforce customer support.

Business account information consists of company name, type, company website, industry, annual revenue, billing and shipping addresses, account record owner, date of creation and modification, and so on.

> **Naming convention for accounts**
> Having consistent account names is essential to ensure clean and accurate account data. It can be useful to adopt an appropriate account naming policy to be used by all users in Salesforce. One way to achieve this is to ensure that accounts are named using their full legal name wherever possible.

As described earlier in this book, accounts are also the primary mechanism used in the organization of records.

They are used within the record sharing and ownership hierarchy and are the parent object for standard objects, such as contacts and opportunities, and so on. When changing ownership of account records, you have the options to re-assign these child records as shown in the following screenshot:

Contact management

Contact management is performed using the facilities found in the **Contacts** tab. Contacts are the individuals that your users want to keep in touch with. For the sales team, this is likely to be people such as purchasers and key decision makers. For the marketing team, this may include the CEOs and CFOs and other influencers. For support, the contacts could be any of the users of the product or service that your organization provides.

Salesforce CRM provides the facility for users to store, view, sort, filter, delete, edit, and find contact information which may or may not be associated with accounts. Each contact is recorded with details, such as title, contact details (address, cell phone, work phone, fax, and e-mail address), date of creation and modification, and contact record owner.

Activity management

Activities in Salesforce are made up of tasks and events. Unlike other areas of functionality, there is no access to Activities from the tab, instead they are created and viewed from related lists on other types of records, such as account, contact, case, and so on. Users can view activities both in the context of a relevant item (such as where they relate to an account, for example) or as a standalone mechanism from their calendar and task lists from the Salesforce CRM home page.

The **Activity History** related list of a record shows all completed tasks, logged phone calls, expired events, such as meetings, outbound e-mails, and so on, for the record and any linked records.

Cloud Scheduler

Creating and scheduling appointments with customers is a central activity of most customer-oriented businesses. Marketing, sales, and customer support teams spend time getting in touch with prospects and customers and use a variety of means to agree on a time and place to meet.

To improve this activity, Salesforce provides the Cloud Scheduler facility which is an automated system used to manage the scheduling and presentation of suitable appointment times to individuals through a web interface.

As part of the Cloud Scheduler feature, Salesforce creates a unique web page for the meeting which displays the proposed meeting times. When invitees visit the web page, they can select the times that are suitable for them, and then send a response.

The Cloud Scheduler requires the new user interface theme to be enabled, and is supported with one of the following compatible browsers: Internet Explorer 7 or 8, Firefox 3.0 or higher, Safari 3.2 or higher, and Chrome 6.0 or higher.

All the responses from invitees are then tracked by Salesforce and a date and time that fits with everyone can then be selected and chosen as the confirmation for the meeting.

Cloud Scheduler setup

First of all, the settings for the Cloud Scheduler can be configured by following the path **Your Name | Setup | (App Setup) | Customize | Activities | Cloud Scheduler**. The **New Meeting Request** button for the Cloud Scheduler can be added to page layouts with an **Open Activities** related list such as contacts, leads, or Person Accounts (if enabled).

For users to request a meeting with a Person Account, you may also need to add the **Email** field to the page layout by following the path **Your Name | Setup | (App Setup) | Customize | Accounts | Person Accounts | Page Layouts**.

You can also include the **New Meeting Request** button on the user's home page. This is displayed above the **Scheduled Meetings** and **Requested Meetings** tabs as shown in the following screenshot:

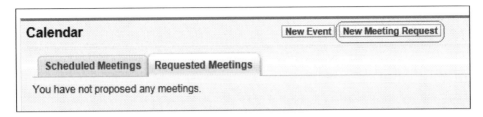

If this section is not displayed on the home page, then **Show Requested Meetings in the Calendar Section on the Home Tab** needs to be selected by following the path **Your Name** | **Setup** | **(App Setup)** | **Customize** | **Activities** | **Activity Settings** as shown in the following screenshot:

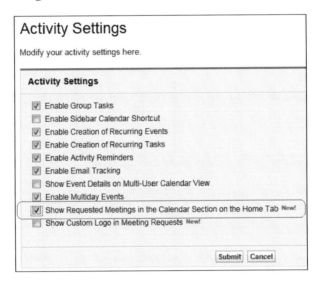

Cloud Scheduler requesting a meeting

The following offers an overview of how users within your organization can request a meeting with co-workers and customers using the Cloud Scheduler.

Requesting a meeting and proposing meeting times

Users can either navigate to the contact or **Lead Detail** page of the individual they want to request a meeting with through the **Open Activities** related list or navigate to the calendar section on their home page. They then click on the **New Meeting Request** button to display the **Meeting Request** page. Here users click to invite other Salesforce users, leads, contacts, or Person Accounts to the meeting, and click in the calendar to propose up to five meeting times, or they can choose to let the Salesforce application automatically propose times, as shown in the following screenshot:

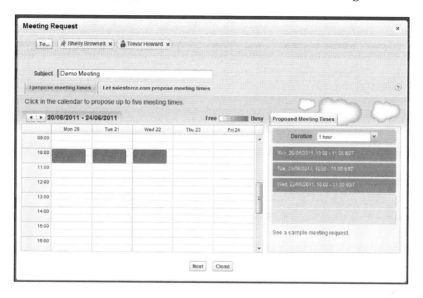

Invitees pick the times they can meet

Salesforce e-mails a meeting request to the invitees so they can pick the times they are available. Within the e-mail is a link which the invitees click called **Respond to This Request** which opens the meeting's web page. Within the web page, invitees can then pick the proposed times that are suitable for them, and then send a reply as shown in the following screenshot:

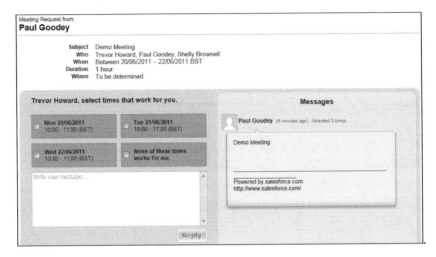

Confirmation of the meeting

Salesforce keeps track of all the responses so users can see when each invitee is available and can then select the best time to meet and confirm the meeting as shown in the following screenshot:

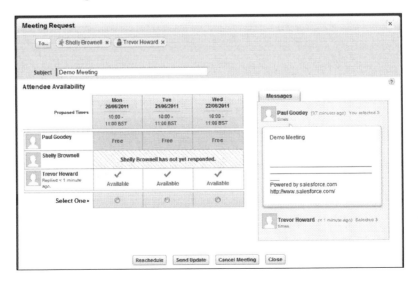

Opportunity management

Opportunity management is performed using the facilities found in the **Opportunities** tab.

Opportunities in Salesforce CRM are the sales deals that the sales team in your organization creates and updates. By adding new opportunities, the sales team is building the sales pipeline which will be used to produce figures for both individual sales forecasts, as well as the wider company sales forecast.

Opportunity records are also important for other users in your organization to track, such as the marketing team who may want to monitor the effectiveness of marketing campaigns, or the customer support teams who may need to have an up-to-date view of customer spending when negotiating support contracts.

Service cloud

At the core of the service cloud in Salesforce CRM is the case management functionality for tracking and recording activities dealing with customer, service, and support automation. Concerned with case management for existing customers cases are associated to contacts and accounts.

A case is a detailed description of a customer's feedback, problem, or question. Your organization can use cases to track and solve your customers' issues. Cases can be manually entered from within the **Cases** tab by the support or sales team after, say, a phone call or e-mail to or from a customer. However, you can also set up more complex Web-to-Case and Email-to-Case to obtain customer responses from your company's website and customer e-mails.

Case management

There are number of ways case records, which may consist of recording phone calls or e-mail communications, can be entered into the Salesforce CRM application. These cases can be entered manually by the users accessing the **Case** tab but there are other methods available for you to consider, which include:

- Automatic creation from an e-mail using Mail-to-Case sent by a customer
- Automatic creation from a web form using Web-to-Case entered by a customer

Email-to-Case

Email-to-Case provides the facility for automatic case creation when an e-mail is sent to a pre-configured e-mail address.

Web-to-Case

Web-to-Case provides the facility where customers can submit support cases online.

 The Web-To-Case feature can be used to generate up to 500 new cases a day.

When setting up Web-to-Case, auto-response rules can be created to use e-mail templates to send an acknowledging e-mail to customers who have created cases using the web form.

Case queues

Queues can be thought of as a storage location to group cases together usually by a geographic region or business function. Cases remain in the queue until they are assigned or accepted by users.

Whenever you create a case queue, Salesforce automatically generates a case list view to enable users to access the records in the queue.

Case records can be assigned to queues manually or automatically using assignment rules. Case queues and assignment rules are very similar to the queues and assignment rules available for leads.

Assignment rules

Only one case assignment rule can be active at any one time, and each rule can contain multiple criteria, up to a maximum of 25 criteria.

Escalation rules

Escalation rules are used to automatically escalate an unresolved case within a certain period of time. This escalation is triggered on the **Age Over** setting (when the **Age** field is overdue).

Modification of a field on a case is the only thing that stops the clock for escalation rules if the rule is set to "disable after first modified" or based on the last modification time of the case.

For each escalation rule you can specify up to five actions, to escalate the case over increasing periods of time.

The **Age Over** field specifies the number of hours after which a case should be escalated if it has not been closed.

This time is calculated from the date field set in the **Specify how escalation times are set** field.

No two escalation actions can have the same time period set.

Sending an e-mail to a customer from the case record does not reset the case escalation. Only when the record is changed, and not a related list, is the case escalation time reset.

Escalation rules use business hours to determine when to escalate a case. The case feature can include business hours in multiple time zones and can associate cases to various time zones.

Each escalation rule can have multiple criteria settings and up to five escalation actions per entry. An example of one such action is shown in the following screenshot:

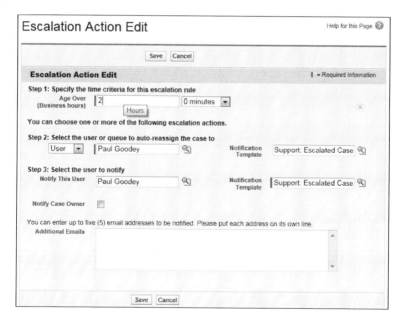

Early triggers

The early triggers mechanism enables case escalation to get expedited to the previous quarter hour slot. The setting is activated for the organization as a whole and is used to ensure that customer **Service Level Agreements (SLAs)** are met.

The early triggers on the escalation box allow you to specify whether Cases should escalate sooner than the **Age Over** time specified.

As an example, we can consider that the escalation logic is currently running on the hour and the escalation triggers are fired every 15 minutes.

Now, say a case is created at 16:16 and the Escalation Rule is set to trigger after one hour, the case will not be escalated until 17:30 because it missed the 17:15 escalation trigger by one minute. This can be an issue when precise escalation is required and hence, by enabling early triggers, this issue can be eliminated.

To enable the early triggers in the escalation box, follow the path **Your Name | Setup | (App Setup) | Customize | Cases | Support Settings**. Now click on **Edit** and set the **Early Triggers Enabled** checkbox as shown next, and then click on the **Save** button:

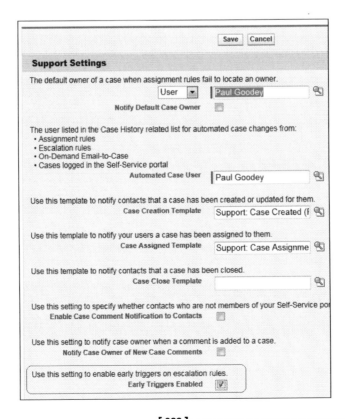

Salesforce Chatter

Salesforce Chatter is an enterprise social networking application that helps users connect with people and share business information. It can be accessed from the App Menu at the top-right corner of the Salesforce CRM screen. Chatter feeds can also be accessed from within the Salesforce CRM record pages.

Chatter is enabled by default for organizations created after June 22, 2010. For existing organizations, you must enable Chatter, as shown next. All users with a Salesforce license have access to Chatter, plus you can create new users that do not have Salesforce licenses but wish to have access to Chatter. These user licenses can access Chatter people, profiles, groups, and files. However, they cannot access any Salesforce object data.

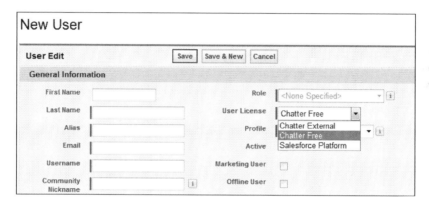

Chatter Only user licenses can be created for users within your company, known as Chatter Free, plus employees not in your organization such as customers, known as Chatter External. These are shown in the preceding screenshot.

A further Chatter license (not shown in the preceding User License selection) is the Chatter Only license. This license is also known as Chatter Plus and is for users that do not have Salesforce licenses but require access to some Salesforce objects in addition to Chatter. This provides access to Chatter people, profiles, groups, and files, plus the viewing of Salesforce accounts and contacts and the ability to modify up to ten custom objects.

You can upgrade a user's Chatter Free license to a standard Salesforce license whenever you wish; however, you cannot change a standard Salesforce license or Chatter Only license for a user to a Chatter Free license.

As mentioned previously, Salesforce Chatter can be accessed from the App Menu by selecting the Salesforce Chatter option within which the following tabs are available: **Chatter**, **Profile**, **People**, **Groups**, and **Files** as shown in the following screenshot:

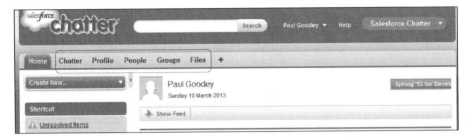

These tabs are available by default in the Chatter app however you can also add these tabs to other apps if required.

Chatter primary features

The following primary features exist in Salesforce Chatter.

Feed

A Chatter feed is a list of recent activities in Salesforce and are displayed on:

- The **Chatter** tab and **Home** tab. Here, users can see their posts, posts from people they follow, and updates to records they follow, and posts to groups they are a member of.
- Profiles, where users can see posts made by the person whose profile they are viewing.
- Records, where users can see updates to the record they are viewing.
- Chatter groups, where users can see posts to the group they are viewing.

Post

A Chatter post is a top-level comment in a Chatter feed.

Invitations

As the name suggests a Chatter invitation is the mechanism to send an invite by e-mail to co-workers (either with or without a Salesforce license) or people outside your company (such as customers).

Chatter settings

Chatter settings provide options for feeds, posts, and invitations. We will first look at the setting to enable Chatter and then in the following sections, we will look through these various settings that you can apply for Salesforce Chatter.

Enabling Chatter

Enabling Chatter also enables the new user interface theme, which updates the look and feel of Salesforce.

When Chatter is enabled, the global search, which allows searching across Salesforce, including Chatter feeds, files, groups, and people is activated.

Where there are 15 or fewer users, all users automatically follow each other when Chatter is enabled. The selection of the **Salesforce Chatter** options can be carried out by following the path **Your Name | Setup | (App Setup) | Customize | Chatter | Settings** (as shown in the following screenshot).

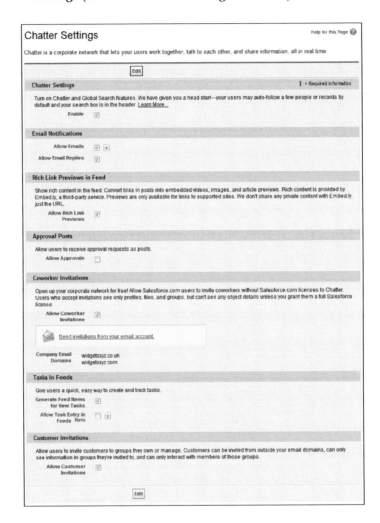

E-mail notifications

Check the **Allow Emails** checkbox to permit users to receive personal Chatter e-mail notifications.

Check the **Allow Email Replies** checkbox to permit users to reply to Chatter posts by e-mail.

Rich link previews in feed

Check the **Allow Rich Link Previews** checkbox to display rich content in the Chatter feed. By enabling this option, links in posts are converted into embedded videos, images, and article previews.

 The rich content is provided by Embed.ly, which is a third-party web hosting service and previews are only available for links to supported sites.

Salesforce does not share any private content with Embed.ly, just the URL.

Approval posts

Check the **Allow Approvals** checkbox to permit users to use Chatter posts within Salesforce Workflow approval processing. By enabling this option users can approve any business process from within their Chatter feed.

Coworker Invitations

Check the **Allow Coworker Invitations** checkbox to enable everyone in your company to access Chatter. This allows all colleagues, even those who do not have Salesforce licenses to collaborate using Salesforce Chatter.

Invited users can access Chatter people, profiles, groups, and files but cannot access Salesforce records unless they have a Salesforce license. To make Chatter available for company colleagues you can either manually add Chatter users or use the **Invitations** option.

Starting in June 2011, invitations are automatically turned on for new organizations and the **Company Email Domains** field is populated based on the first user's e-mail address.

 Salesforce recommends that you do not enter public e-mail domains such as `hotmail.com` or `gmail.com`. Anyone with an e-mail address in these domains could then join and access Chatter features and data within your organization.

You must provide at least one e-mail domain and you can add a maximum of 200 domains. The domains that you enter should be those used in e-mail addresses within your company.

As security, the **Allow Coworker Invitations** checkbox will not be activated if the domain is a free e-mail provider such as yahoo.com, gmail.com, and so on.

Tasks in feeds

Check the **Allow Task Entry in Feeds** checkbox to permit users to create a task directly in a record feed.

Check the **Generate Feed Items for New Tasks** checkbox to automatically generate Chatter feeds whenever Salesforce tasks are created.

Customer invitations

Check the **Allow Customer Invitations** checkbox to permit users to invite people from outside your company network.

Feed tracking

When you enable feed tracking, users will see updates for the objects and records that they follow in their Chatter feed. Many objects and fields are tracked by default, but you can further customize feed tracking to include or exclude specific objects and fields.

You can set feed tracking for users, Chatter groups, and the following standard objects: accounts, assets, campaigns, cases, contacts, contracts, dashboards, events, leads, opportunities, products, reports, solutions, and tasks. You can also configure feed tracking for custom objects.

The selection of the **Salesforce Feed Tracking** options can be carried out by following the path **Your Name | Setup | (App Setup) | Customize | Chatter | Feed Tracking** (as shown in the following screenshot).

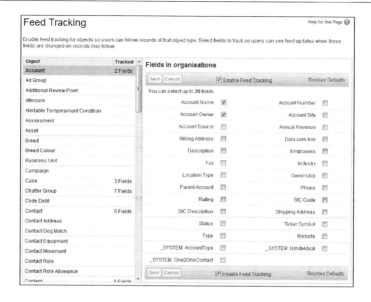

Chat settings

This feature allows users to chat with people they follow in Chatter without having to use external chat clients.

The selection of the **Salesforce Feed Tracking** options can be carried out by following the path **Your Name | Setup | (App Setup) | Customize | Chatter | Chat Settings** (as shown in the following screenshot).

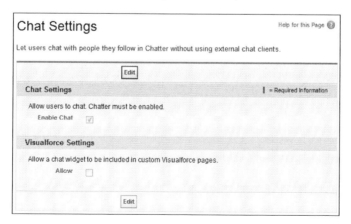

In the **Chat Settings** section, check the **Enable Chat** checkbox to permit users to use the chat facility directly in Salesforce CRM.

In the **Visualforce Settings** section, check the **Allow** checkbox to permit developer and administrators to include the Chat widget within custom Visualforce pages.

Influence

This setting allows you to control how much activity users must have before they are included in influence-level calculations.

The selection of the **Salesforce Feed Tracking** options can be carried out by following the path **Your Name | Setup | (App Setup) | Customize | Chatter | Influence** (as shown in the following screenshot).

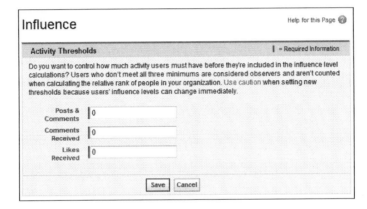

Summary

In this chapter, we looked at the functional areas within Salesforce CRM where we described the process from campaign to customer and beyond which is facilitated by:

- Marketing administration
- Salesforce automation
- Customer service and support automation

Within the functional areas, there are various touch points where the business teams concerned with marketing, sales, and customer service have to agree on roles and responsibilities for aspects of the business processes. Salesforce has developed Salesforce Chatter, a collaboration application that helps in this respect by connecting people and sharing business information.

We looked at how automation can improve the experience for campaign and lead management when producing targets at the start of a campaign, and how the ROI can be measured with statistics and reports at the end.

We also saw how leads can be converted to generate the accounts, contacts, and opportunity records which would be processed through the sales cycle and become the closed opportunity and customer entities.

We described the ways in which Salesforce can be used to support these customers by the customer service and support teams, and the case management features that are associated with the account and contact information to solve problems and answer queries.

In the next chapter, we will look at the ways in which the Salesforce CRM platform can be extended further through the use of customization technologies, such as Visualforce, where you can leverage further benefits for your organization and enhance the system without the need for expensive IT development resources.

8
Extending Salesforce CRM

In this chapter, we will look at how to extend the functionality of the Salesforce CRM application and move beyond the standard pages and functionality that we have looked at so far. Here we will cover:

- Enterprise mashups in web applications
- Mashups in Salesforce CRM
- Introduction to Visualforce
- Creating an example mashup with Visualforce
- Overview of Visualforce controllers
- Introduction to Apex code and triggers

An overview of the technologies and techniques that allow advanced customization will be presented, which will help you gain an understanding of the features and considerations required to create web mashups in your Salesforce CRM applications.

You will discover how, with use of the platform and technologies such as Visualforce, you can extend the core functionality of the application and leverage significant benefits for your organization as well as how to enhance the system without the need for expensive IT development resources.

Enterprise mashups in web applications

A **mashup** is a general term that is commonly used to describe the merging of functionality and content from multiple sources. It is typically applied to describe the merging of web applications where the sources may often be using different technology to provide the service or application, but as part of the distinction for a web application mashup, the common feature that provides the connectivity is the Internet.

The connections between the various sources may require different levels and complexities of integration depending on whether the associated information or content is to be simply viewed or whether it is also to be amended, and therefore whether data is to be distributed across the various systems.

When mashups first started appearing on the web, they were quite simply created to enable the viewing of content from another web source within an Internet browser, and did not transfer any data or functionality between the source systems.

An example of such a mashup is a website that displays a "how to find us" type of page within one of its web pages, such as the contact page. Within the HTML code, there might be an embedded piece of functionality showing a static Google map or a similar web control as shown in the following screenshot:

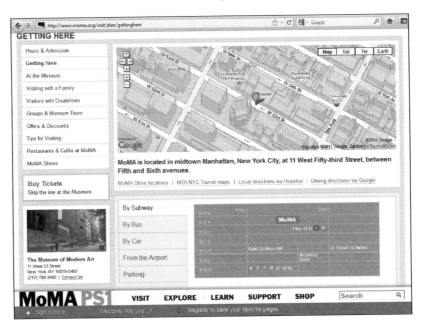

This type of mashup is an example of a simple client-side mashup, where the connectivity occurs inside the web browser. This coding inside the web page provides a way to combine static information from multiple Internet sources and generate an elegant visual presentation.

As mashups have evolved, far more complex functionality can now be achieved. It is possible to have sophisticated integration between web applications where information and functionality are seamlessly shared. As you might expect, this requires more complex coding to achieve, and also may require the use of server-side infrastructures. We will shortly look at the distinction between the client-side and server-side mashups.

Mashups in Salesforce CRM

It may seem daunting at first, especially if you are less familiar with Internet scripting technologies such as HTML, but certain types of mashup can be accomplished by most people and do not require professional software developers or the IT team.

 HTML (Hyper Text Markup Language) is the main markup language for creating web pages and other information that can be displayed in a web browser (`https://en.wikipedia.org/wiki/HTML`).

Before starting out, it is always useful to first evaluate how and where the mashup needs to be done, and in particular, the type of data and service that is to be mashed up. Once this is understood, you can then begin to consider the coding effort and plan the resources required to implement them.

To understand the flavor of mashups as far as Salesforce CRM is concerned, and as suggested, at a high-level, there are two main categories of mashup development, and these can be classed as either server-side or client-side as shown in the following diagram:

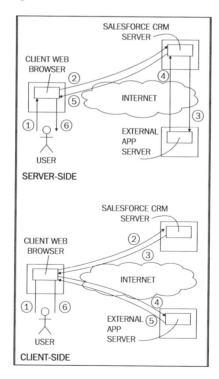

Looking at the preceding diagram, we see that the server-side mashup goes through the following high-level steps:

1. User makes a page request to Salesforce CRM using his/her web browser.
2. The web browser calls the Salesforce CRM servers, which invoke custom Apex code.
3. The custom Apex code in Salesforce CRM calls a function on an external application server.
4. The external application returns the response to Salesforce CRM.
5. Salesforce CRM processes the response and returns the details to the users' web browser.
6. The user's web browser finally presents the overall response back to the user.

Client-side mashups are far more simple, as they use the browser to link the requests and responses required for the mashup, where the following typical high-level steps can be considered:

1. User makes a page request to Salesforce CRM using his/her web browser.
2. The user's web browser requests details from Salesforce CRM.
3. Salesforce CRM returns the response to the user's web browser.
4. The user's web browser requests details from the external application.
5. The external application returns the response to the user's web browser.
6. The user's web browser finally presents the overall response back to the user.

As indicated, server-side mashups often require sophisticated coding and require external infrastructure, which is generally provided by the IT resources. As this book does not aim to be a resource for developers, we will look at server-side technology at a high level, but will not go into the details.

We will, however, cover the use and provide some step-by-step instructions on how you can compose client-side mashups, as well as the tools that are available within your Salesforce CRM application.

Server-side mashups

By way of introduction, and for the sake of completeness, the following section describes the core features of external server-side mashups. We will briefly look, in a little more detail, at the capabilities, features, and implications associated with the use of server-side mashups.

Server-side mashups are a specific example of an external services mashup. This is where external systems may either serve the request for data from Salesforce as a client or use data presented by Salesforce and mash the composite data in an external system.

These mashups typically use web services, and are most often provided by organizations using web APIs, which describe how the service can be accessed by a client application over the Internet, and which are executed on the remote system that is hosting the service.

A more formal definition of a web service is provided by the **World Wide Web Consortium (W3C)**, which as detailed on their web page (`http://www.w3.org`), is "an international community where member organizations, a full-time staff, and the public work together to develop web standards".

The definition of a web service by the W3C is (`http://www.w3.org/TR/ws-gloss/`):

> *A Web service is a software system designed to support interoperable machine-to-machine interaction over a network. It has an interface described in a machine-processable format (specifically WSDL). Other systems interact with the Web service in a manner prescribed by its description using SOAP-messages, typically conveyed using HTTP with an XML serialization in conjunction with other Web-related standards.*

Although the web service definition for the machine-to-machine interaction by the W3C refers to machine-to-machine interaction using SOAP (or simple object access protocol), there is another protocol that is becoming increasingly popular today, known as **Representational State Transfer (REST)**. This is mentioned for information only, and we will not go into any further detail about web services in this book.

Client-side mashups

Within Salesforce CRM, there are typically two types of client-side mashup, namely client-side services mashups and client-side presentation mashups.

Client-side services mashups

Similar to server-side mashups, client-side services mashups can also be used to call web services or consume websites and feeds. They can be used to invoke the Salesforce CRM web services API from within the browser. Client-side services mashups require more complex programming than client-side presentation mashups, and typically rely on the technologies associated with web services.

Client services mashups and external services mashups are useful to organizations that need to access information from various systems that usually serve a business data process and interact in real time. Specifying and developing these types of mashups needs to be carefully evaluated to determine the required effort and resources.

Client-side presentation mashups

Client-side presentation mashups are the least complex mashups, and can be composed relatively quickly. Here, live data and functionality from multiple sources are embedded on a web page, which requires data from the Salesforce platform with which to mashup with the non-Salesforce data and functionality.

Client presentation mashups in Salesforce can be composed using Visualforce, HTML, and JavaScript, which can often be copied-and-pasted by nontechnical users and can immediately add value to a web application.

Having briefly outlined the nature of client-side mashups, we are now going to look at how they can actually be created in Salesforce CRM. As shown earlier, the enabling technology is provided by the Salesforce platform with the use of the web page framework known as Visualforce.

The best way to guide you through the use of new technology is by demonstrating how to use it with an example. Here we are going to compose a client-side presentation that displays a Google News Bar ticker widget that displays Google news information
for a given company.

The News Bar will be presented to the user in Salesforce CRM after selecting an appropriate account record, and live Google news information will be displayed right from within the relevant account detail page. The mashup will be composed by creating a new Visualforce page with the required Google News Bar widget, and then adding a new section to the account detail page where the Visualforce page will be included.

Introduction to Visualforce

Visualforce is the framework in Salesforce CRM, which allows you to further customize your organization's user interface beyond the standard functionality that we have previously covered.

As described previously, using Visualforce, you can combine data from multiple objects, create mashups with data from external web services, and even override some of the logic and the behavior found within standard Salesforce CRM application functions. Visualforce consists of the following three elements:

- **Visualforce pages**: These are used to define the user interface
- **Visualforce components**: These can be thought of as a library of standard or custom-built sections of Visualforce code
- **Visualforce page controllers**: These are used to control the behavior of Visualforce pages, and can either be controlled by standard logic or you can create custom logic to change or extend the standard Salesforce CRM behavior

Visualforce pages

The Visualforce framework allows for the creation of Visualforce pages. These pages are a little like documents that are stored in Salesforce, and are comprised of instructions that specify how the page is to appear and function. Similar in nature to HTML, Visualforce pages comprise of a tag-based markup language, with each Visualforce tag type corresponding to a particular user interface component.

 The maximum size of a Visualforce page cannot be greater than 15 MB.

For the more technical readers, Visualforce performs similar functions as, say, Java Server Pages or Active Server Pages, and is used to manage the retrieval of the data from the Salesforce platform and the rendering of results via the Internet browser user interface.

Creating a Visualforce page

Now that you are aware of the basic building blocks provided by Visualforce, we will describe the creation of Visualforce pages. This section looks at how the creation and modification of pages can be done, and shows the following two ways of doing so:

- Using the Visualforce pages setup page
- Using development mode

Visualforce pages setup page

To navigate to the setup page for creating Visualforce pages, go to **Your Name | Setup | (App Setup) | Develop | Pages**. Now click on the **New** button to create a new Visualforce page. Select an existing entry to view the page, or click on **Edit** to modify it:

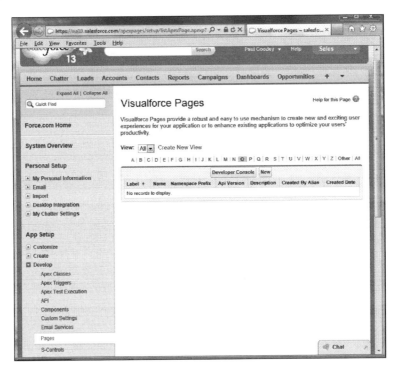

Visualforce development mode

We can also use something called Visualforce development mode to initially create and edit Visualforce pages. This can be a better choice because it provides several useful features that make it easier to build Visualforce pages.

To start using the development mode, it needs to be activated on your user record by navigating to **Your Name | Setup | My Personal Information | Personal Information**. Now click on the **Edit** button, select the **Development Mode** checkbox, and then finally click on **Save**:

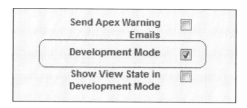

Automatic creation of new Visualforce pages

When in Visualforce development mode, you can create a new page simply by entering a unique URL into the browser's address bar; for example, the URL `https://na10.salesforce.com/apex/FinanceChart` will enable a new page called FinanceChart to be created.

You need to be careful that you are entering the correct URL text, as it is the part `/apex/FinanceChart` in the preceding example that prompts Salesforce CRM to check and create the new page if it does not currently exist. It is also important that the start of the URL is entered correctly. The `https://na10.salesforce.com` part refers to the Salesforce instance for your Salesforce CRM application.

When entered correctly, the following screen will be presented:

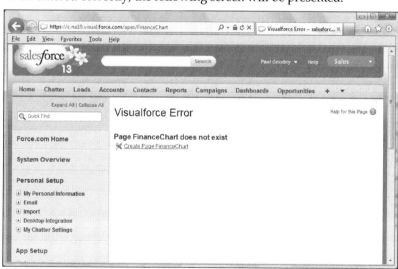

This, as you can appreciate, can save a lot of time when creating a lot of pages, as you do not need to keep navigating to the setup sidebar section, and it saves a number of mouse clicks. The resulting edit page, when you click on the link **Create Page FinanceChart**, is the same edit page as when accessed through the setup route as shown in the following screenshot:

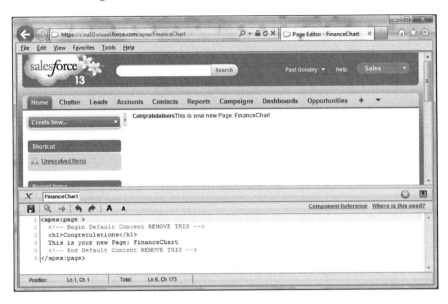

When development mode is enabled, a development section is automatically presented below the Visualforce page that you are creating or editing which displays an editor section. To show or hide the development section, click on the following icon:

The editor allows you to write Visualforce component tags directly within the browser window, and also offers the following features:

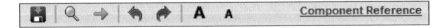

As shown, the seven menu functions are provided for:

- Saving the page
- Searching for text
- Navigating to a specified line in the code

- Undoing changes

- Redoing changes

- Increasing the font size of the text

- Decreasing the font size of the text

Clicking on the **Component Reference** link will navigate to the online documentation, which provides descriptions as well as example code for all the Visualforce components, as shown in the following screenshot:

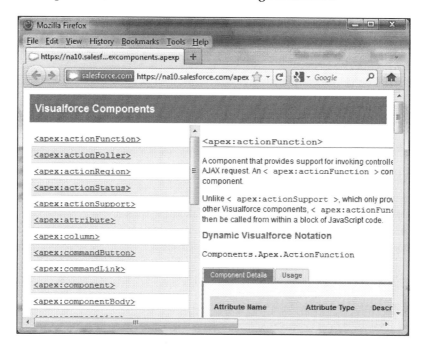

In addition, the page editor also provides highlighting and an autocomplete feature that automatically displays available component markup tags, as shown in the following screenshot:

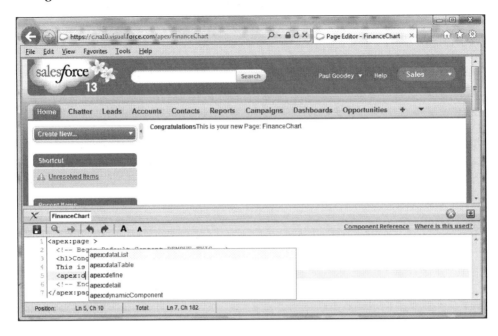

The greatest benefit of having development mode enabled when building Visualforce pages using the Salesforce CRM platform is that as you add component tags and build up the code in the page, you can click on the save icon and view the resulting changes immediately.

 The Visualforce page must be free from errors before the page is allowed to be saved.

Visualforce components

We have seen in the previous section that Salesforce provides a set of standard, pre-built components, such as `<apex:actionFunction>` and `<apex:actionStatus>`, which can be added to Visualforce pages to construct pages of functionality. In addition, you can build your own custom components to augment this library of components.

Similar to the way functions work in a programming language, a custom Visualforce component allows you to construct common code and then re-use that code in one or more Visualforce pages.

Custom components allow you to define attributes that can be passed in to each component. The value of an attribute can then change the way the markup is displayed on the final page and the controller-based logic that executes for that instance of the component.

Visualforce custom components consist of Visualforce markup tags using the standard `<apex:component>` tag, and so rather than repeating the Visualforce markup required for every page that you need the common code on, you can define a custom component that has certain attributes and then uses those attributes to display the functionality on the page. Once defined, every Visualforce page in your organization can leverage the custom component in the same way as a page can leverage standard components such as `<apex:dataTable>` or `<apex:actionStatus>`.

Creating an example mashup with Visualforce

In order to construct our example mashup, we will navigate to the Yahoo! Finance chart code website `http://finance.yahoo.com/badges/`, where we can copy and paste the required financial stock chart code.

 To access the Yahoo Finance finance charts, you will need to either log in directly to Yahoo! or use your Facebook or Google login details.

The URL `http://finance.yahoo.com/badges/wizard/config?style=cq` provides a simple setup wizard that will allow us to obtain the code that will form part of the code that will be entered on our Visualforce page:

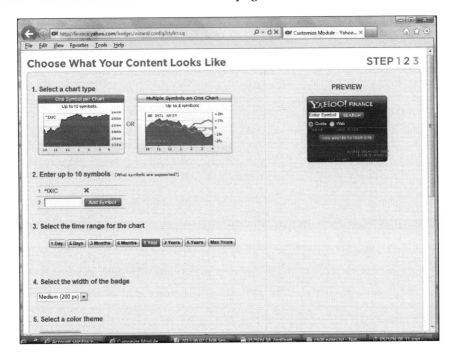

Now apply these settings as shown in the following steps:

1. Select the **One Symbol per Chart** type (the chart on the left).
2. Enter CRM in the **Symbol** textbox (and remove the default ^IXIC).
3. Leave the time range to the default **1 Year**.
4. Select the width of the badge to be **X large**.
5. Select the color theme to be **white** (the chart on the right).
6. Agree to the Terms of Service by checking the **I agree to the Terms of Service above box**.

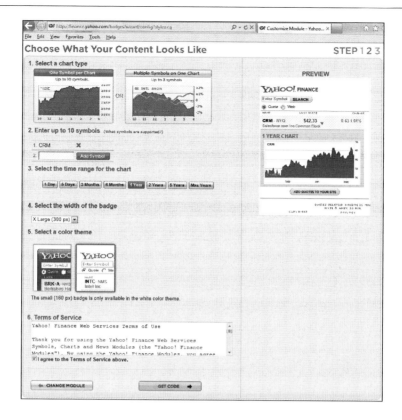

Now click on the **GET CODE** button to display the following:

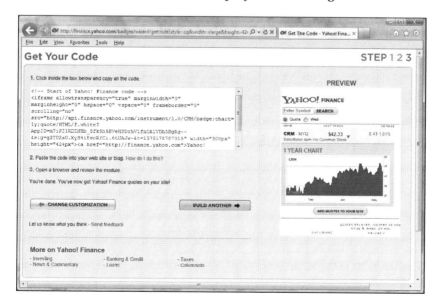

Now we can use the generated code by clicking in the textbox labelled **1. Click inside the box below** and copying all the code. We can then start to copy and paste the Finance Chart functionality into our Visualforce page by following these steps:

1. Delete the default new Visualforce markup content.

2. Change the Visualforce Controller to specify an Account Standard Controller.

3. Add Salesforce-specific merge fields.

Deleting the default new Visualforce markup content

Delete the existing Visualforce page text (lines 2 to 5 in the following screenshot) and leave just the starting and ending tags, `<apex:page>` and `</apex:page>`, as shown:

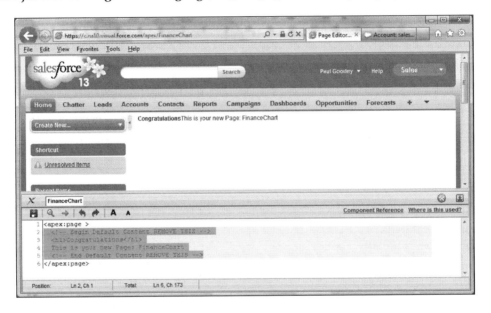

Changing the Visualforce Controller to specify an Account Standard Controller

We also need to change the Visualforce page controller so that we can read the value of the fields stored on the Account record. Controllers will be looked at in more detail later in this chapter, but for the moment, we will change the opening tag `<apex:page>` and add the attribute `standardController`, which allows the call to the Account record, as shown using the code `<apex:page standardController="account">`:

```
<apex:page standardController="account">

</apex:page>
```

Adding Salesforce-specific merge fields

However, it is not simply a case of copying and pasting as it is; we need to make a few changes to complete the mashup and display the account details. The Visualforce feature that allows us to link the account is what is known as merge fields. Here, the syntax for adding a merge field to access the data field in Salesforce CRM is the Visualforce code {!object.Field}, where the expression in between {! and } is evaluated.

For the Account Ticker symbol, which is what we will be passing to the Finance Chart widget, we need to set the code {!Account.TickerSymbol}.

This is done in the following block of code where we highlight the section that is changed:

- **Before**:

  ```
  src="http://api.finance.yahoo.com/instrument/1.0/CRM/
  badge;chart=1y;quote/HTML/f.white?
  <a href="http://finance.yahoo.com/q?s=CRM/">Quote for CRM/</a>
  ```

- **After**:

  ```
  src="http://api.finance.yahoo.com/instrument/1.0/{!Account.
  TickerSymbol}/badge;chart=1y;quote/HTML/f.white?
  <a href="http://finance.yahoo.com/q?s={!Account.
  TickerSymbol}/">Quote for {!Account.TickerSymbol}/</a>
  ```

The following shows the complete code that should appear on the Visualforce page. Note that you will need to use the codes that were generated for the AppID and sig parameters when you clicked on the **GET CODE** button as shown earlier:

```
<apex:page standardController="account">
<!-- Start of Yahoo! Finance code -->
<iframe allowtransparency="true" marginwidth="0" marginheight="0"
hspace="0" vspace="0" frameborder="0" scrolling="no" src="http://
api.finance.yahoo.com/instrument/1.0/{!Account.TickerSymbol}/
badge;chart=1y;quote/HTML/f.white?AppID=[Your AppID Code
Here]&sig=[Your sig Code Here]&t=1370174151909" width="300px"
height="424px"><a href="http://finance.yahoo.com">Yahoo!
Finance</a><br/><a href="http://finance.yahoo.com/q?s={!Account.
TickerSymbol}/">Quote for {!Account.TickerSymbol}/</a></iframe>
<!-- End of Yahoo! Finance code -->
</apex:page>
```

The final code will appear within the Visualforce page as in the following screenshot.

When saving the Visualforce page, the page is rendered immediately, however, at this point, there is no valid ticker symbol to be passed to the Yahoo! Finance Chart widget (this will be rendered properly after we have added the Visualforce page to the Account Page Layout), therefore an error will initially be presented as shown in the following screenshot:

 Notice how with the use of the `<apex:page standardController="account">` tag, the **Accounts** tab is now automatically highlighted.

Adding the Visualforce page to the Account page layout

Now that we have completed and saved the Visualforce page, we can add the **Finance Chart** page to the Account page layout. To add Visualforce pages to Accounts, navigate to **Your Name | Setup | (App Setup) | Customize | Accounts | Page Layouts**. Now select the appropriate page layout. Here we are going to add it to the page layout called Account Layout by carrying out the steps discussed in the following section.

Adding a new section to the Account page layout

The new section has been given the title **Finance Chart** and has been set to **1-Column** width and positioned by dragging-and-dropping below the **Account System and Description Information** section:

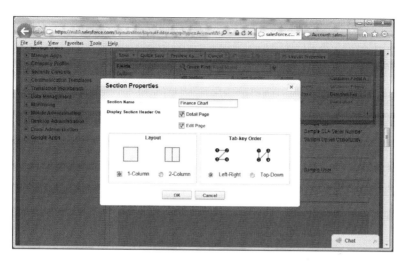

Adding the Visualforce page to the new page layout section

Now drag-and-drop the **Finance Chart** Visualforce page to the **Finance Chart** section on the page layout:

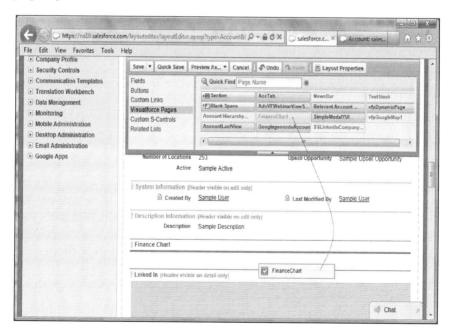

Finally, double-click on the Visualforce page and set the width at **100%** and the height at **400** (pixels), and optionally check the **Show scrollbars** checkbox as shown in the following screenshot:

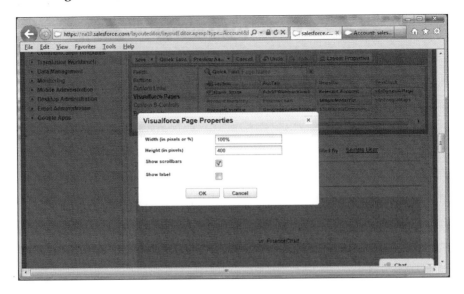

Now click on **Save**; we are ready to test by navigating to an account page.

Running the completed Visualforce page

Navigate to the **Account** tab and select an existing account to verify that the mashup is working as expected.

 You will need to ensure a value is entered on the **Account Ticker Symbol** field. The **Account Ticker Symbol** field is a standard Account field in Salesforce CRM.

Here we have an existing account for salesforce.com with the Ticker Symbol CRM, which presents the following when the account detail page is loaded:

How do I suppress browser security warnings in Internet Explorer?

By default, Internet Explorer displays the following security warning message when a page contains a mixture of secure (HTTPS) and nonsecure (HTTP) content: **This page contains both secure and nonsecure items. Do you want to display the nonsecure items?** When you create a mashup with a nonsecure URL, users may see this warning message depending on their browser security settings. To suppress this warning in Internet Explorer, follow these steps: from the Internet Explorer tools menu, select **Internet Options**, click on the **Security** tab, and click on the **Custom Level** button, and finally, in the miscellaneous section, set **Display mixed content** to **Enable**, as shown in the following screenshot:

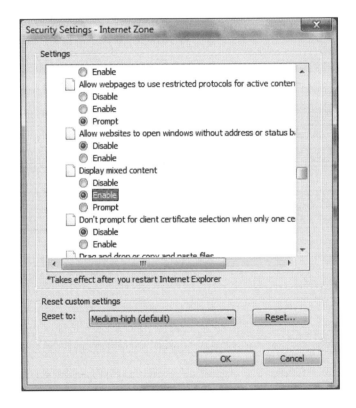

Visualforce page controllers

As described earlier in this chapter, there are three types of controllers that can be used to control the functionality behind a Visualforce page.

Standard controllers

A standard controller provides access to standard Salesforce CRM behavior, and as shown in our example client-side mashup, can be specified using the following tag and attribute as the first line in the Visualforce page:

```
<apex:page standardController="Account">
```

Standard controllers are available for all objects, such as Account, Contact, Opportunity, and so on, as well as custom objects, and provide access to standard Salesforce CRM data operations and behavior for actions such as save, edit, and delete.

Custom controllers

Custom controllers are used for fully customized behavior, and are implemented using the Visualforce tag and attribute as follows:

```
<apex:page controller="CustomAccount">
```

Controller extensions

Controller extensions are used to extend the behavior of standard controllers, and allow the addition of customized functionality. Controller extensions are provided using the Visualforce tag and attribute as follows:

```
<apex:page standardController="Account"
extensions="CustomAccountExtension">
```

Apex code

The Apex code language in Salesforce CRM is based on Java, which is one of the most popular programming languages for Internet and web-based applications, and is executed on the Salesforce platform servers.

Although based on Java, the Apex code and the Salesforce CRM platform is not a general-purpose computing platform that can be used to run any type of program that developers may choose to run. Instead, Apex is kept intentionally controlled and limited and is, therefore, designed with the needs of the business and platform in mind.

 Apex code in Salesforce is not intended to solve every programming problem, and is concerned principally to help developers gain advantages in development time, code conciseness, and reduction in maintenance costs.

Apex is used in Salesforce CRM to develop the code within Custom controllers and Controller extensions, as well as Apex triggers, which we will look at shortly.

Apex is specifically designed for building business applications to manage data and services, and the language provides a highly productive approach to creating applications and business logic. Developers can focus on the functionality required to solve the business problem and domain, and need not be concerned with building the infrastructures such as database connection, error handling, and so on, which is managed by the platform.

It should be noted that since the Salesforce CRM platform is a multi-tenant platform, there are certain limits as to what and how much processing can be performed within certain operations. Such limits are known as Governor Limits, and there are some restrictions and requirements, for example, Apex code must be developed in a developer or sandbox organization and must have test methods to verify each line of code, and only then is it allowed to be deployed to production.

 For successful deployment to production, Apex code must have associated unit test methods that provide at least 75 percent successful code coverage.

Apex triggers

Apex triggers are blocks of Apex code that are executed before and/or after any record action, such as create, read, update, or delete, in the Salesforce CRM application.

Triggers are very powerful and can include complex code to control your process. They are used for complex business logic automation and where such functionality is too complicated to be implemented using validation rules or workflow rules, such as field updates. The development of Apex triggers usually requires the resource of a software developer, as they have certain restrictions and implications for the overall system.

When using multiple triggers, and alongside any existing workflow field updates, there needs to be a thorough understanding of any dependencies to avoid any ripple effect when records are created or updated. As trigger code can make changes to the record being updated within its own operation, any likely recursion effect needs to be understood and avoided.

 It is important to understand the timing, order of execution, and dependencies of the various rules and triggers within an organization.

Summary

In this chapter, we have discovered how easy it is to build a mashup in Salesforce CRM using the Visualforce technology. We looked at how, with the use of Visualforce pages, we can extend the standard page functionality of the Salesforce CRM.

We were introduced to the concepts of mashups concerning both the client side and server side, and the difference between presentation mashups, which are rendered in an Internet browser, and services that require more complex features, such as web services.

We were introduced to the ways in which Visualforce pages can be controlled, where we looked at the use of Apex code, which can extend the functionality within the Salesforce CRM platform.

Finally, Apex triggers were briefly covered, where we considered the need for careful implementation to observe the order of execution for workflow rules and triggers to ensure that no unwanted ripple effects were introduced.

In the next chapter, we will look at ways to improve the experience of users in Salesforce CRM by providing additional functionality using external applications from the AppExchange Marketplace. We will outline methods to improve the **ROI (return on investment)** from the system, and finally, we will look in detail at the various approaches and ways to measure user adoption.

9
Best Practices for Enhancing Productivity

In this chapter of *Salesforce CRM: The Definitive Admin Handbook*, we will look at ways to improve the return on investment from the Salesforce CRM application by adding further values and improving the experience of users in the system.

We will look at user adoption and describe ways to maximize the benefits of CRM within your organization by introducing additional functionality using external applications from the AppExchange Marketplace, such as the **Salesforce Adoption Dashboards** app which is a free app provided by Salesforce (through their Force.com Labs AppExchange listing).

As businesses evolve and processes change, new functionality and information requirements are often identified. Here, we will look at the importance of planning and scheduling the release of changes to your application and provide some best practices relating to change management.

It will be seen how achieving successful user adoption can enhance your business processes and increase productivity, and the more the business's teams use Salesforce CRM, the more valuable the data and information analysis becomes.

We will discuss how successful user adoption can be achieved by empowering users and making their working lives easier. By providing users with information relevant to their daily tasks, keeping data clean and keeping functionality simple, users are not overburdened with unnecessary actions that overcomplicate and reduce productivity.

We will also look at ways to engage users by providing additional tools to help them get their jobs done far more efficiently. For example, users such as field sales and support teams can benefit from Salesforce Mobile, which can significantly improve productivity and user satisfaction by providing access to the application while out in the field.

There is a wealth of solutions to help achieve most requirements available from the Salesforce AppExchange Marketplace, and we will now describe and walk through the process of installing an example application.

AppExchange Marketplace is a website provided by Salesforce.com that enables organizations to select additional applications, known as apps, to add new features to their Salesforce CRM application.

Both the Salesforce CRM application and the AppExchange provide web-delivered platforms for using and building applications. This integrated web-delivered approach allows for the installation of applications and new functionality from AppExchange into Salesforce that is often far simpler and more cost effective than traditional software update mechanisms. The benefits of the AppExchange are that system administrators can easily extend the Salesforce CRM application as your company's business requirements change.

The apps and services listed on AppExchange are provided by the Salesforce community of third party developers and system integrators. Many of the apps are also provided by Salesforce themselves through their team known as the Force.com Labs.

Apps can sometimes incur additional costs, but there are many which are provided free or for a small fee. In general, apps provided by the Salesforce.com Force.com Labs team tend to be free. To access AppExchange, navigate to **Your name | Setup | App Setup | AppExchange Marketplace**, as shown in the following screenshot:

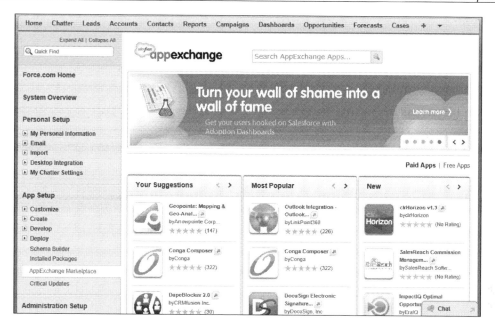

You can also access the AppExchange Marketplace website directly outside of Salesforce CRM by navigating to `http://www.appexchange.com/`, as shown in the following screenshot:

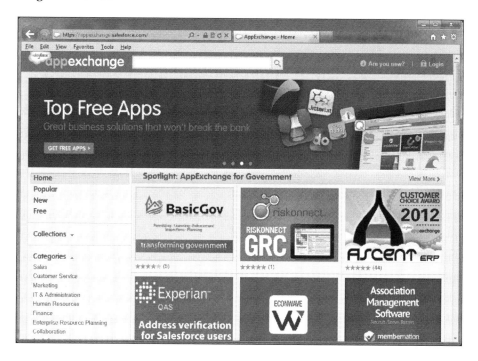

As a directory, Salesforce AppExchange is similar to consumer websites, such as App Store from Apple, in the way that it seeks to provide an open, community-based channel for the distribution, retrieval, and installation of applications.

AppExchange differs, however, in that it provides not only the facilities for third party distribution of apps, but also the listing of services by system integrators. This enables the Salesforce community to search for and review both apps and services from a central site.

Managed and unmanaged packages

Salesforce terms the collection of components and applications that are distributed through AppExchange as a package; there are two types of packages, namely, managed and unmanaged.

Managed packages differ from unmanaged packages by the use of protected components that allow the managed packages to be upgraded by the developers, perhaps to add new functionality or to refactor in any changes in the Salesforce environment. By protecting certain components such as Apex Code, managed packages also serve to protect the intellectual property of the developer organization.

Unmanaged packages, on the other hand, do not protect components, and are therefore static within your organization as they cannot be upgraded by the publishing developer. They allow you to access all of the implemented customization or code and can be useful if you want to change or extend the functionality yourself.

 Users with the permission **Download AppExchange Packages** enabled for their profile can install or uninstall the AppExchange packages from the AppExchange website.

Sometimes the apps are distributed by **Independent Software Vendors** (**ISVs**), which use the AppExchange package as a channel to advertise their presence and to showcase their range of products.

External and third party tools

By showcasing on the AppExchange Marketplace website, ISVs often provide free apps, which help drive traffic and interest in their core products, which complement Salesforce CRM, and are usually provided as web-based solutions in the same way as Salesforce.

These complementary applications are typically deployed alongside Salesforce CRM in support of a specific business process or function. For example, incentive and commission management, project management, product configuration, expense management, address checking, and so on, are all examples of apps for Salesforce which are available from AppExchange.

App security

Salesforce inspects all registered apps to be sure that they have no obvious security risks. However, it is worth noting that since the apps are developed by third party providers, you should also carry out extensive testing and due diligence to eliminate any risk before installing the app into your production instance.

After an app has passed the Salesforce inspection, the core functionality and code can no longer be changed. However, custom links and web tabs are allowed to be changed because they may need to be altered after installation, for example, simple target URLs might need to be changed from one organization to another.

You need to be aware how these links may introduce risks as part of your decision whether to trust the source of an app before installing to production. This is described in more detail as follows:

Before installing an app

The following steps are recommended to help understand more about the app and to determine any risks or need for further setup to your organization before actually installing the app into your production instance:

- Read specifications and reviews
- Review screenshots and customization guides
- Take a test drive

Read specifications and reviews

Before installing, read the specification associated with the app, where you will see the following details: which Salesforce editions are supported, languages supported, components summary, and package details.

It is often also worth looking at the reviews that have been left by others that have attempted to install the app. Although there is no guarantee that the review is 100 percent accurate and may be subjective, it can give an indication of the complexity in use and the successful installation of an app by other system administrators.

Review screenshots and customization guides

Most apps that have been listed on the AppExchange website provide screenshots and guides for any post-install customization that may be required. These are useful and provide a quick indicator whether the app will be of use to you and your organization.

Take a test drive

Apps typically offer a test drive option (especially the more complex apps), where you are directed to an external Salesforce application and can use the app as a read-only user before actually having to install it. A test drive gives you a far better way to determine whether the app is suitable for your organization before installing.

Within the test drive, you have the opportunity to check the app and its components to ensure that they are suitable, and also that they pose no security risks. For example, components such as custom links, formula fields, and web tabs can send Salesforce session IDs to external web services.

 Session IDs are tokens that allow users to access Salesforce CRM without re-entering the login name and password.

Salesforce.com recommends checking all links to external services that include a session ID merge field, because if these session IDs are shared with an external service, then they expose your data, and there can be a significant security risk that we need to be aware of.

Installing an app

The following steps describe the process of how to install an app into your Salesforce CRM application from the AppExchange Marketplace:

1. Get It Now
2. Examine the package
3. Review the security
4. Install
5. Post-install configuration

The best way to guide you through the use of new technology is by demonstrating with an example.

Here we are going to install an application called **Mass Delete**, which has been developed and published by Salesforce.com's Force.com Labs team. This is a free app that provides a set of custom buttons that allow users to select any number of records and delete all of them with a single click.

The **Mass Delete** app from Salesforce.com's Force.com Labs is available from the AppExchange Marketplace directly through the following URL:
`http://appexchange.salesforce.com/listingDetail?listin gId=a0N300000016YuDEAU`

The **Mass Delete** app page looks as follows:

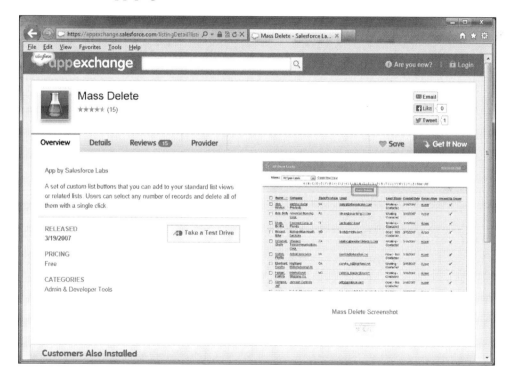

Get It Now

By clicking on the **Get It Now** button, you will start the process of installing the application where you will be prompted to log in to AppExchange using your Salesforce credentials, as shown in the following screenshot:

You will then be asked to select the location for the installation, where the options are to either, **Install in production** or to **Install in sandbox** as shown in the following screenshot:

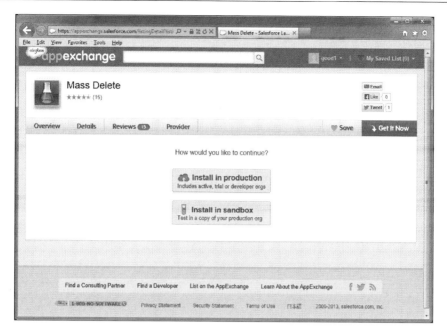

You will then be presented with details of the app that will be installed (listed in the section *What you are installing*) and the Salesforce organization where the app will be installed (listed in the section *Where you are installing*) as shown in the following screenshot:

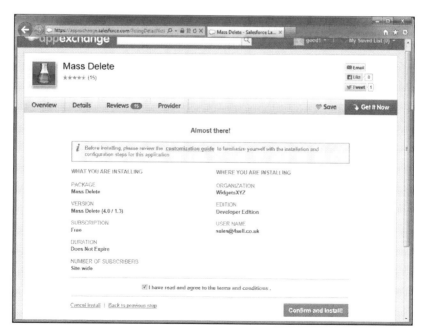

This page shows information about the **Package** and **Version** along with the **Subscription, Duration,** and **Number of Subscribers** information that are a part of the app package.

Click on the checkbox labeled **I have read and agree to the terms and conditions** to confirm that you agree to proceed with the installation and then click on the button **Confirm and Install!** to continue to the next screen as shown in the following screenshot:

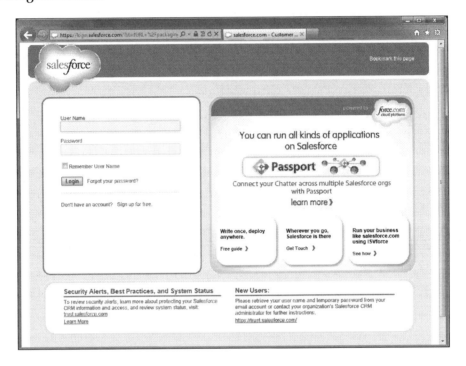

Now enter your **User Name** and **Password** and then click on **Login** to proceed to the next screen:

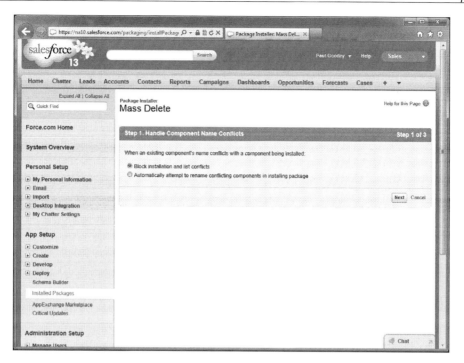

In this screen, **Step 1. Handle Component Name Conflicts**, you are presented with options to handle a situation when an existing component's name conflicts with a component being installed. Here, the options available are **Block installation and list conflicts** or **Automatically attempt to rename conflicting components in installing package**.

Now click on the **Next** button to proceed to the next screen:

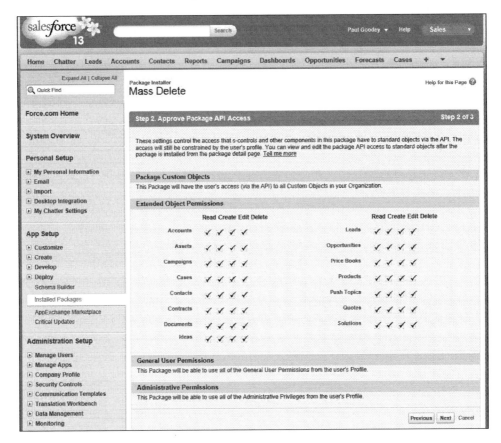

In this screen, **Step 2. Approve Package API Access**, you are presented with a screen showing the **Extended Object Permissions** for the package.

The **Security Permissions Settings** screen displays the package API access that will be applied when the package is installed. Here you should note any settings that require configuration and ensure that they are applied when you have successfully installed the package.

Now click on the **Next** button to proceed to the next screen:

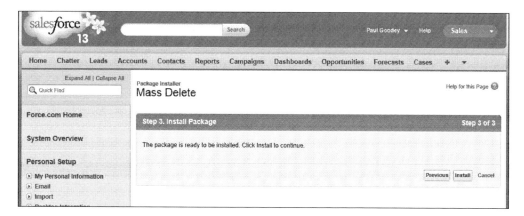

In this screen, **Step 3. Install Package**, you are presented with the final screen with which to start the installation of the app into your Salesforce instance. Here, you need to click on the **Install** button to proceed with the installation:

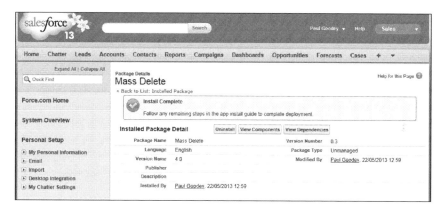

The final **Installed Package Detail** screen shows information about the **Package Name**, **Version Name**, and various other details that make up the app package.

This screen provides confirmation that the app package has been successfully installed.

For large and complex apps, you may not see the **Installation Complete Confirmation** screen straight away. Instead, a screen is sometimes displayed that shows a message that the installation has been scheduled and you then later receive an e-mail notification when the deployment is complete.

Post-install configuration

In this **Mass Delete** app, included in the package components is a PDF guide describing the post-installation configuration that must be applied to the app before the functionality can be used. The guide can be accessed from within the **Documents** tab (which is accessible from the main **Documents** tab) as shown in the following screenshot:

The guide describes how to complete the installation and customization of the app:

Using the guide, we add the custom list button to the **Contacts** related list within the **Accounts** detail page as shown in the following screenshot:

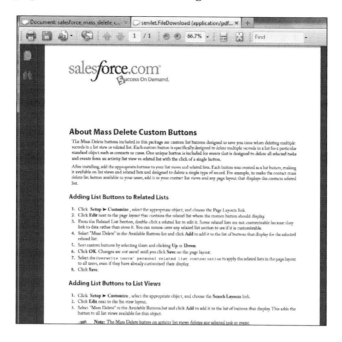

Finally, to verify the installation and customization, we can navigate to the **Accounts** detail page and access the **Contacts** related list section, whereupon we can access the **Mass Delete** custom button and associated functionality:

 In Salesforce CRM Unlimited Edition, you can install an unlimited number of apps. In the Enterprise Edition, there is a maximum limit of 10 apps.

Uninstalling an app

To uninstall an AppExchange app, navigate to **Your name | Setup | App Setup | Installed Packages**, as shown in the following screenshot:

Now select the installed package and either click on the action **Uninstall** or click on the package name to review the details of the package, set the uninstall confirmation checkbox, and finally click on the **Uninstall** button, as shown in the following screenshot:

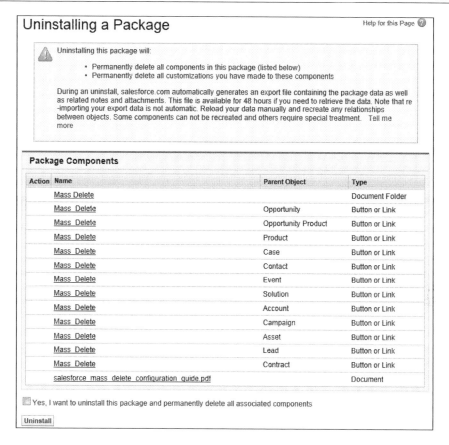

AppExchange best practices

The following best practices should be applied as part of the installation of apps from the AppExchange Marketplace website:

- Clarify that the specification for the app meets the requirements and assess any reviews and comments

- Take a test drive, if available

- Review all the components which are included in the package and be aware of any security issues concerning links and session IDs

- Test the app in a sandbox before deploying into production

- Try to enlist business support to own and validate the app before deploying into production

- Consider undertaking a pilot deployment for selected users if the app is particularly complex

- Communicate the app to the business prior to deployment and activation in production

- Prepare training material for all affected users if the app is particularly complex

Change management overview

As outlined in the section on installing apps from AppExchange Marketplace, you should properly evaluate the functionality and results of deploying an app within your Salesforce CRM organization. This concept is part of a wider concern, which addresses the way changes are applied to the Salesforce CRM application.

With the use of Salesforce sandboxes, you can properly evaluate and perform due diligence for new Salesforce functionality before deciding to roll it out to your users in the production system. In the case of an AppExchange app, if the app proves to be unsuccessful, then it need not be uninstalled.

Salesforce sandboxes

To manage sandboxes in Salesforce CRM, navigate to **Your name | Setup | Administration Setup | Data Management | Sandbox**.

You can view the list of any existing sandboxes that have been created, and clicking on a sandbox name allows you to view details about the sandbox showing when it was created.

In the **Sandbox List**, you can see the sandbox **Name**, **Status**, and **Type**, where there are the following types: **Developer**, **Configuration Only**, and **Full** (as shown in the following screenshot).

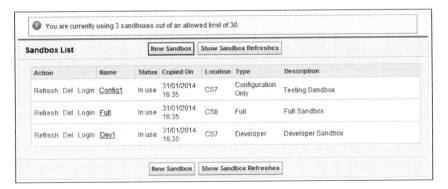

Sandbox availability is dependent on your edition of Salesforce CRM. Some types are provided as standard while others are available for additional cost.

Developer sandbox

A **Developer** sandbox contains a copy of all the configuration setup from your production system. It does not, however, contain any of the data. There is a maximum of 10 MB data storage that can be created. The **Developer** sandbox can be refreshed once per day.

Configuration Only sandbox

A **Configuration Only** sandbox contains a copy of your production organization's configuration setup without any of the production data, similar to the **Developer** sandbox. However, in a **Configuration Only** sandbox, there is a maximum of 500 MB of data that can be stored. Like the **Developer** sandbox, the **Configuration Only** sandbox can be refreshed once a day.

Full copy sandbox

A **Full copy** sandbox contains a copy of your entire production setup, including all the data. Because the data is also copied over during a refresh, there is a limit of refreshing the **Full copy** sandbox to once every 29 days. **Full copy** sandboxes have the same storage limit as the production organization.

 The **Full copy** sandbox is generally used for **User Acceptance Testing (UAT)**.

Clicking on the **New Sandbox** button allows you to create a new sandbox.

The **Show Sandbox Refreshes** button allows you to see the sandbox refresh history, showing when sandboxes were created and who created them.

The **Refresh** button allows you to replace an existing sandbox with a new copy. The existing copy of the sandbox remains available while the refresh completes and until you activate the new copy.

When creating or refreshing a **Full** sandbox, you can reduce the time taken for the refresh by reducing the amount of data that is copied. The following options allow you to reduce the amount of data that is copied:

- The **Case History** option allows you to select the number of days of case history from your production organization to copy to your sandbox. You can copy from 0 to 180 days in 30-day increments. The default value is 30 days.

- The **Opportunity History** option allows you to select the number of days of opportunity history from your production organization to copy to your sandbox. Here, you can copy from 0 to 180 days in 30-day increments. The default value is 0 days.

By default, **Chatter** data is not copied to your sandbox. **Chatter** data includes feeds, messages, and discovery topics. Select the **Copy Chatter Data** checkbox if you wish to copy it.

Salesforce does not recommend increasing the default selections as too much data can cause delays in the time it takes to copy or refresh the sandbox.

The **Refresh** option is only shown for each sandbox that is available for refreshing.

An **Activate** button allows you to activate a refreshed sandbox, which must be done before you can start using the new sandbox.

The **Activate** option is only displayed for refreshed sandboxes that have yet to be activated.

Activating a refreshed sandbox replaces the existing sandbox with the refreshed version and permanently deletes the old version and any data in it.

The **Login** option allows you to log in to a sandbox.

The **Login** button is only displayed for system administrators and may not always be available. Users can log in to an active sandbox by using the following URL: `https://test.salesforce.com` `and entering a modified username`, which is <username> from production, with a suffix for the name of the sandbox. So, for a sandbox called **Test**, it would be `martin.brown@` `widgetsXYZ.com.test`.

Sandboxes that no one has logged in to for 180 days are deleted. Users who have created or most recently refreshed any sandbox within your organization will be notified that the sandbox is scheduled for deletion. These users will receive at least three e-mail notifications over 30 days prior to the deletion.

> Salesforce recommends keeping a sandbox active by logging in periodically to avoid e-mail notifications.

By using a sandbox, you can ensure that changes are deployed in a structured and controlled manner, and any change can be more easily undone. This is known as change management.

Effective change management reduces the risk when introducing new areas of functionality and when making changes to existing functionality. It obviously depends on the amount and complexity of the planned change, but for risk-free and successful implementation of changes in Salesforce CRM, there needs to be a change management strategy, which typically covers the following steps:

1. Change requests
2. Configure, develop, and deploy

Change requests

When working with a change management process in an organization, change requests are typically gathered from ideas and requests from management and application users.

> **Case management for change requests**
> One method of gathering and storing change requests is by utilizing the case management features within Salesforce CRM itself. This feature can be set up to enable users to enter their required changes directly. You can even consider building an approval process so that the change is approved by the user's manager before being considered in any release cycle.

However, the change requests are captured, you need a process to analyze and prioritize the lists of requests and assess the scope of the work required. It can be useful to classify the changes that are requested for inclusion in either an immediate, minor, or a major release.

Immediate release

Change items, which are suitable for immediate release are very small changes that can be quickly implemented; they carry no risk and can be made directly into the production environment. Changes such as new dashboards or reports, or modifications to existing dashboards and reports, and field positioning on page layouts and related lists are considered small changes. This category of release also includes simple data changes, such as data imports and exports.

Changes can be configured, tested, and deployed with minimal impact, and therefore these changes do not usually need to go through the change control process.

 It is worth considering, however, how the changes are applied in any other sandbox such as a developer, user acceptance, or test environment to ensure that all the sandbox environments are kept in sync.

Minor release

Minor releases are for larger changes that can be grouped and scheduled for change, perhaps every 30 or 60 days. The types of change that fall into this category include new fields, new page layouts, new custom objects, and so on, which are more complicated than the immediate release change items.

Minor release change items are medium level changes that can be implemented with minor impact to the production environment and typically require less than a day of additional training for users and overall less than a week of customization or code changes.

 It is worth considering, however, how the changes are applied in any other sandbox such as a **Developer**, **User acceptance**, or **Test environment** to ensure that all the sandbox environments are kept in sync.

Major release

Major releases are large changes that will carry risk and have a major impact to the business or environment. These changes are the ones that require modification to the user interface, to the way data is updated, data migrations, and any integration projects. These types of changes include new or modified role hierarchies, profiles, page layouts, record types, sales and support processes, workflow and approvals, and custom code. These changes can be introduced with the introduction of new AppExchange apps, process-impacting configuration changes, data migrations, and integration.

 Major release change items carry a high level of risk and are obviously more complicated than a minor release change. These changes may require additional time for training users, and in general require more than a week of customization or code changes.

Configure, develop, and deploy

Typical compliance requirements for change management are that changes are appropriately tested and validated and only approved changes are deployed into production.

Configuration, development, and testing should always typically be carried out using a sandbox environment, and a record should be maintained to record the successful testing, validation, and approval of any changes prior to deployment or production. Depending upon the scope and scale of the change request as described previously, you may need to consider using a different environment for development and testing.

A complex change often sees the need for a developer sandbox and separate testing sandbox. When the changes are finished in the developer sandbox, they are migrated to the testing sandbox, and only when approved are they deployed into the production environment.

Only after appropriate review and agreement by the approval authority can the changes ever be deployed into the production environment.

User adoption

In *Chapter 7, Salesforce CRM Functions*, we looked at the core functionality that Salesforce CRM provides and also at how the complete sales process, from campaign and lead capture right through to customer service and support, can be captured. Here, we looked in detail at how Salesforce provides the facilities to obtain a full 360-degree view of customer's past, present, and future relationships within our organization.

We looked at how this information enables marketing to measure the return on investment for marketing campaigns, sales to optimize the sales pipeline and sell more to each customer, support to track customer support incidents, and requests to ensure that each one is resolved appropriately and in a timely fashion.

Having this process in place is one thing, but to ensure that the information is captured to support the process is another issue altogether. After all, processes and technologies are only as good as the people who use them. So, it is vital that users are regularly logging in, creating, and updating information into Salesforce CRM.

CRM technology, therefore, must be easy to use, accessible, and scalable to ensure that the efforts of using the system provide significant enhancements in productivity, efficiency, and information accessibility. Once the business goals have been established and can be measured, organizations generally need to address methods of ensuring or increasing user adoption. Here you can cultivate active product advocates or evangelists from within your business to support certain initiatives for any relevant areas of the business.

A significant factor for successful adoption is to give users incentives to use the system by providing them with functionality that improves the way they work and offers valuable information and tools not available elsewhere within the organization.

Another important consideration is to encourage feedback from the user community. By encouraging feedback and instilling a sense of collaboration, a collective ownership for Salesforce CRM can be obtained that will instill trust. Responding to good suggestions, customizing, and communicating enhancements to the application can lead to better acceptance of changes, and makes people more likely to want to spend their time working with the application.

In spite of the positives mentioned, user adoption cannot be assumed or taken for granted, and your company might need to consider reinforcing adoption with rules as well as rewards.

User adoption seeks to ensure that the business communities, as described previously, are effectively using Salesforce CRM, and that the features that have been implemented are being properly utilized and continue to successfully address the business challenges.

To enable the monitoring of user adoption, there needs to be effective reports and dashboards to capture adoption metrics where the following areas can be considered when building user adoption metrics:

- Usage
- Data quality
- Business performance

Usage

The first key requirement for ensuring that Salesforce CRM is being appropriately used is by measuring the number and frequency of users logging in to the system. You also need to ensure that users are actively and consistently updating data and creating new **Leads**, **Contacts**, **Opportunities**, and/or **Cases** depending on their roles in the organization.

Having a well implemented business application should help to make business processes simple and hide complexity; this all helps to increase user adoption. However, making a computer application appear simple often requires a considered approach, and sometimes takes far more effort than leaving it in its natural complex state. Removing obstacles and unnecessary features takes time and effort, but it is time and effort well spent, and will yield results and hopefully result in higher adoption rates.

Simplicity

As a platform, Salesforce CRM has proven to be highly successful since its conception a decade ago, and the number of organizations and subscriptions to the service grows year on year. Much of this success can be attributed to the simplicity, ease of use, and focus on user productivity that the platform affords.

While you may feel justified in introducing new mandatory fields and enforcing data capture requirements into the application, this can sometimes make the system less user-friendly. Sometimes, applications that offer the simplest solution for a given problem are more likely to be rewarded with acceptance and adoption by your Salesforce community.

Connectivity

Enabling users to connect information from other tools, such as Microsoft Outlook, and fully integrating Salesforce CRM with other such business systems provides a mechanism to access all the information users need.

Salesforce Mobile

In the past, mobile devices that were capable of accessing software applications were very expensive. Often these devices were regarded as a "nice to have" accessory by management, and seen as a company perk by field teams. Today, mobile devices are far more prevalent within the business environment, and organizations are increasingly realizing the benefits of using mobile phones and devices to access business applications.

With improved mobile handsets, field teams can utilize Salesforce Mobile, which is a client application installed on the mobile that exchanges data with Salesforce over the mobile carrier network.

The device application stores a local copy of information in its own database on the mobile device and provides mobile teams with flexible working, where they do not need to be connected through their laptop to be productive.

 Salesforce Mobile supports mobile devices including BlackBerry®, Treo™, iPhone™, and Windows Mobile®.

Users can edit local copies of the Salesforce records that they have access to whenever the wireless connection becomes unavailable, and when the wireless connection becomes available, the changes are duly transmitted onwards to the Salesforce CRM application.

For mobile access, users require a Salesforce Mobile license, which provides access to accounts, assets, contacts, content, opportunities, leads, tasks, events, price books, products, cases, solutions, notes, and custom objects.

While the local data is updated wirelessly, Salesforce Mobile does not maintain an open web connection and communicates with the Salesforce platform using the web services API. As a result, not all of the features in Salesforce when accessed through a web browser are supported in Salesforce Mobile. Here, the following list outlines the capabilities and limitations of the mobile application:

- Dashboards are available in the BlackBerry and iPhone client applications, and reports are available in the BlackBerry and Windows Mobile client applications.

- Reports in Salesforce Mobile are sent to the device in the Excel format and are displayed in a basic table. Here, the report viewer does not support sorting, summaries, subtotals, or grouping.

- BlackBerry users can log e-mails sent from Salesforce Mobile, e-mails sent from the native address book and contact manager, plus incoming e-mails. Windows Mobile users can log e-mails sent from Salesforce Mobile and incoming e-mails.

- BlackBerry and Windows Mobile users can export Salesforce contacts and accounts to the address book application on the respective device. Conversely, they can both import entries in the device's address book to Salesforce.

- BlackBerry users can import Salesforce events to the BlackBerry calendar and export BlackBerry events to Salesforce. The Windows Mobile calendar, however, does not integrate with Salesforce Mobile.

Salesforce Mobile is included for Unlimited Edition organizations and is an extra cost for Enterprise Edition users. There is also a free version of Salesforce Mobile called **Mobile Lite**, which is available to both Enterprise and Unlimited Edition organizations.

Mobile Lite is a restricted version of Salesforce Mobile that is available to any Salesforce user who does not have a Salesforce Mobile license. As the name suggests, Mobile Lite does not provide all the functionality that is available in Salesforce Mobile; it supports fewer standard objects, does not provide support for custom objects, and does not allow administrators to customize or create mobile configurations.

With the Mobile Lite Version, users can only view, create, edit, and delete **Accounts**, **Contacts**, **Leads**, **Opportunities**, **Events**, **Tasks**, and **Case records**. Custom objects are not supported in Mobile Lite.

Communications

Users are far more likely to adopt Salesforce CRM when they know that their peers and colleagues are achieving results from its use. By communicating both the business and personal results, for example, an increase in company sales and the resulting sales commissions paid to the sales team, you can encourage others to adopt the system.

Data quality

Data quality is a valuable metric for measuring adoption. Although outlined previously, it is advisable not to over complicate the entering of information with needless validation; it is important that any critical fields are completed.

When certain fields are consistently filled out, user acceptance will increase as it provides good data integrity and reliability that translates into higher user confidence and higher adoption.

Business performance

Usage should also reflect business performance and compliance metrics that are used to ensure that users are not just using the application, but are using it in a way that enhances business effectiveness. Here, metrics can be built that will uncover patterns and trends that track performance levels, and can then identify areas that need improvement.

This has been a quick overview of areas that can be used to generate metrics that you can track and there is an enormous quantity of metrics that can be generated.

There is a balance, however, in getting accurate views without overcomplicating and spawning too many metrics. Here, it is often best to create the minimum number of metrics that can adequately capture and track the success of the business performance objectives.

Certain performance indicators can be established to identify the business sales revenues, which are listed as follows:

- Compare the current fiscal year against last year's sales by month, say, to measure cyclical variances.

- Compare sales from existing customers against new customers to measure what customer type revenue is coming from and enhance CRM activities accordingly.

- Compare won and lost sales ratios to measure the effectiveness of deal closure, see why deals are getting lost, and learn from the reasons.

- Measure the sales pipeline by sales stage to identify where new opportunities are appearing.

- Measure key opportunities in the sales pipeline to identify the current key opportunities to ensure they get the right attention.

- Measure closed sales actuals against quota. Here, you can introduce a closed sales leaderboard to identify who your top deal-closers are. This can sometimes be seen as a way of shaming bad performers, but sales management can use this information positively to get the top performers to share knowledge and best practices to help the organization.

For marketing specific metrics, the following examples can be performed:

- Measure campaigns by **Return On Investment (ROI)**, Actual ROI, by campaign type and average opportunity amount per campaign

- Measure lead conversion rates

There are many dashboards that you can install from AppExchange that give metrics for how Salesforce is being used. The following is called **Salesforce Adoption Dashboards**, which is an example from Salesforce.com Force.com Labs:

The **Salesforce Adoption Dashboards** app from Salesforce.com Force.com Labs is available from the AppExchange Marketplace directly through the following URL:

```
http://appexchange.salesforce.com/
listingDetail?listingId=a0N30000004gHhLEAU
```

Summary

In this, the final chapter of *Salesforce CRM: The Definitive Admin Handbook*, we have looked at ways to improve the experience of users in Salesforce CRM by providing additional functionality using external applications from AppExchange.

We looked at the importance for planning and scheduling the release of changes into the Salesforce application and provided some best practices relating to change management.

We looked at how the ROI in Salesforce CRM can be improved by adding extra functionality and attempting to make the user's lives easier when entering information into the application. We were also introduced to the concept of Salesforce Mobile, which can significantly improve the productivity of field-based users.

We looked at how a significant factor for successful user adoption is to give users incentives to use the system by providing them with functionality that improves the way they work, and offering valuable information and tools not available elsewhere within the organization.

We also looked at ways to measure user adoption and how to fully ensure user adoption; Salesforce CRM should be easy to use, accessible, and relevant to user's daily tasks.

By keeping data clean and keeping functionality simple, users will not be overburdened with unnecessary actions that overcomplicate their tasks and reduce productivity, which leads to far greater adoption.

Index

Thank you for buying
Salesforce CRM: The Definitive Admin Handbook Second Edition

About Packt Publishing

Packt, pronounced 'packed', published its first book "Mastering phpMyAdmin for Effective MySQL Management" in April 2004 and subsequently continued to specialize in publishing highly focused books on specific technologies and solutions.

Our books and publications share the experiences of your fellow IT professionals in adapting and customizing today's systems, applications, and frameworks. Our solution based books give you the knowledge and power to customize the software and technologies you're using to get the job done. Packt books are more specific and less general than the IT books you have seen in the past. Our unique business model allows us to bring you more focused information, giving you more of what you need to know, and less of what you don't.

Packt is a modern, yet unique publishing company, which focuses on producing quality, cutting-edge books for communities of developers, administrators, and newbies alike. For more information, please visit our website: www.packtpub.com.

About Packt Enterprise

In 2010, Packt launched two new brands, Packt Enterprise and Packt Open Source, in order to continue its focus on specialization. This book is part of the Packt Enterprise brand, home to books published on enterprise software – software created by major vendors, including (but not limited to) IBM, Microsoft and Oracle, often for use in other corporations. Its titles will offer information relevant to a range of users of this software, including administrators, developers, architects, and end users.

Writing for Packt

We welcome all inquiries from people who are interested in authoring. Book proposals should be sent to author@packtpub.com. If your book idea is still at an early stage and you would like to discuss it first before writing a formal book proposal, contact us; one of our commissioning editors will get in touch with you.

We're not just looking for published authors; if you have strong technical skills but no writing experience, our experienced editors can help you develop a writing career, or simply get some additional reward for your expertise.

Salesforce CRM Admin Cookbook

ISBN: 978-1-849684-24-8   Paperback: 266 pages

Over 40 recipies to make effective use of Salesforce CRM with the use of hidden features, advanced user interface techniques, and real-world solutions

1. Implement advanced user interface techniques to improve the look and feel of Salesforce CRM

2. Discover hidden features and hacks that extend standard configuration to provide enhanced functionality and customization

3. Build real-world process automation, using the detailed recipes to harness the full power of Salesforce CRM

Salesforce CRM: The Definitive Admin Handbook

ISBN: 978-1-849683-06-7   Paperback: 376 pages

A comprehensive power-packed guide for all Salesforce Administrators covering everything from setup and configuration to the customization of Salesforce CRM

1. Get to grips with tips, tricks, best-practice administration principles, and critical design considerations for setting up and customizing Salesforce CRM with this book and e-book

2. Master the mechanisms for controlling access to, and the quality of, data and information sharing

3. Take advantage of the only guide with real-world business scenarios for Salesforce CRM

Please check **www.PacktPub.com** for information on our titles

**Force.com Developer
Certification Handbook (DEV401)**

ISBN: 978-1-849683-48-7   Paperback: 280 pages

A comprehensive handbook to guide Force.com
developers through important funfamentals and
prepare them for the DEV401 exam

1. Simple and to-the-point examples that can be
   tried out in your developer org

2. A practical book for professionals who want to
   take the DEV 401 Certification exam

3. Sample questions for every topic in an exam
   pattern to help you prepare better, and tips to
   get things started

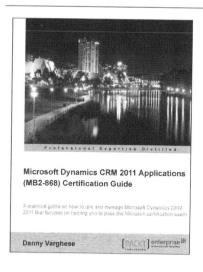

**Microsoft Dynamics CRM
2011 Applications (MB2-868)
Certification Guide**

ISBN: 978-1-849686-50-1   Paperback: 344 pages

A practical guide on how to use and manage
Microsoft Dynamics CRM 2011 tha focuses on
helping youto pass the Microsoft certification exam.

1. Comprehensive step-by-step guide to help you
   prepare for the MB2-868 exam

2. Loaded with screenshots and key points to help
   you pass the certification exam

3. Sample a 75 question practice exam to test
   your knowledge before you participate in
   the real exam

Please check **www.PacktPub.com** for information on our titles